I Ask You, Ladies and Gentlemen

Reviews

There is an intimacy here, even though it is a memoir of displacement and mass murder. The big picture of a genocide — such a cold word for such unfathomable horror — is told from the vantage of a small boy, who remembers the smells and sounds of his hometown. Leon Surmelian evokes the textures of a lost world, the bravado of the young, and the bewilderment of the elders, angry with God. Is it a memoir or a novel, the fragments of the past recalled and woven into a narrative? It is a story of the luck and courage that preserved young Leon and his brother and sisters, saved by Greeks when there was no escape. From the graveyard of Western Armenia, Surmelian migrated to Caucasian Armenia, witnessed the coming of the Soviets, travelled as a stowaway from Batumi to Istanbul, discovered that he was a poet, and in a cheap new suit and brown Oxfords he eventually reached America, the "real" America, Kansas. The memories of Trebizond and those lost never leave him, even as he celebrates his new country.

Ronald Grigor Suny

William H. Sewell Jr. Distinguished University Professor of History,
University of Michigan, Ann Arbor

Leon Surmelian wanted his bestselling and widely translated memoir to be known as "a universal story, the timeless legend of boyhood." It is that, but it is also an astonishingly rich and nuanced portrait of an Armenian world lost to war and genocide. With fierce intelligence and beautiful prose, Surmelian tells his own tale of survival and renewal, and at the same time illuminates the tragic history of his people.

Nancy Kricorian

Author – *Zabelle; Dreams of Bread and Fire; All the Light There Was*

Leon Surmelian's I Ask You, Ladies and Gentlemen remains a vivid reminder of man's inhumanity to man and the impact of genocide on a human soul. With a great command of detail, this masterful memoir recounts the horrors he witnessed as a child and the struggle to find a home. The lyricism and beauty of the prose enrich our understanding of the effects of diaspora on the Armenian people. This masterpiece deserves to be widely read. I ask you, ladies and gentlemen, please ensure this book never goes out of print again.

Vartan Gregorian

President, Carnegie Corporation of New York

The republication of this vivid and tragic memoir of a boy's experience of the events of the Armenian Genocide and its aftermath is very welcome. Leon Surmelian's book is beautifully written, told with poignancy and humour and deserves to be a best-seller.

Thomas de Waal
Author – *Black Garden*; *The Caucasus: An Introduction*

Reading the book made me immeasurably sad about the spectrum of violence especially the young survivors of the Armenian Genocide had to put up with, in loss of family, friends, home, possessions, stigmatisation by the Turks and the constant threat of death. I will work with all my might to ensure such a tragedy of humanity does not happen ever again.

Fatma Müge Göçek
Professor, University of Michigan, Ann Arbor

A most interesting & almost certainly true story of an Armenian boy from Trebizond who, after losing both his parents in the 1915 deportations/massacres, eventually ended up in the U.S.A.

Sir Denis Arthur Wright
Former British Ambassador to Iran and former Vice-Consul in Trabzon
(handwritten note on flyleaf of 1946 UK edition)

Surmelian's delight in little things is exciting and catching. He presents a truly wonderful picture of his old country. One literally smells and touches it. Exotic is an overworked word, but it fits here. The customs and characters he brings forth are enchanting. I think that here I touch on the secret of the pull of the book. Another, unquestionably, is the author's ability to dramatize himself. He is appealing, a little ludicrous (as he should be and wants to be), and there is no difficulty in getting him. His New Year's Eve oration to the ladies and gentlemen, to cite one chapter, is a little masterpiece. Surmelian has got the stuff.

Louis Adamic
Author and Editor – *From Many Lands*; *Common Ground*
(review published in the 1945 US edition)

Leon Z. Surmelian

I Ask You, Ladies and Gentlemen

THIRD EDITION

FOREWORD
Richard Anooshian

PREFACE
Susan Pattie

INTRODUCTION
William Saroyan

**ARMENIAN
INSTITUTE**
ՀԱՅ ՀԻՄՆԱՐԿ

London, United Kingdom

The current edition of *I Ask You, Ladies and Gentlemen* faithfully reproduces the text of the
longer UK first edition (1946) whilst utilising the American orthography of the first US edition (1945).

Published by Richard Anooshian and the Armenian Institute, London
Copyright 2019
All rights reserved

Armenian Institute
London, United Kingdom
www.armenianinstitute.org.uk

The Armenian Institute (AI) is a registered charity in England and Wales, Charity No. 1088410

ISBN 978-1-9161334-0-2

Designed and typeset by Jennifer van Schoor in 10/14 Baskerville

Printed and bound in the United Kingdom by
Page Bros, Norwich

Contents

Foreword

Richard Mourad Anooshian

The handwritten note "A most interesting & almost certainly true story of an Armenian boy from Trebizond ..." was the first thing that drew my attention when handed a first UK edition of Leon Surmelian's classic *I Ask You, Ladies and Gentlemen*. These words were inscribed on the flyleaf of the book by its previous owner, Sir Denis Arthur Wright, the former British Ambassador to Iran who happened to have served as vice-consul in Trebizond in the 1940s. The second thing that crossed my mind was the question: why had I never heard of it?

I was soon drawn into the personal journey of a nine-year-old boy, a heart-warming autobiographical account presented in a novelistic manner. Set in the beginning of the 20th century, Surmelian begins by painting a lively picture of an idyllic childhood in the multi-cultural Ottoman port city of Trebizond on the Black Sea. The onset of the Armenian Genocide in 1915 renders life as he knows it to an abrupt end. Yet, notwithstanding the multitude of losses personally experienced, this is a narrative devoid of bitterness or anger. What strikes the reader is the eloquent and profoundly sincere account of tragic and transformational events from the vantage point of a young boy. This is a beautiful book written with a great sense of humour and humanity. Furthermore, the dozen or so photographs reproduced at the end of this edition provide a visual record of the characters and places that populate its pages.

One hundred years after the events it recounts so vividly, this timeless book continues to be extremely relevant. It delves into the themes of forcible displacement, loss, trauma, memory, survival and ultimately, rebuilding. *I Ask You, Ladies and Gentlemen* is a gem in modern Armenian and American literatures. A must-read for everyone, it awaits re-discovery among new generations of readers.

Preface

Susan Paul Pattie

"I Ask You, Ladies and Gentlemen is strictly a factual story, the literal truth about my boyhood. Most of it originally appeared in literary magazines, such as Louis Adamic's Common Ground. I should like to see it publicized as the universal story, the timeless legend of boyhood. To regard it in any other light is to miss its point and significance." – Leon Surmelian, 1945.

When Leon Surmelian was a child, the 19th century had recently passed into history and the once great Ottoman Empire was undergoing a long, severe decline. A widely extended imperial power with its mosaic of peoples and religions, the Ottomans had lost possessions to independence movements in Greece and in the Balkans. They feared the intentions of the Russian Empire on the eastern border as well as the encroaching British and French imperial intentions in the Levant, Palestine and Mesopotamia. Brutal repressions and unfair taxation within the Empire became more common and in the 1890s, devastating massacres of Armenians took place under Sultan Abdul Hamid II.

In spite of pogroms and raids, most Armenians continued to hope for better times, staying on the land and in the towns they considered historically their homes, some of which they shared with Assyrians, Greeks, Turks, Kurds and others. Surmelian lovingly describes his town of Trebizond and his encounters with the variety of people living there, young and old. The country village where the family kept a summer home and garden is also part of this affectionate portrayal. He describes his own dawning awareness of a change in attitude among their Turkish neighbours, the sudden reversals of friendships, the spread of fear and the rapid contagion of an ideal of national unity built exclusively on Turkish identity. The Young Turk movement, initially supported by many Armenians, had begun by promising reforms that would enhance the lives of all, including minorities. However, by late 1914, when Ottoman Turkey entered World War I as an ally of

Germany and an opponent of Russia, Armenians were already being targeted, regarded as suspect, not Turkish, no longer loyal subjects. Surmelian's town and others in the Armenian homelands would soon suffer deeply as arrests, deportations and genocide of the Armenian population spread across the empire throughout 1915 and the following years.

In fact, very few Armenians had considered rebelling against the Empire but rather the vast majority were trying to continue with their daily lives. In some places arms were taken up in self-defence but there was little agreement about solutions to the terrifying situation. Discussions and arguments within communities about the best way forward are alluded to in the text and Surmelian's anecdotes touch on many important issues and events of the time. From the start, we realise that his own family is torn between the politics of a daring uncle willing to fight to defend them and the majority of his family and town who wish to somehow just get along. Uncle Leon, with whom Surmelian's father disagreed on politics, was nonetheless his chosen bodyguard at night. Decisions and alliances were not straight-forward but most Armenians continued to hope that the ongoing massacres would pass and life would return to normal. Sadly, by Surmelian's time, "normal" had become a powder keg existence.

As an adult, looking back at these times, Surmelian writes about how the Armenians he observed had difficulty hiding their hoped-for alliances and dreams of being saved by the European/Christian powers. He writes, "The Turkish comic paper *Karagoz* had truthfully said, *If you want to know the situation in the Dardanelles, look at an Armenian's face.* The Turks were very different from us; one could never tell what they really thought, what they really knew. They kept their secrets to themselves, and if they talked, they often meant the opposite of what they said." As the war went on, deportations increased and the genocidal aim became apparent. Armenians had indeed put their hopes on outside powers but by the end of the WWI, followed by the Turkish war of independence against the occupying Allied forces, over a million Armenians were dead, their culture destroyed and erased in its homelands. The survivors, like Surmelian, spread across the world, creating new homes, remembering and honouring the old.

Surmelian's memoir takes some people by surprise, wondering at the seeming impossibility of his escapes and travels. Could he really have done all the things he said he did, seen such tragedy and survived with a sense of humour and the soul of a poet? The zest for life that permeates

Surmelian's writing does not negate or deny the seriousness or sadness of his experiences but instead is something that also propels many others who are less gifted at writing their own tales. As a child, I grew up hearing survivors of the Armenian Genocide describe their own feats of endurance and astonishing escapes and have lived with laughter and joking from these same people. Their bone-crushing hugs spoke of an appreciation of life, love and family that could hardly be imagined by those of us who grew up taking it all for granted.

Later while doing ethnographic fieldwork with other survivors, similar narratives emerged: stories of scavenging, even stealing to stave off starvation, hiding from enemies, seeking for family and friends, a little bragging about a particular exploit, quite a few tears and some memories only mentioned aloud at a life's ending. These people, like Leon Surmelian had traveled however they could, wherever they could, often or even usually, on foot. They had crossed long distances, sometimes backtracking or circling around until reaching a place of temporary respite, often helped en route by kind and brave members of the same ethnic groups who were killing them.

Today, unfortunately, we have hundreds of thousands of contemporary examples of people engulfed by war and other forms of violence. Thanks to modern media, we also witness the same audacity and courage of those struggling to survive, willing to try anything to escape their situation. Some of the more intimate documentaries also demonstrate how quickly refugee children grow up and take on responsibilities for themselves and for others, how they learn to grab or even create opportunities, assess their possibilities, move onward, imagine new dreams.

This is the world that Leon Surmelian describes with open-hearted gusto but also with a more private, deep and unveiled grief. The chapter sharing the book's title embodies this discomforting contradiction. The ironic, witty tone of I Ask You, Ladies and Gentlemen does not hide his anguish but simultaneously delivers a love letter to the disappeared world of his childhood and an ode of appreciation to the country that welcomed him and where he thrived.

"There are millions like me, tonight, in free, happy America, haunted by their early years, which are always, everywhere, the happiest. The world is full of sorrow and memories, of stories that cannot be told, of poignant images that have no stories. Forgive me, ladies and gentlemen... I must have another drink."

If other refugees had Leon Surmelian's talent for writing, many of their stories would share a similar combination of traits. Survival depends on luck, strength and practical sense but thriving surely requires all of this and more. As Surmelian also makes clear, the refugee child's quest had been nourished by his own family but also by strangers, by Turks, Greeks, Kurds, Armenians unknown to him, and in the US, a farming family in Kansas, utterly different from his experiences and yet, his conduit to feeling utterly at home once more.

Surmelian has written that this is the "literal truth about my boyhood". I leave it to our readers to decide if, given these historical circumstances, the book you are reading is also, in the author's own words, a "timeless legend of boyhood". In its charming presentation of the sense of adventure felt by a young boy with no real idea of the broad implications of his daily travails, it is certainly found in other homeless, displaced boys and girls through history and in our world today. Thus it is also a timeless and poignant narrative of survival and rebirth, of thriving while living with a hole at the center of one's life. It is also a timeless reminder of the need to help these desperate children.

Introduction to First Edition

William Saroyan

This is a solemn, gentle, civilized book, full of innocence, comedy, and that kindly power which is the possession of men who are truly alive and cultured.

Leon Z. Surmelian is one of the many Armenian children of war years who fooled the enemy and didn't die. The story of these children is by now well-known to everyone. Franz Werfel tells part of it in *The Forty Days of Musa Dagh*, and Elgin Groseclose tells a little more in *Ararat*.

Here, however, for the first time is the *full* story, by one of the children himself. Their world was destroyed, but not their lives. Many of them are now in Soviet Armenia, Russia, Persia, Syria, Greece, Canada, Mexico, South America, and America. Many are dead in the old country, with the world that was destroyed. Their comrades, who were tougher or luckier, will never forget them. Their enemy was not any particular nation or any particular people. Their enemy was Evil, as abstract as Evil might be in any parable. These children were certainly innocent. If they belonged to any nation, it was to the nation of children. They had wronged no one. And yet Evil in men sought to destroy them, and as if they were real only in a fable, rather than in reality itself, these children lived.

Leon Z. Surmelian came out of the old country to America, and proceeded to mend the wrecked legend of his life.

This book tells the story of that mending.

It is a story without hate, for hate and death are partners, and this is a story of life.

I Ask You, Ladies and Gentlemen contains some of the finest writing I have ever read. The whole book is almost a lyric poem. Surmelian's style is simple and unaffected, warm and humorous, and at the same time full of the melancholy of the civilized and intelligent.

I can't imagine anybody being disappointed with this book. It is one of the most beautiful and exciting stories I have ever read. I say this in spite of the fact that Leon Z. Surmelian is my friend.

I know a great and good book when I see one.

Maps

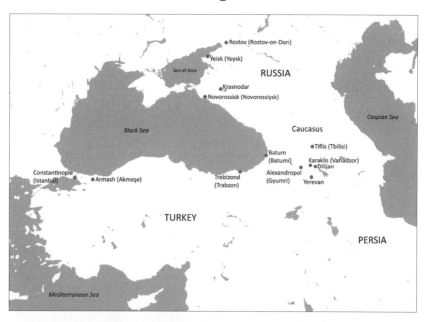

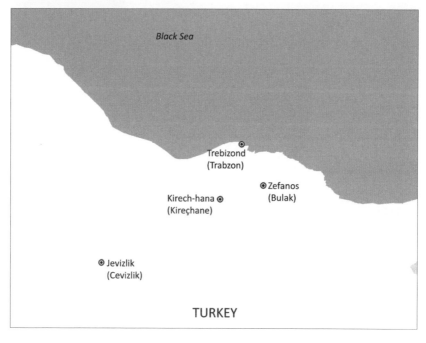

I Ask You, Ladies and Gentlemen

CHAPTER 1

Introduction to Mortality

One bright autumn morning, when I was almost eight years old, my mother took me to Grandmother's because Uncle Harutiun had come back from Paris. I must have seen him a few times, but I did not remember him. All I knew about Uncle Harutiun was that he had sent, from Paris, a little dachshund to Uncle Leon, who was a great hunter, a member of the Armenian Revolutionary Federation, and my childhood hero. The pomegranates were bursting with crimson joy in the gardens of Trebizond, it was the season for oranges and lemons, and itinerant vendors sold roast chestnuts and corn in the streets. A warm wind blew from the sea; the air was crisp and dry. It was like a holiday for me, but my mother was unusually sad and thoughtful.

Relatives and friends gathered at Grandmother's house to welcome Uncle Harutiun home. But strangely enough, all had serious, mournful expressions. My grandmother, a queenly lady, presided over this gathering with an officious smile which could not hide from me the grief in her breast. We all anxiously waited for Uncle Harutiun to arrive from the harbor, and presently a phaeton drew up at the gate, and Uncle Leon alighted from the carriage with a very tall, thin man. Grandmother embraced him and kissed him on his cheeks, Mother and the others did the same, and all pretended to be very happy, but I knew that there was something wrong in this reception.

Uncle Harutiun was a year or two older than Uncle Leon, and must have been in his twenty-third or -fourth year. He had a small, pointed brown beard, like a French artist's, and walked with the stooping shoulders of very tall men. There was that air of distinction about him, possessed by those who belong to the aristocracy of the spirit. The fine dignity which distinguished the members of my mother's family was particularly evident in her scholarly brother from Paris. He was not like other men, not like the grown-up male relatives on my father's side, for instance. He would have stood out in any crowd by the nobility of his bearing and the sweet sorrow of his intellectual eyes. He made altogether an extraordinary impression on me.

It seemed that he was very tired and needed rest. They took him upstairs and put him to bed in a sunny room, practically the only one in Grandmother's gloomy house, where the doors of many rooms were locked, the curtains drawn; and there was a characteristic smell which I may best describe by calling it funereal. It was a large old building, the vast entrance hall on the ground floor paved in marble-like flagstones, yellowed and cracked at several places. It was one of the few houses in the city with a Turkish bath of its own — the mark of an aristocratic family. But Grandmother now lived in genteel poverty. In the salon upstairs hung my maternal grandfather's portrait in a massive gilt frame. I can see it now, the kind expression of his eyes, the handsome countenance, and the wing collar and bow tie he wore. Many of the Christian men in those early days still wore the native garb, but my grandfather in the picture was dressed like a European gentleman. When the Turks killed him in a massacre several years before I was born, he was the leader and spokesman of our community before the government, the most influential and progressive of our notables, and the man who had opened the first *fabrica*, or European factory, in Trebizond, a great flour mill where everything was done by machinery to the endless wonder of the populace, both Christian and Mohammedan. That famous *fabrica* was now in other hands, and my mother's eyes filled with tears every time we passed by it. And Uncle Harutiun, who was expected to take the place of his martyred father and to heal the wounds of the past, had come back from Paris and lay in bed in a sunny room upstairs.

He never came out of his bed. He lay there, like Jesus. I visited him with my mother two or three times every week, and his air of distinction now was something saintly and sublime. He would help me with my French lessons, and I would perform before him the semi-military gymnastic drills I had learned in school. In gymnastics all the commands were given in French.

Repos!
Gardez-vous!
En avant, MARCHE!
Un deux gauche droite, un deux gauche droite!

I was always playing soldier, and had a military uniform, with rifle, saber and accoutrements. I was going to fight for Antranik, the Armenian national hero, who with his bands of revolutionaries defied the might of the Ottoman Empire.

Sometimes I found Uncle Harutiun writing in bed, and he had a mysterious bundle of manuscripts which I regarded with awe. He had gone to France to study agriculture for patriotic purposes, though he was born and grew up in the city. My mother's family was an eminently patriotic one, but while Uncle Leon inclined toward the sword, and was always armed, Uncle Harutiun wanted to serve his people with the pen and the plow. I was half-consciously aware of the fact that he was a poet.

And he presented in bed the classic picture of a consumptive poet. In a few months he was reduced to skin and bones. One day Grandmother said to Mother: "Last night he despaired of getting well. He begged Leon to give him his revolver; he wanted to shoot himself. We had a hard time in quieting him. Oh, my God, my God!"

Mother's lips trembled, but when we entered his room she looked bright and cheerful. And he looked to me more than ever like Jesus. Oh, I loved him so much!

Every night on going to bed I prayed to God to make Uncle Harutiun well. Time and again we thought he was on the road to recovery, and my poor mother would smile again. But a relapse invariably followed, and for a few days he would hardly have enough strength to speak a few words. I felt like crying when I caught the haunting, ghost-like glance of his eyes during these recurring periods of relapse.

It was in the afternoon of a magnificent spring day shortly before Easter. I had just returned from school when my mother received a message: Uncle Harutiun was "gravely ill" and doctors were holding a "consultation." She was crying, silently, in her quiet way, as she put on her charshaf, the silk mantle she wore on going out, and taking me along hurried to Grandmother's. Mother almost never went out without me.

When we arrived at Grandmother's house I saw Uncle Leon, alone in the dim drawing room, crying with his head bent down, his black hair disheveled and his face covered with his hands. He raised his head for a moment and looked at us with bloodshot eyes. He did not speak. Mother asked me to stay in the entrance hall, and went upstairs to Uncle Harutiun's room. I felt the gravity of the situation, but it did not occur to me that Uncle Harutiun was in the agony of death. I had never seen anybody die. I had not even witnessed the death of an animal, such as a dog, which is the first experience of many children with the awful concept of death. Stealthily I crept up the staircase, anxious to know what was going on there, in Uncle Harutiun's room, but I turned back on hearing the doctors' voices. After a few minutes my mother came downstairs, daubing a handkerchief on her eyes. "You go home," she said. "Uncle Harutiun is dying. I will stay here tonight."

And so it fell to my lot to carry that portentous news home, to tell my paternal grandmother, brother, and sisters, that Uncle Harutiun was dying. We children cried, but my paternal grandmother, a majestic woman of eighty-six, merely said, "May God illuminate his soul," and continued counting the beads of her chaplet seated cross-legged by the stove in our living room. She was past tears, and serenely waited for her own death, though she could walk from one end of the town to the other, and her eyesight was keener than mine.

We closed the door so that neighbors would not hear us, and besides, grief seeks privacy. Suddenly somebody knocked on the door, and we crying children rushed to open it, wondering who it could be. An old Turkish beggar was calling on us. Turkish beggars did not fare very well in our exclusively Christian street; our old clothes and leftover food usually went to Christian beggars, but we were extremely generous with this man. He might have been Christ himself for all we knew. In fact, I knew a story about Jesus going around disguised as a beggar in order to test the faith of the people He called on for alms. So we filled his sack with food, gave him fresh and not stale bread. He was delighted with our kindness; we treated him as if he were a holy man, and he kept thanking us by saying, "May Allah give you plenty." We were quite certain that God, seeing our good deed, would summon back the angel of death and permit Uncle Harutiun to live.

The swallows had returned to Trebizond and were staging their customary jamboree in our street, as the sun descended over the Promontory of Yoroz, the Sacred Mountain, which extended darkly into the sea. Golden clouds gathered on the fringes of the pale-blue sky, and on the slopes of the Gray Hill that towered over the city was the dazzling pageantry of sundown. For a few minutes our street was magically lighted with a roseate glow and the windowpanes reflected the flaming brilliance of the departing sun. It was enchanting! The muezzin of our neighborhood mosque ascended the soaring white minaret, and putting his hands behind his ears chanted in far-reaching melodious voice, "Allah Ekber! God is Great!" At this hour of the day the children in our street stopped playing and gazed about them and above them rapturously, as if they were looking at the world through bits of colored glass, a favorite pastime with all of us, and especially with me. But now all this beauty of nature made our grief the more poignant. Our beloved uncle, whose name meant Resurrection, was dying a few days before Easter, our greatest and most glorious festival. Images of Christ's crucifixion and subsequent rising from the tomb, on rolling clouds, became interwoven in my mind with Uncle Harutiun, and I felt sadder than I would have felt otherwise.

How I missed my mother that night! She was not in the living room while Father had his customary apéritif before dinner. This was a period of family bliss. When Father poured some water in a glass of raki, which instantly turned it milky white, and tossed it off, we children said together, "May it be sweet!" Father would wipe his mouth with a napkin, and then exhale with a sound of lordly enjoyment. But that night we did not say, "May it be sweet!" and Father did not make that noise. For the first time Mother was not with us at the dinner table. There were seven of us at home, but our house was empty because Mother was absent.

God did not call back the angel of death. Uncle Harutiun died, and wearing our best clothes we children went to Grandmother's to attend the funeral ceremony. The salon on the second floor, now stripped of all its furniture, and a black gauze covering my grandfather's portrait, was thronged with mourners. All the women were dressed in black, and the men wore black bands around their arms. When we four children entered, all heads were turned toward us. As no other children were present we attracted attention. In the center of the hall, placed between two burning candles of enormous size, there was a long, silvery coffin, in which lay Uncle Harutiun, with his hands crossed over his breast and his eyes closed. His face was blanched to a chalk-white color. He was surrounded by a group of women crying on their knees, while Grandmother, waving a handkerchief bordered with black, spoke to him in the most beautiful language I have ever heard.

Her speech was like a series of death ballads, a recitative of deepest motherly love and of grief inconsolable. She reviewed the main events of his life, reminded him of the things he had done and said as a child, how his father and uncles were killed in the massacre, when he was a boy of six, their happiness before that dread event, the summers they had spent in the country. You went to study, she told him, in the great universities of Europe, you wanted to make us happy again, but now you have left us before we could enjoy you. She described the charms of the beautiful girl she had chosen to be his bride, and this part of her sobbing soliloquy was particularly touching to me, small as I was. My grandmother, talking to her dead son, before the portrait of his father, now covered with a black gauze so that he would not see him, was the image of Mother Armenia with all her ancient sorrows; the tears she shed were also the tears of countless Armenian mothers sobbing over the dead bodies of their stalwart sons. And it seemed to me Uncle Harutiun heard and saw it all, but did not say anything.

I could not bear for long this spectacle of death and mourning. Grandmother's words and the sight of my mother weeping on her knees next to her pained me so much that I broke loose and fought my way to the coffin.

"Please don't cry any more!" I pleaded with Grandmother, meanwhile addressing myself to my mother and the other women who formed this circle of woe around the corpse. Grandmother looked at me fondly with her eyes, the saddest I have ever seen, and a wan smile flickered on her lips. The wailing ceased. People carried their handkerchiefs to their mouths instead of their eyes. And I wanted to stay there to keep them from crying, but somebody with strong arms pulled me back, back to the side room where my brother and sisters were, and the lamentation broke out anew.

Suddenly we heard a commotion downstairs. A large cross flashed in the doorway, clouds of incense smoke swept into the hall, and a crowd of death-smelling ecclesiastics made a dramatic appearance, led by our prelate, a distinguished prince of the Church. With firm, resolute steps he advanced toward the coffin as people made way for him and crossed themselves with bowed heads. The wailing women around the coffin got up to their feet. Standing between two acolytes who carried tall copper candlesticks, the prelate read from the sacred book he held in his hands and offered the appropriate prayers for the dead. After this ceremony pallbearers moved forward and lifted up the coffin to carry it downstairs, whereupon Grandmother and the other women let out heart-shattering screams and clung to it desperately, would not let them take it away. This struggle ended with Grandmother's fainting. She was carried to her bedchamber.

Uncle Harutiun was to be buried with all the pomp of the Church, as befitted the son of a prominent family. There were two long lines of wreath-bearers as the funeral procession formed in the street. The bells of the ancient cathedral of the Holy Mother of God tolled the plaintive invitation of death. As the procession wound through the streets many stores had their shutters drawn and suspended business; all Christian men, whether Armenians, Greeks, or Franks, took off their fezzes or hats, and even the Turks looked grave and respectful. On the faces of all, irrespective of their religion, was reflected man's brotherhood and humility in death.

And now the streets were streets of death, the sky was a sky of death, and death sang its everlasting dirge through the voices of the priests and the forty children who formed the choir. Uncle Harutiun was carried to his tomb with the grand and solemn music of the Church, with the profound supplications voiced in the mighty words of the Fathers of our Church and Nation. That music of the soul was now a murmurous tumult, and now swelled into divine intonations of hymns chanted in antiphony.

We children did not go to the cemetery, which was a few miles outside the town. We went home after the requiem mass in church. Uncle Harutiun was the first person I had seen die, and I pondered upon the mystery and grandeur of death. I was troubled, deeply troubled. And on our way back from church, I asked my brother, Onnik, two and a half years older than I, many questions about death. He remarked that everybody would sooner or later die.

"What!" I exclaimed, terrified. "Do you mean to say that Father and Mother will die too, that you and I also will die?"

"Yes," he said. "Father and Mother, you and I, all of us, everybody will die some day."

The wholly innocent and utterly happy phase of my childhood was over. And I did not have the consolations of philosophy as I thought about death, trying hard to comprehend its infinite mystery. A new secret world, visible only to the inner eye, was revealed to me, and my child-mind wandered into the regions of eternal solitude. This tragic end to which all of us were doomed, as my brother asserted, meant that neither my mother nor my father, absolutely nobody, could protect me from death, that I would be separated from them, or they from me, and all of us would face death alone and helpless.

But I could not, no matter what my brother said, imagine myself dead, like Uncle Harutiun. Others, perhaps, would die, but not I.

"I'll never die," I declared.

"You think you won't!" my brother replied sarcastically. "You will just close your eyes and die like the rest of us."

"But I won't close my eyes!" I protested, indignant. "I'll always keep them open," I insisted. "I'll never close them, never, no matter what happens, no matter how sick I am. Tell me, how can I die if I always keep my eyes open?"

I believed I had discovered the secret of immortality.

CHAPTER 2

The Shame of Maundy Thursday

Easter in Trebizond! What a holiday that was! The schools closed for two weeks, and there was goodness and happiness on the faces of people as they prepared to rejoice in the resurrection of Christ. Holy week was the busiest week of the year.

I had joined the church choir. They gave me the most coveted and difficult piece, the solo part from the *Book of Daniel*, to read on the night of Holy Saturday. And I was one of twelve boys whose feet our prelate was going to wash on Maundy Thursday. That was something to remember all our lives.

"So the prelate is going to wash your feet!" people would tell me. "Be sure they are clean."

On the morning of Maundy Thursday we went to the bathhouse, my brother and I carrying two bundles containing such family heirlooms as Turkish towels, clogs inlaid with mother-of-pearl, a silver bowl for pouring water. We always went to the bathhouse of the Infidels — the Giaour Hamami, originally a Byzantine church. When the mighty poet-sultan Mohammed II conquered Trebizond eight years after his conquest of Constantinople, he had the largest and most beautiful church buildings in the city transformed into mosques and public baths for the eternal glory of Allah.

Both Christians and Turks bathed in the Giaour Hamami, but never together. There were separate days for each. Women and children bathed during the day, men at night. It was situated in a maze of medieval lanes, with white and red roses climbing garden walls. A small gate led into a wood

yard where you could see the huge furnace in the basement — a fearful
sight. It made me think of the fires of hell. The great boilers were kept
furiously hot day and night. Crossing this wood yard we entered the cool
outer, or dressing hall, of the bathhouse. The manager, a handsome,
passionate-looking Turkish woman with a milk-white face, sat cross-legged
in a railed dais at the door furnished with rugs and cushions, smoking a
cigarette. She might have been the reigning queen of a sultan's harem. She
welcomed us with all the polite, poetic phrases of the ceremonious East,
inquiring after our health and showering compliments on us, which Mother
duly returned.

The outer hall was round, with an elevated double gallery on three sides
divided into open compartments and a few rooms. The rooms were furnished
with better mattresses and had gilt-framed mirrors and accordingly cost a
little more. In the center of the hall there was a decorative fountain with a
fish pond. In an alcove an old and withered Turkish woman wearing clogs
and *peshdimal*, a sheet of striped cloth tied around the hips and reaching
down to the knees, was busy with her copper coffee pots. Pink, languid
Greek and Armenian women wrapped in fluffy snow-white towels lay on
their mattresses in the gallery, resting after the rigors of their baths. Every
time the thick, heavy door that gave access to the inner hall was pushed
open the outer door resounded with a sudden blast of ringing uproar and
steam, abruptly shut off as the door closed.

We undressed, and walking carefully along a slippery vestibule entered a
vast, torrid rotunda, filled with clouds of steam and an infernal din composed
of women's voices, babies' screams, children's shouts, the clash and boom of
metal bowls, and the constant splashing of water over the marble slabs. For
a few minutes it was almost impossible to breathe that steam-laden air. The
bathing compartments consisted of a marble basin with faucets of hot and
cold water and two marble slabs to sit on. There were small chambers
affording privacy, but the air was unbearably hot in them. Women retired to
those blistering cells to henna their hair and have leeches suck their blood,
which was not very pleasant to see.

In the center of this rotunda was an octagonal platform of colored tiles,
over which a few women lay at full length, and the Turkish bath attendants
rubbed and massaged them with rough gloves. The women of Trebizond
are famous for their beauty. Rubens should have been in our bathhouse. I
can see those nude women now — their swelling, voluptuous figures — I can

see the slender virgins running with their long hair streaming down their backs. We children were stark naked, but the women and older girls wore *peshdimals*. We boys played tag, a dangerous game on those slippery marbles, and jumping on to the octagonal platform blew soap bubbles. They floated through the vaporous air like balloons, and the light that fell from the glass apertures of the lofty dome directly above it tinted them with all the colors of the rainbow.

From time to time we had to return to our respective compartments and suffer the unspeakable tortures of being rubbed and washed by our merciless mothers. A thorough rubbing and three soapings from head to foot were required before Mother pronounced me cleansed. And, of course, everyone joked about my feet, said they were dirty, no matter how hard I washed them.

This bathing lasted four or five hours, after which, wrapped in towels and wearing clogs, we returned to the dressing hall. It was like getting out of the heat of the deserts of Araby and entering the cool, delicious paradise of Allah. We did not dress immediately; that would have spoiled the luxury of our bath. We reclined on the mattresses in indolent repose, refreshed ourselves with fruit and lemonade, appeased our hunger with *halva* and *simits*, or sesame rings. And leaving the bathhouse had its special etiquette. Mother again exchanged the customary compliments with the manager as she paid her.

Late in the afternoon, our cheeks still flushed with the characteristic bathhouse glow, we went to church for the most solemn rite of the washing of the feet. I put on my surplice, red, with a blue cape of velvet, and took my place in the choir, proud and self-conscious. I knew that my mother watched me approvingly from the women's gallery.

While the prelate was being appareled in the vestry, our precentor sang the stately and monumental hymn, *"O Mystery Deep!"* with the rest of the choir humming a deep drone in antiphony.

"O mystery deep!"

"Hummmmmmmm"

"Incomprehensible, eternal!"

"Hummmmmmmm"

"Who hast set up Thy heavenly throne in unapproachable light, in splendid glory of brilliant celestial spirits!"

"Hummmmmmmm"

"Thou who didst spread Thy creating arms to the stars, make our arms firm with power, to intercede when we raise our hands unto thee."

"Hummmmmmmmm."

At the end of this hymn, the singing of which took fully ten minutes, the prelate came out of the vestry with a deacon and subdeacon, with the crown on his head, looking like a Byzantine emperor. He wore a shimmering chasuble and the buckle of his belt was studded with jewels. One of the deacons swung a censer before him walking backward and bowing continually, while the other carried a small basin and a pitcher of water. The prelate washed his hands before us and then addressed the congregation, telling them how much he had sinned and begging them to entreat God for him. He then turned around and went up the stairs of the sanctuary accompanied by his two acolytes. The curtain was drawn.

Toward the end of the interminable mass the singing ceased suddenly. Everybody stood still. Men who had been prostrating themselves, touching the floor with their foreheads, rose to their feet and did not move. We twelve boys representing the twelve disciples of Christ went up the stairs of the sanctuary in single file and took off our shoes and socks in a side chamber. A large basin of water was placed on the platform of the altar. I peeped out from behind the curtain to see my mother, grandmothers, aunts, and other female relatives who had come to see the prelate wash my feet. I was nervous, palpitating, but immensely proud. Not only could you hear a pin drop, so profound was the silence, but to use the Armenian idiom, there was no place to drop a needle, so large was the crowd. The cathedral was jammed full with a congregation eager to witness the most dramatic ceremony of the church. I saw a sea of faces.

The prelate, who was a towering bishop, took off his crown and chasuble, and rolling up his sleeves knelt humbly by the basin. I went to sit on the stool before him and held my foot over the basin. He dipped a rag in the water and, murmuring a prayer, squeezed it on my foot, after which he put consecrated ointment on my toes. I didn't know what to do next.

"Kiss and go," he whispered.

I raised my foot as high as I could and stretching my neck as far down as it would go, tried to kiss the holy ointment he had put on my toes, but I could not reach it with my lips.

A multitudinous murmur swept through the cathedral, which grew louder and louder and became peals of laughter. I was very good in gymnastics, but one had to be an acrobat to do what the bishop asked. The more I struggled with my foot the louder became the mortifying laughter. The thought that I should be the cause of this appalling and sacrilegious uproar in the house of God was so crushing that I wished I could fly away and disappear forever. I knew they were laughing at me, but didn't know why. In the delirium of my confusion and despair, the cathedral was rising in vast billows of blazing lights and faces, faces, faces, dissolving into space. Angels wheeled over this terrific and catastrophic tumult and an angry God watched me from his throne with his bushy white brows drawn together. The bishop assumed the proportions of a gigantic phantom, became an oppressing shadow before me, above me, and all around me.

I finally gave up my acrobatics and looked helplessly at his wrathful face. "Kiss the cross, the CROSS!" I heard him saying.

So it was the cross I had to kiss, and not my foot! It lay on the stool at my side with a large, silver-mounted Bible, a heavy jeweled episcopal cross. I fell on it with devout lips and hobbled away in a hurry, to find the other choir boys rolling behind the altar and gasping for breath as they held their sides. This was the most humiliating of all.

"Fool!" one of them said.

I could make no reply. There was a stinging sensation in my burning ears.

On the night of that same disastrous day clergy and congregation, dressed in black, lamented the crucifixion of Christ in a long dolorous service. All the lights, except one or two on the altar, were put out, and the usual bright curtain of the sanctuary was removed and replaced by a black funereal one. This midnight service was faithfully attended especially by those women who like my mother were in mourning.

On Good Friday Mother dyed eggs by boiling them with onion skins, and made several loaves of paschal cake, each weighing about two pounds, baked in our neighborhood bakery. On the morning of Holy Saturday I confessed, with a group of other boys. We knelt in the vestry of the church and the priest read the appropriate prayers over our bowed heads, enumerating all the sins human flesh is heir to, and begging forgiveness from God. Every minute or two, changing the tone of his voice, he told us under his breath: "Say, 'I have sinned, O Lord!'"

"I have sinned, O Lord!" we all exclaimed piously.

"May God grant ye remission," the priest said, and began reading the next list of sins.

Guilty or not we had to say, "I have sinned, O Lord!" We did not know the meaning of many sins. The language of our Bible and liturgy was in ancient Armenian, which only the old folks and highly educated people could understand.

After this group confession we boys went around and asked those whom we had wronged or injured in any way to forgive us. Old scores and feuds were now settled in a spirit of true Christian humility and brotherhood, as we got ready for the communion. Boys who were not on speaking terms shook hands and became friends. There were, however, a few louts who sputtered with laughter every time they saw me, and grabbing their feet tried to kiss them.

The festival of Easter began with a grand mass, the Lighting of Lights, late in the afternoon of Holy Saturday. I read my scroll from the *Book of Daniel* with a vengeance, "like a bulbul," people said later, even though among my schoolmates I could never live down the shame of Maundy Thursday. We went home and had our traditional meal of fish, with colored eggs and paschal cake, beggars being our honored guests. I was so happy to round up groups of them in the churchyard and take them home with me. They ate for the salvation of Uncle Harutiun's soul. On Ash Wednesday we children had hung an onion from the lamp in our dining room, with seven feathers stuck into it. Every week we had plucked out a feather, and now joyously removed the last one. It was our Lenten calendar.

Sunday morning we went to church without eating breakfast, or even drinking a drop of water, because we had to take the communion. The altar was lighted brilliantly and decorated with flowers. The picture of the Virgin and Child was replaced by an old painting showing the resurrection of Christ. There were new faces in our choir, men who had worn the surplice in their younger days.

Our precentor struck his tuning fork, gave the signal, and we sang with glad ringing voices the Easter introit, as he clashed his cymbals together.

> Christ is risen from the dead! By His death He overcame death and
> by His resurrection He has granted us life. Glory be to Him forever! Amen.

From behind the new curtain, woven in heavy golden threads and sparkling with sequins, the bishop glorified the resurrection in exultant words, to which we responded by singing:

Christ is risen from the dead; alleluia.

Come, O ye people, sing to the Lord; alleluia.

To Him Who is risen from the dead; alleluia.

To Him Who has enlightened the world; alleluia.

The veteran choristers who had joined us were the day's soloists, and vied with one another with their vocal talents. The bishop delivered one of the sermons for which he was famous, denouncing young women who wore décolleté gowns and copied the sinful modes of Paris. He held his episcopal staff as he spoke, with its double-headed silver snake.

We sang the *Lord's Prayer*, the blessed, unleavened bread was passed around, and at last a deacon called out to the congregation:

"Come near with awe and communicate with holiness!"

The crowd surged forward. Holding the golden chalice high in both hands the bishop turned around, uttering words of rapture, and descended the altar steps, to squat at the edge of the platform, a candle bearer standing on each side of him. He broke a piece of the consecrated wafer, soaked it in the wine of the chalice, and put it in the communicant's mouth, who made the sign of the cross as he swallowed it.

As people came out of the church, the crowd in the churchyard became thicker. Hundreds had to stand outside during the service, for lack of room in the church. All were in their Easter best, and even the children of the poorest families wore at least new shoes. Outside, in the crooked narrow street, the Turkish *simitjis*, men in purplish baggy breeches and red sashes, handkerchiefs tied around their fezzes by way of a turban to distinguish them from fez-wearing infidels, did a lively trade selling crisp sesame rings as we famished children swarmed around them with coppers and nickels in our hands.

At home we had our customary Easter dinner, an entire roast lamb stuffed with rice, raisins and pine nuts being the main course. Father, who never observed the Lent, let us children have half a glass of wine each, thinking he was doing us a great annual favor, not knowing I had drunk from his big wine bottle many a time, when nobody was around to see me. Refilling his wine bottle in Mr. Persides' distillery was one of my chores. We tapped colored eggs: you won the egg you cracked.

After dinner Onnik and I took our rockets and fire-crackers, which we had bought with our savings of several weeks, and staged a noisy celebration in our street with Elevtheraki Persides and other Greek boys. And then, with Mother's permission, we went to the cinema to see a picture on the life of Christ. It caused a riot as some boys, excited by the scenes of Christ's sufferings at the hands of the Jews, attacked a lone Jewish boy in the theater and began to beat him. There was only one Jewish family in our town, or at least I knew only one, a pale contractor, from whose yard we boys stole barrel hoops to roll them.

The next few days were spent in making and receiving calls, people greeting each other with the Easter salutation:

"Christ is risen from the dead."

"Blessed is the resurrection of Christ."

We served our visitors Turkish coffee, cognac, liqueurs, raki, candy, cherry and rose leaf jam, citron marmalade — in an elaborate silver set. If our maid Victoria did not know who was to be served first, Mother directed her with her watchful eyes. That was very important. The strictest etiquette of priority was observed. The oldest and most educated people were served first. We received all our guests in the drawing room, which was formally furnished, with French sofas, chandelier with crystals, a porcelain stove, which was imported from France but never kept the room warm and was cracked, piano, round walnut table, and a magnificent Persian rug on the floor. Our living room was a bit *à la Turca,* but our drawing room was fashionably *à la Franca.*

Our parish priest, Der Shaghah, came for the Easter house-blessing with the sexton, the exorcist, the candle lighter, deacons, subdeacons and precentor — a real state visit. We children had to go to the drawing room to kiss his hand. After they blessed our house with an appropriate ceremony, they sat stiffly, partaking of the refreshments in the silver set and conversing with Mother. She was the treasurer of the Ladies' Union, and our maternal grandmother was its perpetual president. Together they raised a lot of money for the church, and sponsored an industrial school for needy girls.

We children had to show them our accomplishments. Nevart played the piano, Onnik his violin. I stood on a chair and recited a poem Der Shaghah's beautiful daughter had taught me in the kindergarten, where she was my teacher, and I loved her very much. I shouted at the top of my voice:

When I grow up
And have mustaches
A soldier brave
I will be.

"Very good, very good," Der Shaghah said, when I finished. He patted me on the head.

"He can repeat the sermons of the Holy Prelate," Mother said, pleased.

"I know!" the precentor said, with a cautious little laugh. "I have caught him doing it — with a broomstick in his hand." He praised my singing and reading.

"God's key opened his mouth," Der Shaghah said, smiling at me. He had put the key of our church door in my mouth when I had reached my third year without learning to speak. A miracle was performed, and after that, I more than made up for lost time. I stuttered when I became nervous, Mother told him, and he said God would cure me of that too. No mention was made of the awful incident on Maundy Thursday. They spared my feelings. I was anxious to redeem myself in their eyes, but the shame of it, I knew, would always cling to me, and nobody who saw me trying to kiss my foot before the altar would ever forget it. When they rose to go, Mother slipped into Der Shaghah's hand a gold coin, to be divided among the members of his party, according to their rank. The others pretended not to see it.

"God bless you all," the priest said again at the door, and murmured another benediction on our house.

CHAPTER 3

The Fiery Horse

Fortune and history have favored the first-born among the male, and it is they who have been deemed worthy of inheriting the kingdoms of the world. My older brother was favored over me in a hundred different ways, even though I was as tall as he, and just as strong, I insisted. I fought with him almost every day, to prove it. In school too, even though he was always first in his class, I didn't do badly either. I got good grades, and I was never punished. No teacher ever rapped my hands for being late or not knowing my lesson, or made me kneel alone in the corner, with my face to the wall, for shooting a paper swallow.

And now another summer had come, no more school for three months! With other boys in the third grade I was given my certificate and turned loose. We celebrated our freedom in the traditional manner — smashing our ink bottles on the cobblestones as we ran up a steep street with cries of joy. From time to time, as I ran, I glanced up at the blue sky, thrilled with the thought of another vacation in the country. I could see myself finding a bird's nest in the still heart of the woods, with five little eggs in it, warm to the touch, covered with blue dots or delicate coffee-colored stripes... I could see myself bringing down a sparrow with my slingshot... wading through a stream. Too bad few boys in my class could go to a village in the summer.

My mother was busy sewing on her Singer machine when I dashed into our house, with my rolled-up certificate. I gave it to her proudly. She gasped when she saw I had received 10, the highest mark, for Conduct.

"How you fool them!" she said. "I am going to see your director and ask him to change it to zero."

I was terrified. "But Mother, I behave in school, I really do!"

I was always conscious of my responsibility to uphold the honor of my family among outsiders.

My mother relented and agreed not to complain to the director on my promise I would behave myself also at home — and I could make no bigger promise than that. And then, as if to reward me for it, she said, "Here, try these on." She held up a pair of blue pants on which she had been working. I took one look at them and recognized them as Onnik's. She blushed and looked embarrassed. Her trick didn't work. She had altered them and tried to pass them on to me as new.

"Look at this patch in the seat," I protested, indignantly.

"But it's no bigger than a pinhead. Nobody would notice it. You can wear it in the village."

Father was frankly partial to my older brother and sister Nevart. He never refused them anything. He was always boasting about their accomplishments to his friends. But he never boasted about me: I could not play a musical instrument, I could not read and understand classic Greek, I got poor marks in arithmetic — and music, Greek and mathematics were the only subjects that mattered, according to Father. All his Greek customers knew that Nevart was first in her class in a *Greek* school. He was a great admirer of the Greeks, their language and culture. We lived in a Greek street, and some Armenians sarcastically said we were more Greeks than Armenians.

And now Mother has done something that hurt me worst of all. If Nevart and Onnik were "Father's children," I and my baby sister Eugenia were "Mother's children." The balance was all in Nevart's and Onnik's favor, because Father's word was law in our home.

Wearing Onnik's discarded pants was the climax of all the discrimination and neglect I had suffered. I wore them only because I thought of the poor and beggar children who would have been very glad to have them.

"See, how nicely they fit you," Mother said, pulling them up. My pants were always on the verge of falling down, I was so thin, while Onnik was plump.

I stood before the mirror and sighed. "I wish I were good looking like Onnik and Nevart," I said to myself. But I was the ugly duckling in my family. I was dark, and my black hair stood up on top of my head, I could not keep it laid down no matter how much I wet and combed it. Onnik, on the other hand, was light, with soft brown hair, and Nevart was blonde. Everybody said I didn't look like them at all.

Onnik came in, with his violin under his arm, looking important. He had two tutors; I had none. Nevart also had two tutors. Father spent so much money on them. But he ignored me. Nobody took me seriously. I didn't count. Ever since he received a basket of pears from the Patriarch Zavén, the supreme primate of our Church, for reciting a poem before him, Onnik thought he was somebody. Why, I could recite better than he. Only he knew a poem with a lot of hard words in it, being two classes above me in school, and having two tutors.

"The vegetable man didn't come today," Mother said. "I want one of you to go to the grocery and bring me an oka of peas and three bunches of parsley."

"I've to practice my violin lesson," Onnik said, excusing himself.

So of course I had to go. It was I who always went on errands. And after I brought the peas and the parsley, I had to carry two pails of water from the public fountain — as if I had no pride. At last I was free to play. Anthula and Penelope Persides asked me to play hopscotch with them.

Anthula, pale and gentle, was my sweetheart. I was going to marry her when I grew up. There were six girls in the Persides family, our Greek neighbors across the street, and each one of them could have posed for Praxiteles, they were all so perfectly beautiful. I was reluctant to play with Anthula and Penelope. After all, I was a boy, and I wanted to assert my male superiority. They begged me, and I finally consented.

Their older sister, Helene, being twelve, was already past the playing age. She sat on the doorstep of their house, watching us.

"Look at the mirror, the mirror!" I laughed, pointing to her panties. That was the expression naughty boys like me used on seeing the panties of the girls. Her cheeks flushed, and she pulled down her skirt.

"Oh, pull it up," I said, "let me see the mirror again."

Helene stuck out her tongue and gave me, what you would call, the raspberry.

I picked up a clog — a heavy wooden shoe with a leather strap — somebody had left in the street, and threw it at her, not really meaning to hit her, but out of sheer deviltry. To my surprise, the clog struck her right on the eye. She jumped up screaming. Blood flowed down her face. I stood staring at her, petrified with fear and remorse. Did I blind her? Anthula and Penelope were speechless. They said nothing. They were too well behaved. Perfect little ladies.

Our game was over. Everybody ran out to see what had happened. "Oh, my God!" Mother cried, ran back into our house, and rushed out with bandages and a bottle of iodine to dress Helene's wound. She threatened to call the police. "Even the jail is too good for you!" she said. "May you go to the bottom of Gehenna!" Nevart was wringing her hands and apologizing to everybody.

"Wait until Father comes home," she told me.

"Stupid!" Onnik said.

"Kurd! Savage!" Nevart added.

I fled into our house and dashed upstairs to my bedroom, slamming the door behind me.

I was now an outlaw, and I knew nobody would speak to me again. Lying in bed flat on my face, I waited for the police to come and take me to jail.

All the policemen were Turks, wearing grey lambskin caps with a crescent and star, huge pistols at their sides. There was a police *karakol* close by our street. I had seen gangs of prisoners with heavy chains tied to their feet. I had even witnessed the hanging of criminals in the Maydan, the central square of the town, and could now see their bare feet dangling from under their white robes, with official papers enumerating their crimes pinned on their breasts. The Turkish judge would sentence me to jail, and then they would tie those dreadful chains to my feet. Well, let them hang me, I said to myself. I would die like a hero. I could see myself walking down our street handcuffed, escorted by two policeman — but my lips tight, and my chin up. I could hear people saying, "He's a bad boy, but brave."

A swallow flew into the room through the window, fluttered against the walls, circled round and round, twittering to me, and then flew out. It was *my* swallow, one of a pair that had built their nest in our entrance hall upstairs, for in the spring we left our doors and windows wide open. That swallow was the only friend I had now. It told me, in its language, that it would visit me in my prison cell, carry messages for me, like the swallow in a story in my Armenian reader, *The Happy Prince*. I was so touched by that tender and beautiful tale!

The room glowed in the lurid light of the setting sun. I screwed up my eyes, and watched the teeming luminous things in the darkening air — things that I could see, and yet could not see, things that were by turn a hundred other things: now large butterflies — now floating balloons — now purple smoke blown away by some secret wind — now showers of pink petals falling upon me from strange blossoming trees — now swift, leaping lights, artful, pellucid, spider-like forms that spun around me their ethereal webs.

Presently I heard Father's voice and footsteps downstairs. He had come back from his pharmacy! In the evenings I always waited for Father and ran down the street to meet him. Now I could hear him asking about me at the door, and Nevart, Onnik, Mother, all telling him about the awful thing I had done. I decided to run away. I would go to another city, and perhaps to Russia. I was through with school! I thought I could make my living by working as an apprentice in a grocery store, or shoe store, or by selling matches and cigarette paper in the streets.

At nights, after work, Father was always gay. When he took his apéritif in the living room, he would shout, "I am a lord, lord!" Meaning an English lord. He would pat himself on the back and call other men cross-thieves. "Here is my woman, here are my children — what else can a man want?" he would say. The word "woman," as he said it, would embarrass Mother. It sounded like "wench." Father liked to clown. His humor was Rabelaisian. He enjoyed shocking the modesty of the ladies.

After his apéritif, Father would lead us children in an impromptu musical program before we went to the dining room. We had to sing some of his favorite songs, as he stamped his foot on the floor, keeping time. Onnik had to play his violin, with Nevart accompanying at the piano. Sometimes he himself would play the violin, and would amuse us by singing a church hymn, imitating all the shakes of old-time psalmists. He would boast of his past glories in mathematics. In his time, the Armenian school was a real school. When he entered the classroom, all the boys stood up and hailed, "Here comes our master mathematician!" Nobody could give him a problem he could not solve. Yes, sir, they had some real teachers then, not asses and bashibozuks, he would say.

But now the silence downstairs was ominous.

I heard them rising and going to the dining room. I was hungry, but nobody cared. I could smell the peas, and the boiled ox tongue, which Father maintained was a royal dish, and the fish, and the tea. Nobody, nobody loved me. I wanted to die.

I got up and stealthily watched from the window our Greek neighbors across the street. They too had gathered in their dining room and were eating. Helene's head was bandaged. I had not blinded her, but the wound would leave an ugly scar, and nobody would want to marry her, I thought miserably. At the head of the table sat her stern father, Mr. Persides, a distiller. I was afraid of him, but not as much as his own children were. He was an eminently respectable citizen. I could see Mrs. Persides and Delesila, Androniki, Theanon, the three oldest girls, and their brother, Elevtheraki, who was my chum. An older son was studying in Paris. No doubt, they were talking about my crime. I was a disgrace to my family, and my nation, too.

Gradually the room became pitch dark. I was sure there was a burglar under my bed, and another one was hiding in the clothes closet. And there were ghosts. I wanted to yell for help and run downstairs. But I was supposed to be a fearless soldier, a revolutionary, like my Uncle Leon. And he was never afraid.

After I heard them return to the living room, our gorgeous maid, Victoria, came up, lamp in hand.

"Father wants to see you," she said, gravely.

"Is he very angry?"

She nodded. I followed her downstairs and entered the room with my head bent so low I could see only the designs on the rug. Nobody spoke. Seeing Mother's feet in a corner I slowly moved toward her, not daring to raise my head.

"*Esh!* Ass!" Father said, his strongest word of contempt. His nervous arms, trembling, came down on my back. I collapsed to the floor. This was the first time he had struck any of us children. I felt as if God Himself had struck me. I was so crushed, humiliated, though it didn't hurt me physically at all. I was so sorry for him. His hair was turning gray, he worked so hard for us, spared nothing for our comfort and health, sent us to country resorts every summer, while he himself stayed in the sweltering heat of the city, compounding drugs.

I struggled to my knees, hiding my face, not daring to look at him or at anyone else in the room. Crawling up to my mother, and forgetting that I was a brave soldier and revolutionary, I burst into tears in her lap. She let me cry for a while, and then took me upstairs and put me to bed, tucking me in after I said the *Lord's Prayer* in my nightshirt and crossed myself with a shaky hand.

"Tomorrow you must go and apologize to Helene."

"Y-yes, M-Mother."

After she left the room I bawled under my quilt. I felt I could never outgrow this disgrace. About fifteen minutes later Aunt Azniv, our maiden aunt, who was like a second mother to us children, and had recently returned from her pilgrimage to the Holy Sepulcher in Jerusalem, came in and sat down by my bed. Onnik was her favorite also; they slept in the same room.

But she had brought me a little mandolin from Istanbul inlaid with mother-of-pearl, and had sent me a French postcard from Beirut — Napoleon on his horse, a great, subtle compliment.

"*Shad char es,* you're very naughty," she said, with a note of despair in her kindly voice. "Why can't you be like Onnik? He isn't *char* like you."

"But even if he were, Father would never beat him," I said, smothering a sob in my pillow. "I'm the only one who is always p-punished. If a g-glass is b-broken, I b-broke it. If anything is missing, I t-took it. N-no t-tutors, no m-music lessons for me, I have to carry water, I've to go to the grocery and bakery, it doesn't m-m-matter if I wear pants with a p-patch in the seat. Onnik and Nevart can do anything they like."

"They are older, dear. But I'll tell you a story."

Once upon a time, she said, a man had three sons. A thief was stealing their crop at nights, and he asked them to capture him. The first night the eldest son guarded the field, but he fell asleep and the thief stole their crop again. The second night the second son guarded the field, but he too fell asleep, with the same result. The third night it was the turn of the youngest son, Manug. His brothers laughed at him and said he couldn't even catch a fly.

Manug waited for the thief. He cut his finger with his pocket knife and rubbed salt in the wound to stay awake. At midnight he heard a roaring wind-like sound in the sky, and looking up, saw a fiery horse. It had flaming wings, lightning flashed out of its eyes, and it left clouds of sparks behind its hoofs as, flying fast, it made straight for the field. The earth shook when its hoofs struck the ground.

This strange horse began eating the crop. Manug watched it from behind a bush. So this was the thief! He crept toward it and jumped on its back, pulling his rope tight around its neck. The animal stamped furiously, reared on its hind legs, tried to throw him off, but could not. Realizing that it had found its master, the horse pleaded:

"Please let me go! I'll never eat your crop again. And I promise to repay you for your goodness some day. If you ever need me, whistle and say three times, 'Fiery Horse!' I'll be with you at once."

"Very well," Manug said, "I believe you."

He released the horse, and it flew away and disappeared in the sky. Returning home, he told his father and brothers that he had caught the thief, but let him free on his promise to stay away from their field. His brothers called him a fool. But from then on no thief entered their field.

The king had a very beautiful daughter whom he wanted to give in marriage to the best horseman in his kingdom. He sent messengers to all parts of the country to announce a great festival on the palace grounds, at which horsemen would compete for his daughter's hand. She would be seated in a window of the palace, wearing a ring. Whoever jumped high enough with his horse to pull the ring off her finger would win her hand.

And so horsemen from all parts of the kingdom hastened to enter this contest. Manug's older brothers also wanted to compete, as they were good horsemen, and handsome. They wore their finest clothes, mounted their best horses, and galloped off, leaving Manug behind. They wouldn't take him along. "Stupid," they said, "what chance would *you* have?"

Manug had no horse, wore the cast-off clothes of his brothers, and he knew he wasn't handsome. He was despondent, when he suddenly remembered the fiery horse. He went out to the field, whistled, and called out three times, "Fiery Horse!" Instantly, there was a sound like earthquake, and, as if springing out of nowhere, a splendid horse stood before him, with a silver saddle on its back.

"I'm your friend, the fiery horse," it said. "What can I do for you?"

"Take me to the king's festival, please."

"With the greatest pleasure."

As soon as Manug got on the horse, his appearance changed. He looked like a handsome knight. He raced to the festival at top speed. The contest had already begun. When his turn came, he jumped higher than any of the other horsemen, missing the ring only by inches. A tremendous cry of admiration rose from the crowd. "Who is he? Who is he?" everybody asked. But Manug did not wish to reveal his identity. He wheeled around and disappeared.

In the evening, at home, his brothers related to their father the exciting events of the day, and wondered who was the mysterious knight who almost won the prize. Manug, who had changed to his former wretched appearance again, listened and smiled to himself.

But his brothers were not discouraged. On the second day they tried again. And again Manug surpassed them all. He jumped high enough to reach the window and touch the hand of the princess, but failed to pull off the ring. He rode off and vanished before the crowd could learn his identity.

On the third and final day of the contest, Manug snatched off the ring! "He got it! He got it!" people cried. "Hold him! Let's see who he is!" But he was off in a flash, and disappeared again. He thanked the fiery horse, turned it loose, and went home with a rag tied around his hand, to hide the ring. He pretended to have cut his finger.

The royal messengers commanded all the people to another great festival. Everybody had to go on pain of death. So Manug's brothers let him go with them this time. The king's daughter, acting as a hostess, took pity on Manug when she saw him. "What's wrong with your hand?" she asked him. "It's nothing," he replied. "I just cut my finger." "Let me bandage it for you," the princess said. "You are very kind," Manug said, and removed the dirty rag.

The princess drew back as she saw her ring, which had the biggest diamond in the world, gleaming on his finger. Then she smiled, and he smiled back. She took him graciously by his arm and led him before the king. "Father, meet the bridegroom," she said, as Manug bowed.

"Ah!" the king exclaimed, shifting his gold sword to one side, and twirling his mustaches. "So you are the winner! My daughter is yours, take her."

"Thank you, sire," Manug said. "I love her dearly."

In his regal garments, with a gold sword hanging by his side, Manug looked the handsomest man in the kingdom, as he was the luckiest. His marriage to the beautiful princess was celebrated for seven days and nights.

I forgot all my woes as a younger brother when Aunt Azniv finished her wondrous tale. And from then on I was always riding a fiery horse. I owe much to it, even my life.

CHAPTER 4

In an Armenian Village

The ringing sound of horses' hoofs and the rough voices of the drivers roused me from my sleep. Jumping out of bed, I pulled off my nightshirt and wriggled into my clothes, quivering with excitement. And I put on my new shoes with upturned toe-ends for country wear, so light they made me feel like flying. Sliding down the balustrade I dashed out into the street to see the horses.

They moved awkwardly on the flagstones. Horses seldom entered our street, for it was barred to traffic by a wall at its end, between the Persides house and ours. I watched them with a proprietary interest. Two were gray, two chestnut-red, one white. I liked their healthy animal smell mixed with the pungent fragrance of leather, saddlebags, and feed bags filled with barley and straw.

Day was just breaking. A large pale star still glimmered over the Gray Hill, which looked like a monk's cowl now. The rock-hewn Byzantine monastery at its top, ascending like a white aerial stairway to the throne of God, was becoming visible. I was delighted by the freshness and purity of the world at this early hour: a cool blue-gray light. A few swallows were already darting this way and that, swooping up and down, with shrill ecstatic cries.

Shouting and twirling their ropes the drivers — Laz daredevils — had invaded our house. Handsome, well built, of medium stature, they were quick like cats on their feet — wildcats. They wore their tribal costume, gray or black: tight breeches with balloon seats; a smart jacket with two cartridge pockets across the breast, embroidered around the edges and left unbuttoned in front; a cloth-hood wrapped around the head, with the two ends left flapping over the shoulders; shoes with upturned toe-ends like mine. Each carried a dagger or a knife.

Our house was thrown into a flurry of activity. Father had already gone
to his pharmacy and Mother supervised the packing. Kitchen utensils and
provisions were put in baskets, and then covered with rugs and cushions for
us to sit in. Dishes, glassware, a couple of clocks went into bales of bedding,
securely wrapped in carpets or rugs, the drivers jumping all over them as
they pulled their ropes. I ran up and down the stairs, from one room to
another, giggling to myself. From time to time I helped carry a few things.

"Mother, let's take it to the village," I said, holding our stereopticon.
We had an album with pictures of *Barbier de Séville*, *Le Mariage de Figaro*,
Opéra-Comique; buildings and street scenes in Paris. They came to life with
a magic glow in our stereopticon.

"No, it will break," she said curtly.

Rummaging around I dug up under Mother's bed a woman's plumed hat
in a cylindrical box. I did not know Mother had ever worn a "Parisian" hat!
She always put on her somber Turkish charshaf on going out.

"Mother, is this hat yours?"

"Yes," she sighed.

"Why don't you wear it any more? I wish you would!"

She did not answer. I suspected why she no longer wore a hat. She was in
mourning, had been many years. For the same reason she never played our
piano, which was hers, her father had bought it for her when she was young.
There were also pieces of velvet and silk cloth in the cylindrical box, and I
pulled out a little wool bootee, light blue, with a fluffy white pompon.

"Whose is this?" I asked. "Eugenia's?"

"No, it's yours," Mother said, smiling sadly.

I was incredulous. "Did I ever have such tiny feet? Why, I can't even push
my hand into it." I rubbed it dreamily against my cheek, trying to remember
the time when I was so small.

But Mother was annoyed, and she ordered me out of her way.

"A regular mouse. He will dig out everything, you can't keep anything
from him in this house," my paternal grandmother said. She was not going
to the village with us, she was too old for vacations, she said. Neither was
Father, for he had to keep his pharmacy open, but he had promised to visit
us a few days. Our cat was also staying behind.

Neighbors and relatives came to bid us good-bye. The Persides children
watched our preparations enviously, for they did not go to summer resorts as
we did. Helene's head was still bandaged, but I had apologized to her and

we were friends again. The noisy drivers began loading our baskets and bales on their horses.

Sitting in the half-filled baskets, we started off — a ridiculous way of traveling, but the only way to go to the village. A dozen handkerchiefs waved us good-bye.

"Drink milk for us too!"

"Don't forget to bring us a big pumpkin when you come back!"

"And roasting corn!"

"Don't get too fat!"

As we rode down the street, windows opened and the rest of our neighbors waved their hands or handkerchiefs, wishing us a happy vacation.

We passed by our store in the center of the town. I read proudly its name, "Central Pharmacy," written in gold letters on its broad windowpanes in French, Turkish, Greek and Armenian. We could see the Turkish women, their faces covered with black veils, seated on the rush-bottomed chairs, meekly waiting for their medicines, or to be examined by Dr. Metaxas in the back room. Seeing us from behind the prescription counter Father stepped out into the street with Dr. Metaxas, and both were smiling. On Father's swarthy face was the beaming, proud expression: See how I take care of my woman and children!

As we got out of town we rode for a while along the beach, then turned into the mountains. The primitive road coiled through the Pontic Alps.

"Close your eyes," Eugenia said, who was on the same horse with me, in the other basket. She seemed to have made a wonderful discovery. I did, and the horse started going backward. When I opened my eyes again, I saw we were going in the right direction.

"The horse goes back, doesn't it?" Eugenia said.

Both of us were puzzled. And we amused ourselves by closing and opening our eyes.

"Eugenia, look!" A rabbit jumped into the bushes. I began reciting a poem I knew about a rabbit, which always grieved me, because at the end the hunter shot it.

Sometimes Eugenia or I was suspended over a terrifying abyss, a foaming mountain torrent roaring below. A single false step would have hurled us down into the white, raging stream, but our horses moved with the nonchalance of tight-rope walkers, and their drivers sang monotonous Turkish ditties.

I launched my boat,
I am from Rizeh, Rizeh;
I take into my lap
A pretty one like you.

The horses responded to their singing with spirited snorts, which I
would imitate.

It was a full day's journey to the village. And until we approached its
boundaries we were afraid of the drivers. The Lazes were a lawless people
given to piracy and brigandage. They were also Turkey's best sailors and
soldiers. Though fanatic Moslems, they were different from the Turks
proper, were more like the Georgians, and it was said that at one time they
used to be Christians like us.

Once in the village, however, we felt perfectly safe, for we were in
Christian territory there. Father had rented a cottage with a pear tree in
front of the door, already loaded with big yellow pears, and an avenue of
young poplars planted across the lawn. There was a tobacco and cornfield
in the back, sloping down to the wooded bank of a tumultuous stream. After
unloading our goods and receiving from Mother the remainder of their pay,
with the expected bakshish, the drivers departed with their horses, and we
settled down for three months of vacation.

Mother rented from our landlord three sheep and one goat. He was to keep
them with the rest of his flock, but their milk belonged exclusively to us. He was
very respectful and kept saying, "You are welcome on my head, it's an honor."

This village was famous for its healthful climate and drinking water. Its
pears melted in our mouths like some heavenly sugar. Its cheese and butter
were prized in Constantinople. It produced much tobacco and hemp, and its
"chestnut" pumpkins were the biggest of all, each weighing over a hundred
pounds. Boiled pumpkin was a treat for us on long winter nights. And baked
in the oven, it was sold in the streets of the city like roast chestnuts.

Early in the morning the young shepherds gathered the village flocks and
drove them to mountain pastures. Their return at sundown was a great daily
event. Everybody was out, waiting for them. The peasant women cackled
away on the flat earthen roofs of their huts, their fingers busy with distaff
and spindle or knitting needles. The city women, wearing shawls, for
evenings were chilly, strolled up and down the main street, if street it could

be called. The eyes of all fixed on a bold, rocky hill with an ancient chapel and hermits' caves at its top.

We first heard a faint, distant concert of bells which grew louder and louder. And before long the sheep appeared on the hill. We boys let out a yell and raced to meet them, riding on our stick horses. The flock spread down the hill and then surged through the street, led by an advance guard of bearded wise goats, whose larger bells made a hollow mournful sound — like French horns in this pastoral symphony. The torrent of woolly backs and pattering feet branched off left and right. The sheep trotted to their separate pens, their udders so full that their hind legs crooked outward at the hocks. Curly-coated, long-legged lambs hopped along merrily with ewes. We would embrace these darling May lambs, hugging them in our arms.

When the milking started the village became very quiet. We children watched the milking of our sheep and goat by the wife and daughter of our landlord. The daughter would carry a bucketful of warm, rich milk to our cottage. She herself was full of milk, her baptismal cross dangling over the joyous swell of her breasts. Few city girls could compete with these village lassies in looks, envied their blooming complexions. Typical of them was our maid Victoria, born in a near-by village. She had cherry-red cheeks, soft chestnut hair, and a marble-like perfection of face and figure. Victoria had been taken into our family when she was a young girl of nine, and now, at eighteen, she was a real city lady to her village sisters. They were deferential with her, impressed by her clothes, her gold heart, brooch and bracelet. Victoria was indeed elegant. She was like our eldest sister, wasn't treated as a servant, and she took French lessons with Nevart.

There was a former shepherd boy living next door to us who had only one leg, having lost the other in some accident. He watched wistfully the coming and going of the flocks, and played heart-rending music on his pipe. He could not herd sheep any more, that rocky hill was too steep for him to climb with his crutches. An expert gunsmith, he made rifles for us boys out of a piece of board, a wire and an empty cartridge shell. We used real powder, and they sounded like Turkish army rifles when we fired them.

"Watch out the gendarmes don't come," Mother would say, plugging her ears. But we knew there were no gendarmes anywhere near us.

We wanted to pay him for our guns, but he would accept nothing but cigarettes. Consequently Mother could never find out what happened to the cigarettes in our fez-shaped porcelain bowl. She filled it periodically for visitors, and periodically I emptied at least half its contents into my pockets. He liked to smoke them. Made of Baffra tobacco, they had gold tips. It fascinated me to watch him light a cigarette by striking two flints together.

By the middle of June the peasants were harvesting their wheat, and a period of fun began for us boys as we rode on the threshing sledges — two long boards joined together, their underside studded with flints. When the tail of an ox went up, we immediately held a manure pan under it, thus keeping the threshing floor clean. The peasants winnowed their grain by shoveling it up into the air at the close of the day. The wind carried off the chaff and the grain fell to the ground in gladsome showers. But only the more prosperous villagers could afford to eat wheat bread. Most of them ate corn bread, which was cheaper. White city bread was a rare delicacy for them, as their corn bread was to me.

When Uncle Leon came to the village he fired his revolver into the air as he rode to our house, to announce his arrival, as was his custom. I hung from his arm as he entered our cottage. Mother's eyes brightened.

"Let me hold your revolver," I begged him.

"Don't you give that thing to him!" Mother said. "And you had better be careful yourself."

Uncle Leon, however, let me hold parts of his revolver as he cleaned and oiled it. He had just come back from a trip to Constantinople, and brought gifts to all of us. Mine was an ivory pencil, shaped like a feather.

The leaders of the village youth came to greet him. "Welcome, Comrade Leon," they said, proudly shaking his hand. They were fine, brave fellows, with keen, sensitive faces, in Laz costume. Uncle Leon had taught in the village school, and these young men were members of his party. He had "organized" them. They talked for a while about conditions in the village: the tax gatherer had again ruined several families; agrarian disputes with a Turkish village threatened to cause more bloodshed; the tobacco crop promised to be good, but filberts didn't bear so well; there had been letters from villagers who had migrated to Russia and were growing tobacco there.

"The whole village wants to move to Sukhum," they said. "Soon Russia would produce more tobacco than we do."

"Comrades," Uncle Leon said, in a disturbed voice, "you must persuade them to stay. That's exactly what the Turks want us to do. It weakens our forces here. I think better days are ahead for us. In talking with our party leaders in Constantinople I told them of the situation in our region. The new political developments are encouraging. The Great Powers are behind us, and, as you know, the Turkish Government has signed an agreement with Russia for introducing reforms in the eastern provinces."

They questioned him eagerly about these "reforms" — a word I had heard so often. Does Russia really mean business this time? Aren't the Turks up to their old tricks again? Or do they sincerely intend to carry out such measures guaranteeing equal rights to Christians and Moslems? Is it true that government laws would be published also in Armenian, and our language would be acceptable in the courts? Is it true that a Norwegian inspector-general is coming to Trebizond to supervise the execution of this agreement?

And Uncle Leon who had talked with the party leaders in the capital gave them reassuring answers. "Only Germany is against us," he said. "Cilicia isn't included in this scheme, because the Germans consider Cilicia within their sphere of influence. It lies directly on the Berlin-Baghdad railway. So they want no reforms in Cilicia."

"But our last kingdom was in Cilicia," one of the village youths protested, who apparently knew a lot about Armenian history.

"What can you do? Germany is afraid of Uncle Russia, and so is backing the Turks," said Uncle Leon. "The Germans know better than the Turks that reforms in Cilicia would so strengthen the Armenians there that we would soon take things into our own hands. Or, who can tell? Uncle might decide to come down from the Caucasus and bathe in the warm waters of the Mediterranean, thumbing his nose at Germany.

"Russian will be taught in our city school next year," Uncle Leon added.

Nothing had ever excited our school as much as this. We were taught French and Turkish along with our mother tongue — but the implications of studying Russian were so breath-taking, that we felt our mighty Uncle was surely on his way to Trebizond.

Uncle Leon had brought from Constantinople the latest issues of the party newspaper, *Azatamart* (*Battle-for-Liberty*), and *Droshak* (*Banner*), which was published in Switzerland. These young country intellectuals seized these publications eagerly.

"But what's the real attitude of the Ittihad?" one of them wanted to know.

Uncle Leon was again reassuring. "It's common knowledge in Constantinople that the Minister of the Interior, Talaat Pasha, dines and plays backgammon with our party leaders," he said. "And the Ittihad does what he says. Jemal Pasha, the new Minister of the Navy, is also friendly."

"How about Enver?" That was the most magic name of all for the Turks.

"Enver had nothing but praise for our soldiers during the Balkan War. It wasn't easy for our boys to fight against the Christian Bulgarians — with Antranik serving in their army. Well, Dikran, you went through the Battle of Chatalja." Dikran nodded, grimly.

"If it weren't for Dikran, Antranik would have taken Constantinople," one of his friends said, and they all smiled.

But Uncle Leon, though bringing such good news, had also words of caution for them from the party leaders.

"We can dine and play backgammon with them, but we must never cease to organize. They can fool us again. The governor-general pretended to be my father's bosom friend just before they killed him in the Maydan. No, you never know when we may have to use this." He slapped the holster on his hip, in which he had replaced his revolver.

And now their conversation became cryptic. It was evident that they wanted to discuss something very secret. Uncle Leon suggested that they go out for a walk, he wanted to see the new flour mill, he said. I wanted to go with him, but I suspected he had some other news for them which was none of my business to know. Of late he had been engaged in shady dealings, mysterious shipments of goods to the villages and to other towns, received from abroad, which worried Mother no end. Quite a few of these goods went to Van, where I knew the Armenians were especially well "organized." Uncle Leon had opened a wholesale tobacco and grain store, but I was sure it wasn't tobacco or grain he was smuggling, but something in which his party was very much interested.

Onnik and I got up early the next morning to go swimming and fishing with Uncle Leon. Not far from our cottage there was a lovely pool with a waterfall. We undressed and splashed around in the pool, and then Uncle Leon clambered down the rocks and stood directly under the waterfall, letting it strike against his expanded, hairy chest. Onnik and I followed his example, but the huge weight of the water flattened us to the bottom, and laughing, we rolled over in the rushing stream. It was full of fish, and we returned home with a string of trout which Mother grilled for breakfast. U'm, were they delicious! Mother was glad to see Uncle Leon resuming his normal summer-time activities, instead of brooding like her over Uncle Harutiun's death.

Uncle Leon had brought his double-barreled shotgun to the village. Every time he went hunting he came back with his mesh bag bulging with partridges and quail, which Mother fried for supper, and sent some to our relatives and neighbors. After supper, we often sat out on the porch. And while Mother and Aunt Azniv knitted and Victoria crocheted her exquisite laces Uncle Leon told thrilling tales of Armenian revolutionaries: how some of our village young men had fought against Lazes and gendarmes, and won fame even among the Bulgarian comitadjis in Macedonia, for their bravery; how revolutionaries seized the Ottoman Bank in Constantinople and threatened to blow it up unless reforms were granted; how the great David Beg in Karabagh routed the Persians, Turks and Kurds; how the peasants of Zeitun, in the mountains of Cilicia, turned back a Turkish army of fifty thousand men, and did not lay down their flintlocks until the Great Christian Powers intervened and promised to protect their rights.

"Zeitun was never conquered by the Turks," Uncle Leon said. "And Sassoun is just as brave."

I would get so excited by these tales that I fought these battles all over again, shouting "Boom! Boom! Boom!" as I ran around madly.

"There he goes crazy again," Mother would say, with a half smile.

Uncle Leon would always stop at a critical climax in the story. Onnik and I were dying to know what happened next, but he would not tell — until next night, after supper, thus keeping us in suspense. We three males slept in the same room, and when jackals came and howled in our yard, Uncle Leon would grab his shotgun and fire at them through the window. They would stay away from our neighborhood the rest of the night. He never killed one, though, and I never saw a jackal.

There was a merry round of card games, visits, table-tipping séances, hikes and picnics and much group singing at night in the village square. A few of us children gave a play, in which I was cast as a soldier, with a fierce black mustache painted clear across my face with burnt cork. The grown-ups consented to attend our performance in an improvised theater, paying a copper penny for admission.

On Sunday afternoons the peasants danced in the village square, the men in Laz costume, the women in wine-colored velvets and green silks, their red velvet disk-like caps bedecked with gold coins, silver buckles on their red shoes. They danced in a circle, holding each other's hands, or arms thrown over each other's shoulders, advancing and retreating, the leader waving a handkerchief and doing the fanciest steps of all.

Sometimes the men separated from the women, and holding their arms above their heads, their little fingers interlocked, danced on their toes, their individual expressions vanished and their faces beaming in a group ecstasy. Their rhythmic circle now contracted, and their breasts with their cartridge pockets touched each other's — now expanded wide. They would crouch on one knee, then jump up crying *"Alashaghah!"* and crouch on the other knee, jump up again with the same war-like cry, and continue dancing round and round at a furious pace, quivering all over. The quivering was the most characteristic feature of this men's dance. Meanwhile the music of bagpipes and drum would reach its most martial shrill notes, firing the blood of peasants and city folk alike. Occasional shots from firearms added to the gaiety of these dances, which often resulted in a new engagement or marriage, or celebrated one.

At last Father also came to the village, riding on horseback in his funny manner, his legs sticking forward, and his heart in his mouth, so that we could not help laughing when we saw him. It was a miracle he wasn't thrown by the horse on his way, for he was the worst rider in our town. He was accompanied by my two grown cousins, George and Vertanes, both of them pharmacists. (As was their father, Uncle Stepan. Pharmacy was our family profession.)

Father was determined to have all the fun he could, after a year's hard work with not even Sundays off. He spent two days visiting friends, including those at a Greek village, clowning everywhere. His every visit was a hilarious affair, and there were many humorous stories told about him which embarrassed us. I went to the Greek village with him and saw how enthusiastically his Greek friends received him, protesting they did not know he was coming otherwise they would have butchered and roasted a sheep in his honor. They called him "Karapetis," adding a Greek suffix to his name, Karapet.

After he had visited and entertained his Greek friends — they somehow always came first — Father was free to go on an all-village picnic with us. He was very fond of picnics. The fattest sheep was butchered for this occasion, and with our provisions loaded on two donkeys, we started out in the morning, headed for a ferny field near a sacred "milk fountain." Nothing but sweet, cool water flowed out of this fountain, though. We went up a flinty path and then crossed a grassy plateau sprinkled with little globular flowers of yellow gold we called "the Tears of the Virgin." According to the legend every year

St. Mary wept in these mountain meadows — I thought because there were so many poor people; children went to school without overcoats and galoshes in the winter, and our chapel-strewn land was under Turkish rule.

It was from this plateau, with its tears of the Golden-Headed Virgin, fleecy clouds clinging to dark mountains at a level or below us, and the tinkle-tinkle of distant sheep bells floating in the air, that I first perceived the towering beauty of our land. There was a holy incense-like fragrance in the air, coming from flowers and herbs which possessed miraculous healing qualities and bore in their Latin names the title of *Pontica*.

On reaching our camping place we children scattered in various directions, gathering firewood. The sheep was barbecued whole on an open fire, a man turning the spit with many exclamations of delight. After performing our chores, including that of carrying water from the milk fountain, we children picked wild flowers and wove them into wreaths for our heads, and magnificent baldrics and belts. Tablecloths were spread on the grass, under giant shade trees. The baskets were opened. Every family had contributed something special for this outdoor feast. Mother modestly exhibited a loaf of *pât d'Espagne* she had baked, Father's favorite cake. No mean achievement in a village, for the temperature of the oven had to be just right, or the cake burnt.

We children could hardly stand on our feet, we were so hungry, when the meat was finally done to perfection and we all sat down to eat. The lamb fairly melted in our mouths. Raki glasses were filled and toasts were drunk. We ate vine-leaf rolls stuffed with spiced rice and raisins and cooked in olive oil, boiled eggs, salted anchovies, sardines, black and green olives, salad and pickles, homemade *halva*, fig, quince, sour cherry, rose-leaf preserves. Meanwhile jokes and stories were told, especially those of Nasreddin Hoja. I knew a few myself. We appreciated the humor of that semi-mythical Mohammedan schoolmaster, who was never worsted by others, and was always ready with a quip. Once, for instance, Nasreddin Hoja borrowed a kettle from his neighbor, and returned it with a small pan, saying the kettle had given birth to it while in his house, and the neighbor was glad to accept it. A few days later Nasreddin Hoja borrowed the kettle again, and did not return it. When the neighbor wanted it back, he said, "Sorry, my friend, but your kettle died." "How can a kettle die?" the neighbor said angrily. "If you believe the kettle can give birth to a pan, why don't you believe it can also die?" To which of course the neighbor had no answer, and the wily schoolmaster, a poor man, kept the kettle.

The older girls got together and played *vijak*, or fortune. They filled a clay pitcher with the water of the milk fountain, and each girl threw an earring, or ring, or bracelet, or some other personal article into it, meanwhile making a wish. The mouth of the pitcher was closed with seven different flowers. The girls sat in a circle on the grass, the youngest among them holding the pitcher in her lap, seated in the center. They sang a special song — making fun of young men. Then one of the girls made a prophecy by quoting a popular saying or proverb, while another drew out an article from the pitcher. The prophecy just pronounced was to come true in the life of the girl who owned the article, and as it had to do with romance and marriage in most cases, there was an outburst of feminine shrieks and applause every time an article was drawn.

At dusk we gathered armfuls of dried ferns and made a big bonfire. We boys leaped through the flames. Father proposed that everybody sing *Come, Armenians!* He beat time with his foot and waved his arms as we sang:

> Come, Armenians, let us march forward
> And salute again the Constitution...

That was his favorite song. His voice, husky from much smoking, was terrible.

"A solo, Karapet effendi!" people urged him, laughing at his comicalities.

"I wore the surplice when I was a boy," he boasted. "I haven't been to church for fourteen years, ever since I married, so I don't know how they sing in church now. But we did some real singing in my time!"

Clearing his throat he broke into a nasal hymn, imitating all the trills and shakes of old-time psalmists. Even Mother was smiling now, he was so funny.

The difference in their temperaments was never more apparent than during festive occasions like this. Father was always the life of the party. Mother was reserved. She never spoke much. She was thirteen years younger than he, with long brown hair and a milk-white skin, taller by a few inches, and her carriage, looks, the way she walked, everything about her had a noble dignity. She was "like a Circassian" in her youth, and it was common knowledge that a member of the royal Austrian house who had been exiled to Trebizond — an extremely handsome young prince — had fallen in love with her when she was eighteen. But four childbirths, and many shocks and sorrows, had left their marks on her face. She could never forget the murder of her father and uncles in the Massacre, though twenty years had passed since then. The Turkish Government had imprisoned the youngest brother of her father as a revolutionary and condemned him to death by hanging. But before the execution of the sentence a pardon came from the Sultan and he was released from prison, thanks to the efforts of the British consul, who was a personal friend of his. He had previously visited America and could speak English, "hobnobbed with consuls and pashas," as I had heard him described. Banished from Turkey, he went to London, where he married an English woman, and died in exile.

There were so many deep, silent sorrows in my mother's heart. I had seen her crying alone in our kitchen when Father gave a party on his name day, complete with champagne and orchestra. He would shout the French orders for quadrille. Mother never took part in the festivities Father loved. And now, during that picnic, as I saw her smiling, I smiled also. I always suffered, silently, with her, and nothing made me happier than her smile.

We sang all the way back to the village, with Roman candles in our hands, which filled the night with fountains of sparks. We all knew the Turkish march:

> *Yashasun hurriet, edalet, mussavat,*
> *Yashasun millet!*

> Long live liberty, fraternity, equality,
> Long live the people!

Brass-band words borrowed by the Young Turks from the slogan of the French Revolution. That such words should exist in Turkish, we thought... Yet the music was good, and we sang it lustily, with imitations of various band instruments.

Before Father went back to the city the inevitable happened: a political argument with Uncle Leon. The newspaper Father read was the *Byzantion*, which criticized everything *Azatamart* published. To the readers of *Byzantion* the readers of *Azatamart* were hot-headed, irresponsible men, with dangerous ideas about socialism and such things; the readers of *Azatamart* looked down on the followers of *Byzantion* as old fogies and cowardly effendis. The prudent *Byzantion* was careful not to antagonize the Turks, and could be safely read by merchants and bishops.

What was all this nonsense the leaders of his party were spouting? Father demanded. What kind of "high diplomacy" were they playing with the Ittihad, the so-called Committee of Union and Progress, the dominant Turkish political party?

Father was strongly for Armeno-Turkish friendship, and the only Armenian in Trebizond critical of Russia, but to him the Europeanized Turks were far more sinister than the conservative, old-school Turks. He heaped again his scorn and sarcasm on the Armenian Revolutionary Federation.

"It's destroying our nation! It has ruined our schools, disunited our people. What do your leaders know about international politics? Wasn't it all this revolutionary foolishness that caused the Massacre?"

Father was now very serious. A formidable foe in argumentation, he was more than a match even with our scholarly bishop. What could Uncle Leon do against him? He tried to defend his party, but he could never speak his mind freely, out of respect for Father's age and position. Even my cousins George and Vertanes did not dare smoke in his presence — and George was thirty-five and bald. Uncle Leon was only twenty-two.

My mother was on the verge of tears, as Father, in ridiculing our socialistic revolutionaries, recalled an incident connected with her oldest brother Avedis, who had died a few years before Uncle Harutiun. At seventeen or eighteen Avedis, an artistic youth who loved to paint, was the secretary of the local committee of the Armenian Revolutionary Federation — as was Harutiun after him. Avedis had tried to organize the first trade union in Trebizond, and staged a demonstration on May Day by unfurling a large red flag on the Gray Hill, and then with a band of his comrades, mere schoolboys, marching into the city singing *La Marseillaise* and an Armenian socialistic song.

The Turks thought the Armenians of the city had risen in revolt, to establish a kingdom of their own — their old bugaboo — and a mob of Laz cutthroats, dervishes, theological students, and other such patriots, armed to their teeth, gathered in the Maydan, the central plaza, to "suppress" this new rebellion of the infidels. Fortunately the town commandant happened to be a more enlightened man and knew something about May Day celebrations in Europe. When the alarmed leaders of our community appealed to him for protection, he sent troops to disperse the murderous mob, and a massacre was narrowly averted.

"If the Turks had attacked us, we would have defended ourselves," Uncle

Leon said, while Mother got up and left the room. These political arguments in our home made her acutely unhappy.

"Defended with what?" Father shouted.

"Our party had eight hundred members in our region."

"All right, you had eight hundred heroes against how many Turks? — eight hundred thousand, with millions more behind them. Did you expect the British fleet to force the Dardanelles to come to your help — and climb maybe to the top of Mount Ararat? Or did you think the Russian Emperor would declare war on the Sultan because Avedis was waving a red flag and singing socialism?"

I did not know what socialism meant, I did not understand half of what they said. Though it seemed to me that Father was right — he was too smart to be wrong — and though George and Vertanes agreed with everything he said, and disagreed with every thing Uncle Leon said, I was nevertheless heart and soul for Uncle Leon.

In fact I resented my cousins. George — or Brother George, as we children called him — was hardly on speaking terms with Uncle Leon, because of past party quarrels. He had been a member of a rival revolutionary faction, the Hunchak, or Bell, and still had a revolver. But he had resigned from the party, disillusioned and bitter, and withdrawn from all political activity.

Vertanes was popular with us children, and he had taken us on many gay phaeton rides on Sunday afternoons, but he did not even have a revolver. He had never belonged to a party. He was a handsome, debonair cavalier, always flirting with the girls, always involved in some secret romance. His hobby was reading American detective stories, and his heroes were Nat Pinkerton and Nick Carter. A graduate of the French university in Beirut, he had opened the newest pharmacy in the city, and half a dozen matchmakers were busy trying to find him a wife, for he was already twenty-seven. They said he was too particular, he should go to Constantinople to find a wife.

They were three against one. I wanted to ask Father, "Then why do you call Uncle Leon, and not Brother George or Brother Vertanes, to protect you with his revolver when you go out at night?"

Father was in terror of the Turkish toughs who attacked Christian pedestrians in the streets, robbed them, beat them, and sometimes knifed them to death. The main street, from his pharmacy to our home, was fairly safe, but the dark, crooked, narrow side streets were not. We had to carry a lantern when we ventured into these perilous alleys on visiting our relatives. When it was Father's turn to keep his pharmacy open until past midnight, or when he went out after supper, Uncle Leon had to accompany him as bodyguard.

Father and my two cousins returned to the city. Uncle Leon followed them a week later. We continued our vacation, and then suddenly there was a war in Europe. The Great Christian Powers were fighting among themselves. And Turkey, backed by Germany, saw her chance of settling old scores with Russia and her allies — our friends.

As if to signal the approach of our doom there was a total eclipse of the sun at this time. Old women in the village shook their heads and said gravely:

"It's an ill omen. May God protect us."

We found the city a veritable war camp in September, with ships in the harbor unloading troops and supplies, and Turkish soldiers, trained by German officers, marching off to war goose-stepping. Men and materials were being rushed to Erzurum, the great fortress breasting the Russian Caucasus.

There was a general mobilization. Vertanes, wearing the uniform of a Turkish lieutenant, came to bid us good-bye. He, too, was going to Erzurum. He let me play with his sword. I practiced drawing the long, heavy blade out of its scabbard. If he was worried, he tried not to show it. He knew he looked well in his uniform. The ends of his black mustache were waxed and twisted up like Enver Pasha's. He was in the medical corps. He asked Nevart to play the piano for him once more, and when she finished her number, he clapped his hands and cried, *"Bis! Bis! Repetez!"* with his customary enthusiasm. He acted as if he had done nothing all his life but attend concerts.

Uncle Leon, being a widow's sole support, was allowed to pay an exemption tax of forty gold pounds — half of which he had to borrow from Father.

"Before long they will take me too," Father said gloomily. "It's going to be from seven to seventy." The schools opened as usual, but Trebizond was not the same city any more.

CHAPTER 5

My Turkish Playmates

The frog said to the heron, "Please take me up with you, friend heron. I am tired of living in this slimy water."

The heron replied, "Very well, friend frog. Hang on with your mouth to this stick in my beak. Take care not to say anything while we are in the air. Be sure to keep your mouth shut."

"I will not say a word," the frog promised.

So they went up together. The heron flew over fields and mountains, and the frog was delighted. But soon it forgot its promise, and as it opened its mouth to speak, it fell to the ground and was killed.

Our Turkish lesson that day was about the frog that talked too much.

There were many stories with a moral in our Turkish reader. This particular lesson made me think of what my father often said: we Armenians talked too much; we did not know how to keep our mouths shut. Thus we proclaimed our love for Russia, England, and France from the house tops. The Turkish comic paper *Karagoz* had truthfully said, *If you want to know the situation in the Dardanelles, look at an Armenian's face.*

The Turks were very different from us; one could never tell what they really thought, what they really knew. They kept their secrets to themselves, and if they talked, they often meant the opposite of what they said.

Just a few days before, we pupils of the Armenian National School had given three Russian prisoners an ovation. They were Cossack officers and had the faces of tigers. They acknowledged our applause and shouts of admiration by bowing politely and smiling, while their Turkish guards no doubt gnashed their teeth, but said nothing.

Our instructor of Turkish, Mr. Ohanian, was a distinguished-looking man with graying temples and pince-nez glasses. He spoke in a deep resonant voice. We were very proud of him. When Enver Pasha, the Minister of War, came to Trebizond on his way to Erzurum to drive the Russians out of the Caucasus, Mr. Ohanian had surpassed all the Turkish orators by the grandiloquence of his speech at an outdoor patriotic meeting in which we also had participated, carrying little Turkish flags in our hands and singing the new Turkish war song, *"Illeri! Illeri! Forward! Forward!"*

Enver Pasha thanked and complimented Mr. Ohanian. His was the most high-flown and incomprehensible speech, and the Turks were greatly impressed, for the less they understood a speech, the better they liked it. Mr. Ohanian had used many poetic Persian and Arabic words, which moved his Turkish listeners to patriotic raptures, though there were not five men in the city who could understand them.

Now, in the classroom, he took off his glasses and wiped them with a silk handkerchief. Then replacing them on his nose, he said in his magnificent Turkish, "We shall next have an exercise in orthography."

Immediately we opened our copybooks and tested our Turkish reed pens by pressing them against the inside of our thumbs. Turkish orthography was difficult, for, as in shorthand, we had to omit most of the vowels, but the decorative wiggles and tails of the Arabic alphabet were most pleasing. We wrote Turkish from right to left, with special reed pens. In perfect, respectful silence, we took down Mr. Ohanian's dictation, and only the scratching of our reed pens could be heard in the classroom.

Suddenly a terrific explosion shook the windowpanes. Mr. Ohanian frowned. He got up from his chair, stepped down from the platform, and looked through the window.

"I am afraid a munitions dump in the harbor has blown up," he said.

Another explosion, more violent, followed these words.

The school bell rang the fire alarm. We ran down the stairway into the playground, while the mysterious explosions became one continuous thunder.

"The Russian warships are bombarding the city!" our director cried out excitedly. "To the church! Everybody go to the church!"

And to the church we ran, joyously. Here we felt perfectly safe, for its cross was clearly visible from the sea, and we imagined the Russians were Christian warriors coming to save us from the Turkish yoke. Perhaps the

Russians were already landing troops! We thought that under Russian rule Trebizond would become a modern port, a real European city with straight streets and electricity. There was no more magic word in our vocabulary than "electricity." It summed up all the glamor of Paris, London, New York.

I was in heaven, listening to the thunder of the Russian guns. The bombardment lasted about an hour, and was followed by a deathly hush, as if a volcano had erupted like Vesuvius and buried the town under the rumbling torrents of its lava, although the Christians were somehow miraculously alive, while all the Turks were dead.

Presently a mob of hysterical women were clamoring for us at the gate. Aunt Azniv had come to take my brother Onnik and me home.

"Were you afraid?" she asked, pressing us to her.

"Not a bit," I assured her. I was disgusted. I saw a platoon of Turkish soldiers marching down the street. "I thought the Russians had landed troops," I said.

"Shsh! Be careful! Remember what Father said. The walls have ears," Aunt Azniv cautioned me, carrying a finger to her lips.

On our way home German army trucks loaded with Turkish soldiers roared down the main street. The war had brought the first automobiles to Trebizond, and the Turks believed they were driven by *shaitans*, devils, but I knew better. Automobiles were like electricity, products of modern civilization, of European science.

As we passed by the French school, now converted to a Turkish military hospital, we saw a group of German army nurses, young women with pink cheeks and determined chins. They had red crosses on their white caps and arm bands. This strange Alliance of the Christian cross with the Turkish crescent disturbed and puzzled me.

"Have the Germans become Mohammedans?" I asked Aunt Azniv.

"No, my dear, I don't think so. But they might as well be," she added indignantly.

The next day we went to school as usual. Many boys exhibited pieces of Russian shrapnel, and asked big prices for them. I got one by trading for it a Nestlé chocolate premium, a pocket mirror with the picture of a pretty girl on the back of it, and two rare stamps. That lovely piece of jagged steel was now my prized possession. It symbolized the might of Christian Russia.

We were so restless and distracted in the classroom that even Mr. Ohanian had to rap for order and attention. Well, sooner or later the Russians would be in Trebizond. The Turks weren't going to stop them. Why, one of those Cossacks could cut down fifty Turks!

Two months later the Russian fleet bombarded Trebizond again, and this time it seemed they would really land troops and occupy the city. The new bombardment lasted five hours. Buildings were crashing down all around us. It was a terrifying, yet glorious experience. But the Russian warships steamed away at nightfall, and from the balcony of a neighbor's house, in the shell-proof basement of which we had taken shelter, we watched them disappear.

The next day both Turks and Christians fled to villages. We moved to Zefanoz, where my grandmother had an estate. It was a cold, rainy day in February. On reaching the village we found both of Grandmother's houses requisitioned by a prominent Turkish official, Remzi Sami Bey. His uniformed orderlies had taken the keys from the caretaker and were busy cleaning the buildings. His wife and children were expected to arrive momentarily.

We stood in the rain, shelterless. It was revolting. But what could we do? To oppose a government requisition was a crime punishable by death. We wondered whether his wife belonged to the old bigoted or the new "enlightened" class of Turkish women.

Happily she turned out to be of the latter. She was unveiled, which meant she was emancipated and civilized. She and her two sons, riding on horseback, were accompanied by a few soldiers. Pale, slender, chic, she was extremely attractive. She told us that she was born and educated in Constantinople. We relaxed.

Her name was Selma Hanum. She apologized in exquisite Turkish phrases for the inconvenience she had caused us, and she said she did not know the houses had been requisitioned without their owner's knowledge and consent. She was sorry. However, because of her husband's official position, which necessitated many important conferences in their home with high German and Turkish officers, they had to live in this village, which was close enough to the city, yet out of the reach of the Russian guns. Perhaps we could rent to her the large house? *Rent?* We could hardly believe our ears. She was a real lady. With mutual thanks and compliments an agreement was reached.

She talked with us freely and without covering her face, for we had no menfolk with us. Father had to remain in the city to keep his pharmacy open, as required by law, and Uncle Leon was to join us in the village a few weeks later. She expressed the wish, patting my head, that Onnik and I would play with her two sons, Mahmut Bey and Shukri Bey. As their father was a bey, they were beys too, and she called them by their titles. Both were fair, good-looking boys, in European clothes. We had never played with Turkish children before, but now we shook hands and talked like friends.

We got the small house back. It rained for several days in succession, and we were kept indoors. I was so restless that Mother said to me, "What's the matter with you? Have you worms in your blood?" I couldn't sit still a minute. Grandmother dug up an old copy of *Robinson Crusoe* in Armenian translation, with calf binding, and gave it to me to read. I was nine years old, and was pleased by the compliment. I had never read anything but my textbooks before. I knew the story of Robinson Crusoe — every boy in our school did — but now I learned all its exciting details. And no other book I have read since then has given me so much pleasure.

Selma Hanum paid us a ceremonious visit, which we duly returned. After this exchange of diplomatic courtesies, we became good neighbors, and Onnik and I played with Shukri Bey and Mahmut Bey. Their mother would watch us approvingly. Mr. Ohanian was also in the village, and she engaged him as Turkish tutor for her sons. I was very happy because he was a poor man and had a family to support. We had no idea Turks could be so nice. Selma Hanum won us over completely.

In a few weeks the winter was over. The crocus bloomed. The vendors of charcoal who came to the village with their donkeys had clusters of that bright flower tucked under their headgear or the turban of their fezzes, indicating the arrival of the spring. By the middle of April the plums and sour cherries were ripe in Zefanoz. We boys played from morning to night; the days were simply too short.

I awoke one morning with the gay riot of sparrows under the eaves of our roof. Onnik threw a pillow at me. I threw it back at him, and we chased each other on all fours, growling and barking like dogs.

"Stop that racket!" Mother cried. "You can take an example from Shukri and Mahmut. See how gentlemanly, how well behaved they are."

We had to agree that they were. We were pretty wild and rough compared to them. They wore long pants, too, though they were not older than we.

"Onnik! Zavén!" Shukri and Mahmut called us from the lawn, standing under the windows of our bedrooms. *"Sabahunuz hayir olsun!* May your morning be felicitous!"

"Sabahunuz hayir olsun!" we returned, leaning out of the window.

Mother smiled. They were so glad to see us. It seemed they couldn't get along without us.

"Come on down, and let's play tip-cat," Shukri begged. He sent a small stick flying through the air with a blow of his bat. "See how I have improved!"

"You certainly have," we agreed. We had taught them the game. We were their only playmates in the village; they did not associate with other boys, not even Turks. Dressing in a hurry, we ran downstairs. What a gorgeous morning! Not a speck of cloud in the sky, butterflies with yellow or spotted blue wings hovered over the rhododendrons and blackberry bushes, the laurel trees were heavy with purple clusters, and the blackbirds whistled here and there. The sea was as blue as the sky. In the east rose the sharp crest of Lazistan, and behind it, in the hazy distance, we could see the silvery, cloud-like pinnacles of the Caucasus mountains.

I had planted some beans under an acacia tree, and dashed over to see if they had sprouted. Clawing the earth back, I felt them with the tip of my finger. They were firm. They had taken root!

"My beans are growing!" I shouted excitedly, and grabbing Mahmut whirled around with him. He was happy too.

"We have sunk another English battleship," he said. "Father got the news last night."

"Our soldiers in the Dardanelles are eating English chocolate," his brother Shukri added, laughing.

But what was good news for them, was bad news for us. I became glum. Mahmut sang *"Illeri! Illeri!"* and marched across the lawn. He was always playing soldier, like me. But while I aspired to be another Napoleon, his idol was Enver Pasha. He maintained that Enver Pasha was greater than Napoleon and would clean up Russia, England, and France. I was careful not to betray my feelings too much, and did not argue with him.

After breakfast we played tip-cat with them, and then watched the Turkish recruits drilling on our lawn. Remzi Sami Bey had transformed part of our lawn into a drill ground. The Christian soldiers were not given arms any more and were herded in labor battalions. For them life in the Turkish Army was hell. But even the Moslems suffered. I felt sorry for these recruits. They were such a miserable, submissive lot, just resigned to their kismet. They never joked or laughed. Some of them were barefooted. They lived on bean soup and brown bread, but the soup was like dishwater, and lucky was the man who fished out a bean. They were starving. This group was almost ready to go to the front; they had finally learned which side was left, and which side right. The sergeants had an awful time teaching them that. I knew the commands much better than they.

While we were watching them drill, and the air was filled with the hoarse shouts of the sergeants, the telephone rang. Telephones were strictly for high official use, and Remzi Sami Bey had installed one in the large house. This particular call was for Shukri and Mahmut, and came from another village. They ran to answer it, and then told us proudly that they had just talked to the sons of the governor-general, who was coming to spend a week with them. Their fathers were close personal friends.

The guests arrived in the afternoon, on horseback, with a few orderlies. I disliked them intensely the minute I met them. The three sons had mean faces, and were loud and spoiled. Shukri and Mahmut included us in all their plans for the week, but their guests could barely hide their contempt for us. We were nothing but giaour dogs in their eyes. We were afraid to antagonize them; otherwise we would have preferred not to have anything to do with them.

The youngest, about my age, was the meanest. We played marbles and knucklebones, and he flew into a rage when he lost. In the running game, "taking prisoner," I purposely let him catch me a few times, though I could run faster than he. When I caught him, he insisted he had not crossed my boundary. We had an argument. I was willing to let him have his way, since his father was governor-general and our lives were in his hands. I wanted to be diplomatic, since we were living in dangerous times, but I lost my patience.

"Giaour dog, you can't talk to me like that!" he shouted in my face. "You don't have many more days to live anyway. We will cut your throats. We will massacre all of you. We will not leave a single Armenian alive!" He moved his hand across his throat and showed me how they would butcher us.

Onnik and I were stunned. We left the game, and stared at them with wide-open eyes. None of the other boys denied it, though they did not repeat the threat themselves. I looked at Shukri and Mahmut, hoping they would say it wasn't true and would apologize. They had always been so courteous to us, but now they acted as if we were complete strangers. So it was true then. So they all knew it. Even Shukri and Mahmut knew it. They had heard their fathers discussing it in their "conferences." They had heard them planning secretly to massacre us, and had not breathed a word to us about it! We had been playing together all these months, we had become almost like brothers, while they knew all the time our days were numbered.

"Don't say a word," Onnik cautioned me. "Let's go home."

And unable to give vent to the rage that shook my rebellious soul, to make a single gesture of defiance, I went home with my brother, with bowed head.

Our elders took this threat very seriously. The indiscreet child had let out a family secret. They began to talk of the massacre twenty years before, during the reign of Abdul Hamid. I sat on the divan in the living room, listening to their grave, worried conversation. Cold blades wielded by turbaned fanatics, wild-eyed mullahs and dervishes flashed before my eyes, and I kept feeling my throat with my fingers. Massacre became an imminent reality, and not a vague concept of something dreadful that had happened in the remote past. We were doomed to die, to be butchered, all of us. The governor-general and Remzi Sami Bey had decided in their "conferences," in the presence of Selma Hanum, Shukri, and Mahmut, to cut our throats, not to leave a single Armenian infidel alive. And all this time our neighbors had smiled at us…

I remembered the lesson in our Turkish reader about the heron and the frog.

CHAPTER 6

My Mother Turned Me Over to the American Flag

A Turkish soldier with fixed bayonet stood at our door. A Turkish soldier was stationed before every Armenian house in the village and we saw numbers of them guarding the roads, their bayonets flashing in the early morning sun. The sparrows were chirruping under the eaves of our cottage as usual, my beans were opening their fuzzy leaves, the blackbirds whistled, and in the blue bays of Lazistan lateen-rigged sailing boats floated like graceful white swans in painted lagoons. But the Turkish soldiers kept watch on us like grim sentinels of death.

Our alarm increased when we saw that the door and windows of the large house in our lawn were closed and all the curtains drawn. The Turkish family which rented it from us apparently did not want us to appeal to them for help.

"Go downstairs and see if the soldier will let you out," Mother told me.

But he would not, even though holding up my pants I told him in Turkish I had to hurry to the toilet.

"*Yasak der,* it is forbidden," was his answer.

"Why are you standing here?" I asked him innocently, as if I were too young to comprehend anything.

He ignored my question. I went upstairs. "The soldier says it is *yasak der* to go out," I told Mother.

Uncle Leon, who had been watching this mysterious siege from behind a window, snapped his fingers and exclaimed under his breath:

"They are searching for arms. That's it! They are going to disarm the Armenians in the village. Look at those *chetas*. They are entering Uncle's house."

We saw a party of men in top boots and lambskin caps going into the house of Mother's uncle.

"The dogs!" Mother said.

The *chetas* were the party troops of the Ittihad, mounted irregulars composed of highway robbers, pirates, cutthroats and degenerates of all types released from the prisons. Instead of fighting the Russians at the front they were charged with the responsibility of maintaining "the internal order and security" of the country... We could distinguish them from the regular soldiers by their ferocious appearance and Circassian clothes.

"Where shall I hide my rifle?" Uncle Leon said to Grandmother and Mother.

I did not know he had a rifle. The possession of a rifle by an Armenian was too terrible to even think of. But Uncle Leon was a fearless hero.

After a brief anxious consultation they decided to hide it under the roof. Uncle Leon produced a Martini rifle from our bedroom. I had never seen it! He wrapped it up in a blanket, climbed through an opening in the ceiling and hid it away under the roof. His Mauser revolver, bandoliers and a small heavy tin box of ammunition were also pushed into various cracks and holes.

Presently the *chetas* came to our house. They deposited on the lawn a pile of antique horse pistols, flintlocks, curved Persian swords, shotguns, meat knives, and walked in, the proud guardians of Turkish law. The leader, a towering Circassian speaking with a strong guttural accent, said to Uncle Leon:

"We have orders to search you. So hand over your arms and save us, time."

"You are welcome to search me," Uncle Leon said. "I have no arms."

The blood-red eyes of this formidable ex-pirate or highway robber narrowed to a murderous gaze. "If we find any weapons on you or in this building we would have to arrest you. Armenians who conceal their arms will be shot immediately."

I marveled at Uncle Leon's coolness as he replied with a quick smile:

"Yes, I know."

"Search him!" the leader said to his men.

Uncle Leon raised his arms, and two of these cutthroats felt around his waist and pockets. Then they made us unroll our bedding and carefully examined the mattresses, quilts and pillows. They emptied out the contents of every drawer, trunk, box and closet they saw, and even shoveled out our charcoal. They removed the rugs from the floors and everything that hung on the walls. I think during this systematic search, especially when they looked at the ceilings, Grandmother and Mother died a few times. But they could not find anything and had to be satisfied with our meat knife in the kitchen.

By noon the guards withdrew and we were free to go out. Our Turkish neighbors opened their doors and windows, but Shukri and Mahmut no longer ventured to our side of the lawn.

A feeling of apprehension, nay, of panic, seized all the Armenians in the village. Even those who had maintained that a massacre was unthinkable, that the days of Sultan Hamid were over and Turkey had made much progress since then, were convinced this was a very bad sign.

Even though traveling for Christians was forbidden, and going to the nearest town required a passport which no Armenian could hope to get, and mail service had ceased, yet somehow news of events in Constantinople, Van, Erzurum and elsewhere in Turkey reached us in Zefanoz. All the outstanding Armenian intellectuals in the capital, hundreds of poets, journalists, teachers, doctors, lawyers, pharmacists, and even members of the Ottoman parliament, had been rounded up by the police in one night and sent under heavy guard to the interior, nobody knew exactly where. They had disappeared and had not been heard from. In Van an Armenian uprising had taken place after their leaders were treacherously seized and murdered by the governor-general Jevdet Bey, who was Enver Pasha's brother-in-law, and the entire Armenian community there was threatened by a general massacre. The Turks were bombarding the Armenian quarters of Van from the fortress. The Van Armenians were famous fighters and Uncle Leon was confident they would resist to the last man.

In Trebizond the blow first fell on the Russian subjects, several of whom were in Zefanoz, and we had relatives among them. They were summoned to the palace of the governor-general to hear an "important message" — and never returned. We understood they were put in boats and deported to Kerasund, in the custody of gendarmes and *chetas*.

About a week later a proclamation by the governor-general was posted in the streets of the city and announced by town criers. Copies of it reached

Zefanoz and Mr. Ohanian, our instructor of Turkish, read and translated it to the anxious people who gathered around him. He wiped his pince-nez glasses with a silk handkerchief exactly as in our classroom before he started reading that lengthy edict. It went like this:

> Our Armenian fellow-countrymen, having allied themselves with the enemies of the state and religion, and being in revolt against the government, are to be deported to special districts in the interior and shall have to remain there for the duration of the war.
>
> We hereby order every Armenian in the province of Trebizond to be ready to leave in one week, June 24 to July 1. Every Armenian without a single exception is subject to this decree. Only those who are too ill and too old to walk will be temporarily exempted from the deportation and taken care of in government hospitals. Armenians from this day on are forbidden to sell anything and are allowed to take with them on their journey only what they can carry with them. No carriages can be supplied.
>
> In spite of their ingratitude the government will not deny its Armenian subjects its usual paternal care and protection, will keep their houses and stores under seal, and restore them to their owners when they return from their temporary exile.
>
> We are forced to take this extreme measure for the defense of the fatherland as well as for the good and security of our misguided Armenian fellow-countrymen. If any Armenian opposes this decision of the government by armed resistance or otherwise, or tries to hide himself, he will be taken dead or alive. All those who hide an Armenian or give him food, shelter or aid of any kind will be punished by hanging, whether they be Moslems or Christians.

Mr. Ohanian wiped off the beads of perspiration that had sprung up on his scholarly brow. The color was completely gone from his face.

"I devoted my life to the teaching of the Turkish language," he said in a voice charged with emotion, "and now I have to read and translate a proclamation like this."

People discussed the implications of this order and I listened eagerly.

"The Germans have deported thousands of Belgians, but this is not a mere copying of German methods. This accursed government wants to destroy our nation."

"Calling us ungrateful when Armenians have built Turkey! We have built the palaces in which their bloody sultans live, we have built their greatest mosques, we have sewed their clothes and made their shoes and treated their sick and even taught their children how to read and write their own language. We have built and they have destroyed. And now the Ittihad is going to solve the Armenian question by exiling all of us, men, women and children."

"Where are they going to send us?"

"To the Arabian deserts. That's where they are sending the Armenians of Erzurum. We have to walk to Mosul and Baghdad."

"It would take us at least four months to reach Mosul."

"This is wartime and the government is disturbed by what has happened at Van, so wants to remove the Armenian population farther away from the front as a military necessity. I think, on the advice of the German high staff. We shall suffer, yes, but deportation is better than massacre."

"What we should do is to escape to the mountains, as many of us as possible, and fight our way to the Russian lines."

This proposal thrilled me. Oh, boy, how I would fight!

"Don't talk nonsense. It will be sheer suicide. Fight with what? Can we muster up fifteen rifles?"

They argued pro and con. Uncle Leon summed up the discussion by saying out of the corner of his mouth:

"Whatever will happen will happen to us men." Meaning the government's intention was to kill the men, but merely deport the women and children.

And that seemed to be the general belief.

Uncle Leon was one of the few known revolutionaries in the village and, being a marked man, friends urged him to take his rifle and go join the band of peasant deserters in the mountains, among whom was his cousin Barnak. But he shook his head:

"I can't leave my mother alone."

"Don't worry about me," Grandmother said. "I have lived long enough. You run away and save yourself."

"I am going to stay with you no matter what happens."

When in the evening Remzi Sami Bey, who had been extremely busy that week with conferences in the city, returned to the village, a delegation of Armenian women headed by Mother appealed to him to spare the women and children.

"We don't know where to turn, whom to appeal to except you. You are our neighbor, you know us," Mother said, blushing.

Others, more frank and voluble, raised their voices, half protesting, half begging him to exempt the women and children. At his request this meeting took place on the lawn next to ours. His wife and sons kept discreetly out of sight. Standing like a god before us the mighty bey listened to these appeals, and then gave his official answer in a thundering voice.

"Ladies, *Hanum effendiler!* The Armenians of Van revolted to stab our heroic army in its back, while the regiments of Armenian volunteers in the Russian army are carrying on a war of extermination against us. We were obliged to withdraw from Van, and the unprincipled traitors there who have taken up arms against their own government have committed terrible atrocities on the peaceful Turkish population."

He paused, surveyed the crowd before him, and throwing back his big, handsome head roared louder. "The Russians have set up an Armenian government in Van under the presidency of the chief of those bloodthirsty fiends, and the very existence of our fatherland is threatened! We are very sorry, but we have to remove all Armenians without exception to the interior in order to protect the rear of our army. I give you my word of honor that our gendarmes will protect you on your way and no harm whatever will come to you. The Ottoman State is magnanimous. After the war, which cannot but end by the complete victory of our arms, you will be permitted to return to your homes and receive back all your properties and goods. The day will come when you will realize that Russia and your own comitadjis are your worst enemies, and you will thank the government for securing the freedom and safety of the country and your own future happiness and prosperity by the expedience of temporary exile."

He turned on his heel, and strode back to his house.

For some reason I visualized the Armenians of Van as human warriors living and battling in a red sky. Oh, if I could only be at Van! If I could somehow fly on a fiery horse to those red clouds! The word "Van" constantly hammered in my mind as I lay in bed that night, unable to sleep.

The next day all the Armenians in the village were busy preparing for departure. Women and girls sewed knapsacks, breeches and caps as if they were going on a vacation. Mother hoped we might be exempted from the deportation, Father being a pharmacist. The government surely could not afford to deport him when epidemic diseases killed more soldiers than enemy bullets and pharmacists were even scarcer than doctors. We were quite certain Father would attach himself to an army hospital or do something like that to save us. There were many influential Turks among his friends and clients, and he was known to be a conservative man, opposed to our political parties.

While the women were busy packing up, we boys raided the hazel groves to cut walking sticks. The shoots we had envied in vain — strong, straight, marvelously flexible — now fell under the blows of our pocket-knives. We scraped the bark off with a bit of glass, and carved our initials and various elaborate designs on the handles. Thus we felt fully equipped to travel to Mosul or Baghdad. I was ready to walk clear around the world, like the Danish globe trotter I had met in school, and whose autographed picture I prized so highly.

In a reckless, cheerful mood we boys invaded the cornfields, slashing at the young corn and crushing it under our feet. We did not want the Turks to gather the crops planted by Armenian peasants. Then we broke into the orchard of Mother's aunt. Her sour cherries were ripe, and we devoured fistfuls of them. She appeared in the doorway of her cottage, a severe old dame dressed in black.

"Hey! You good-for-nothing rascals! Get out of my orchard!" she cried. "I was keeping those cherries to make jam."

"Jam?" We burst out laughing.

"Do you want the Turks to come and eat them?" I asked her, swinging merrily on top of a tree.

She realized that this was not an ordinary cherry season, that in a few days we would be on our way to Mesopotamia, and she need not worry any more about serving her guests the sour-cherry sherbet of which she was so proud. And, shrugging her shoulders, she went in.

On the afternoon of that same hectic day Mother received a note from Father. Unlike the other families we did not make any preparations as we did not know what Father wanted us to do. His note was laconic and gave us no hope of a possible exemption. He asked us to take only a few blankets with us and return to the city, to Aunt Shoghagat's house.

We looked like a group of forlorn refugees as we left Zefanoz. We did not lock the door of our house, knowing the futility of doing so. Turkish peasants, sensing the rich booty in store for them, had already gathered like vultures around the village. Since we were forbidden to sell anything and had to travel to Mesopotamia on foot, our possessions were of no earthly use to us anyhow. We were not so naive as to believe the government would keep them under seal, in spite of Remzi Sami Bey's assurances.

What I regretted most leaving behind me was my potted pink carnation. I watered it for the last time and hid it on the roof. I would have asked Shukri and Mahmut to water and take care of it during my absence, and also to be kind to my beans, but their door and windows were closed again. All departures make one not only sad, but forgiving. I wanted to shake their hands and say good-bye, but they did not come out of their house.

On our way back to Trebizond we met a Turkish family, obviously going to a village for their summer vacation. The women rode astride on donkeys holding their little ones in their laps, while the men jogged along the dusty road, big checkered handkerchiefs tied around their perspiring necks. We were curious to know how the rank and file of the Turks, families like this one, took the deportation order. The women were veiled and we could not see their expressions, but the men seemed to tell us with their sad eyes: "Why should such things happen? Isn't there room enough for all of us to live in peace? You have done us no harm, and we wish you no harm. Allah be with you."

The city was dead. Practically all the stores were closed, the streets deserted. Now and then a Turk passed by, grave and silent. We almost wept when we saw the shutters of our pharmacy drawn too, in broad daylight. That was something we had never seen before. Poor Father! What was he thinking of, what was he doing, now that they had taken his pharmacy away from him?

Aunt Shoghagat, Father's sister, older than Aunt Azniv, lived in a Turkish ward. We went down a very narrow street that descended like a winding stairway to the beach, a ghostly lane impervious to the sun, cool as caverns and smelling of the refuse of the sea. Life in this Turkish street was so very different, so somber and mysterious, with latticed windows and exhortations from the *Koran* carved over the façade of an old public fountain. Here we saw a few women fill their brass ewers, different in shape from those Christians used. They had longer and narrower necks. These women were shrouded and bundled in the mystery of the East, and only their fingertips tinged with henna were uncovered. As they walked before us clitter-clattering in their clogs we could not tell whether they were toothless old hags or beautiful girls and brides.

Toward the lower end of this gully-like street where it made a sharp, precipitous turn for the beach was Aunt Shoghagat's house. Whenever we visited her it was my privilege to pull the bell-wire that stuck out through a crevice in the wall. I reached for it and pulled it a few times. The bell rang at the other end of the wire, in the front room.

"It's Vardanush," my sister Nevart said, as we heard the clitter-clatter of clogs across the cobbled yard.

We could tell by the sound of the clogs who it was coming to open the door, whether Aunt Shoghagat, or one of her two daughters. Vardanush ("Rosesweet") was a tall flat-chested girl with auburn hair, and being twenty-three and still unmarried was considered an old maid. Though she was our cousin we children called her Sister because she was grown up and calling her merely by her first name would have been disrespectful.

Opening the door she greeted us without her customary smile and gaiety. Her eyes were red, as if she had not slept all night or had been crying. But visiting them had always been a treat for us children. Their rickety old cottage overlooking the sea was such a homey, sunny, quaint little place. Pumpkins of the enormous "chestnut" variety grew in the walled-in yard, climbing over the laundry shed. They had a miniature garden in the back over which they lavished much love and care. It was just large enough for one orange and two pomegranate trees, and could be entered only through a trap door on the floor of the living room. They hung on the walls of the rooms ripe oranges and pomegranates with their branches. They raised silkworms, wove rugs and attended the Turkish weddings in their neighborhood. Everything they did was charming and unusual.

We four children, carrying blankets on our backs rolled in soldier style, ran into the cottage, making our usual enthusiastic, noisy entrance. Father had taken his shoes off and was seated cross-legged in a corner of the divan in the living room.

"Hello, Father," we said cheerfully. Tears glistened in his eyes and he turned his face away, toward the wall. I had never seen tears in his eyes before, and his appearance and the way he turned his head made a most painful impression on me. Father's face was gray with a few days' beard, and he had become a silent, shrunken, utterly broken man.

Everybody in the room looked despondent, as if they were living their last days. Uncle Stepan, Father's eldest brother, who for fifty years had been a pharmacist and had always refused to retire, now for the first time was really an old man. He did not tease me, did not tell me "you dropped it, you dropped it," as was his habit on seeing me. (I would look around me,

wondering what it was that I had dropped, while he chuckled.) How was
Uncle Stepan going to walk to Mesopotamia? He was sixty-seven years old
and his hair was all white. My paternal grandmother looked more angry
than despondent. Her muslin kerchief drawn tight over her silver head she
sat cross-legged like Father, counting the beads of her rosary, the same
majestic woman of eighty-eight. She looked angry with God. I thought even
God had to bow and kiss her hand.

We children brought into the room a breath of free nature, remembered
pleasures of vacations in the country, a cheering vitality and anarchy.
Gradually they recovered some of their former spirit and began to talk and
ask us questions, although Father continued to remain silent, as if he would
have cried if he opened his mouth.

"We have heard so much about your doings and sayings in Zefanoz,"
Aunt Shoghagat told me, a faint smile spreading over her dark, homely face.
"Come on, let's see what a good soldier you are."

They urged me to prove my proficiency in Turkish military drill, as if that
were the last thing they wanted to see before they died. And hoping to cheer
them up, since l was expected to be amusing, to do and say odd, entertaining
things, I barked like a hard-boiled Turkish sergeant, and marched up and
down the room, knelt and fired, fell prone on the floor and continued firing,
then leapt to my feet for a bayonet charge, and finally presented arms and
yelled at the top of my voice, *"Padishamiz chok yasha!* Long live our great
King!" (The Sultan.)

I was glad to see that even Father smiled.

At Zefanoz we had a sense of comparative freedom and security and
were ignorant of the terrible events that were taking place in the city. Those
Russian subjects who had been deported a week before by the sea route had
been shot by the gendarmes and *chetas* who followed them in another boat,
and their bodies were thrown overboard. One of the men, the well-known
revolutionary Vartan, was wounded in the head, but was still alive, and as
this massacre had taken place at night the gendarmes had not seen him
when he swam ashore. He returned overland to Trebizond, so crazy that he
was arrested in the streets and sent for "treatment" to the military hospital
where Vertanes worked as a pharmacist. He was isolated from the other
patients and given a poisonous injection, but Vertanes had managed to see
him before he died and thus learned what had happened to him and the
other Russian subjects.

The police were after the revolutionaries, the only men the government feared, and they were already being arrested and deported by the "sea route," although, officially, the deportation order was not yet in effect. Boats sailed away loaded with prominent members of the Revolutionary Federation and after a few hours returned empty. Several hundred other men had been arrested and sent to a concentration camp, the Armenian monastery a few miles out of the town, off the highway to the interior. Our bishop, the prelate, was arrested too, but his "offense" apparently was a much graver one, and he was sent to Erzurum to be court-martialed. He never reached Erzurum. The guards murdered him on the way.

A few Armenians went mad and committed suicide. One man in our neighborhood slashed his throat with his razor and jumped dramatically to his death from the balcony of his house. Uncle Stepan and his family had come back from the village of Tots, where gendarmes had seized the Catholic priests of the Mekhitarist Congregation and shot and bayoneted them in a glen. We had spent a summer vacation in Tots, and I knew those learned priests.

From the beginning I noticed that the other men did not look with favor upon Uncle Leon's presence in our midst. After a conference in the bedroom, my cousin, Brother Antranik, acting as spokesman for the group since we were in his house, said to Uncle Leon:

"The police are looking for the revolutionaries. If they find you here with us, they will take us for revolutionaries too. So you had better go to your house."

Asking the youngest man to go find his own salvation when they knew it was tantamount to driving him into the arms of the police was more than I could bear. But though violently indignant I did not dare voice a single word of protest, nor did Mother.

Uncle Leon turned red, looked embarrassed. He got up and apologized, said he did not know he wasn't wanted, and taking Grandmother by the arm walked out of the room. They were hurt.

Greek friends who might have been able to help us were scattered in various villages. But Dr. Andrew Metaxas was in town, and he came to see us, like an angel sent from heaven. He was our only hope, our sole means of communication with the outside world. It required real courage to visit us in a Turkish street.

Dr. Metaxas had brought us children into the world. His office was in our pharmacy, and he had been Father's closest friend and business partner for twenty-five or thirty years. He was a man of vigorous health and resolute manner, with a sharp gray beard and keen blue eyes sparkling behind pince-nez glasses — the very picture of a surgeon. I was afraid of him. I was afraid of his shining surgical instruments, of his sharp commanding voice. He spoke like a man used to giving orders. Belonging to a well-known Athenian family, he was a Hellenic and not a Turkish subject, which helped. The King of Greece had married the Kaiser's sister. Dr. Metaxas was the most prominent physician in Trebizond, everybody knew him. Among the Greeks his influence was only next to that of their magnificent metropolitan, Archbishop Chrisostome.

The men retired with Dr. Metaxas to the bedroom for another conference, in which it was decided that one of us boys should be sent immediately to his home in Monastir, the Greek monastery where he had moved his family. This isolated monastery in the wild mountains of Pontus was an ideal place to hide an Armenian. Its name was Sumelas.

As they wondered which one of us should go, Onnik or I, I clung to Mother and said, whimpering, "Send Onnik! I don't want to go!"

The idea of separating from Mother was too painful for me, and I could not imagine myself living away from her. Besides, I wanted to be a good sport. They would have sent Onnik anyhow, he being older. He was disguised as a Greek peasant boy and went to Monastir with a Greek muleteer. Thank God, one of us was saved. Onnik would carry on our family name if we all died.

A few hours after Onnik's departure Uncle Garnig and his family arrived from a village. Uncle Garnig ("Lamb") was a red-faced giant from Gumushaneh who had married Aunt Shoghagat's oldest daughter. He was bursting with peasant health, while his wife, Sister Arusiag ("Morning Star") was a pale, delicate woman. Though a saloon keeper by occupation, he was in the intimate circle of our clan. He would have sold the shirt on his back for the education of his children. He had sent Haigaz, his eldest son, to the Mekhitarist college in Venice. But alas, shortly before the outbreak of the war Haigaz had come back for a vacation and was unable to return to Italy. As Haigaz entered the room with a knapsack on his back the women looked at him and sighed. If he had remained a little longer in Venice he would have been saved.

They had seen Onnik at a road inn, but he was so well disguised that at first they thought they were seeing his Greek double.

"He didn't seem to recognize us," Sister Arusiag said. "But I had hardly opened my mouth to call his name when he carried his finger to his lips and signed us not to speak to him."

How like Onnik! How prudent of him! And while the other women praised him, recalled things he had done and said in the past, Mother and Aunt Azniv wept silently. I imagined Onnik grown up and always thinking of us, dead for many years. He would remember that once upon a time he had a soldier brother. Of course he and I had fought a lot, but we had also had so much fun together.

The conversation of the women turned to Haigaz. We felt very sorry for him. Haigaz was silent, and looking at his shy, studious face I was sure he was seeing the Piazza San Marco at the concert hour… the Canal Grande in the moonlight, gay with a long stream of gondolas… magic, scintillating places he had told us so much about. Ah, Venice, happy, happy Venice! If I could only fly to you! If by some miracle I could become a fiery horse, and transport all of us through the air, landing directly at the Piazza San Marco!

None of us, not even I, was hungry. Nobody wanted to eat, and the luscious grapes and pears which Aunt Shoghagat put on the table were left untouched.

What made our ordeal immeasurably more painful was the almost certain conviction on the part of the men and especially of Father, that the Ittihad party or the government — it was the same thing — was seeking the extermination of our race by a systematic plan, the deportation order as a military necessity being merely a ruse and a camouflage. It seemed as though it was the end of the world for us. And yet, while one lives, one hopes and we hoped against hope that we might, somehow, escape this mass death sentence. Perhaps it was the government's intention to kill only the members of our patriotic societies, the "dangerous" elements. Aunt Shoghagat bribed a Turkish neighbor to elicit some information on this point from reliable sources, but we learned nothing. Even the Turks were kept in ignorance of the true intent of the deportation order, or professed not to know it.

One thing seemed certain. Even if we were really deported to Mesopotamia, many of us would die on the road, and it would be hell for all. Father was very pessimistic, and he was too much of a realist not to see the situation in all its inconceivable horror. The only thing he had taken from his pharmacy on closing it was poison. He distributed it to the women in the room, and they sewed it in their dresses. Now that they had this means of ending their own lives, dying inviolate, their faces beamed with an inner peace.

But who could tell? Perhaps some of us might eventually return to Trebizond. And after another conference, the men filled a pot with jewelry and gold and buried it in the basement or garden, I did not know which. I was not let in on the secret.

There is a gap in my memory here. I cannot recall how many days of such anguish I spent at Aunt Shoghagat's, whether one, two or three, and how I was separated from my father.

It was about four o'clock in the afternoon and Mother and I rode in a phaeton.

"Where are we going, Mother?" I asked her anxiously.

"To the American Mission," she said.

"Why?"

She hesitated to answer for a moment, then said with a sigh: "The Americans will protect you, dear. Dr. Crawford has received permission from the government to keep boys of your age in his school."

I knew Dr. Crawford. He looked like the Apostle Peter and spoke a strange Armenian through his nose. With the presentiment that I would be separated from my mother too I touched her charshaf caressingly, which being made of silk gave me a cool, agreeable sensation, and I kept looking into her face. Her white cheeks were more hollowed than usual. I thought of the exiled young Austrian prince from Vienna who, I had heard, had lived in Marco's Hotel across the street from Grandmother's house and had fallen in love with my mother when she was eighteen years old and wore plumed Parisian hats. This thought in turn led to the reflection: if Mother had married the Austrian we would have been exempted from the deportation...

The phaeton drew up before the Mission compound.

"I will be back in a minute," Mother said to the driver as we got off.

At the Mission gate she bent down and kissed me on my head. Her lips were trembling. She tried to say something but checked herself, held my face between her hands and kissed me again on my forehead.

"Go in, darling, and play with the boys." I felt it was not what she intended to say. I had always been sensitive to the slightest nuances in her moods and Mother could never fool me, but before I could open my mouth she turned around and hurried back to the carriage. The driver cracked his whip and the phaeton moved off. I wanted to cry *"Mairig!* Mother!"

and run after her, but I said nothing. I saw that she carried a handkerchief to her eyes and her shoulders shook. My poor mother was sobbing for me. And that was our last parting. I was never to see her again.

I went in through the gate. The Mission compound was crowded with boys who had been brought and left there by their mothers, trusting them to the protection of the American flag which flew on a long pole. I was amazed to find these boys spinning tops, playing marbles and knucklebones, trading stamps and chocolate premiums, as if absolutely nothing had happened. They seemed to be totally unaware of why they were brought there.

But I was grave, thoughtful. In a few seconds I underwent one of those profound inner changes which close one chapter of our lives and open another. The world altered completely. I stared at the trees, the walls of the compound, the decorative plants, at the sky overhead — but they were no longer the trees, walls, plants and sky I had known. It seemed as though I was seeing the reverse, drab side of the world's scenery, that everything had been turned around, and the real, beautiful side was now hidden from my view.

I realized that my happy childhood had ended and I stood on the threshold of a new life, in a changed world, no longer the boy I used to be, but a different person. I felt as if I had grown up, become a man at once. How fortunate, how supremely happy I had been just a short time ago, without knowing it! That not knowing it caused me the deepest regret.

CHAPTER 7

On the Highway of Death

Shortly before dusk a group of well-dressed Turks came to the American Mission. They were members of the Ittihad committee and said Americans had no right to keep us. We, too, were to be deported. I wanted to jump over the compound wall and run away, but it was getting dark and I was afraid.

I didn't know what to do. The Turks were rounding up the boys and the few older girls who, acting as caretakers, had just given us bread and olives to eat. The girls tried to hide in rooms and closets, were panicky. But the Turks found them. I wanted to hide or escape somehow, and kept gazing over a wall at the tiled roofs, which now, at sundown, were a frightfully lurid red.

Another Greek friend of ours, a lawyer who lived in our street and had important connections, secured permission from the government to adopt my two sisters. That was being discussed while I was at Aunt Shoghagat's. When he learned I could not stay at the American Mission, he agreed to adopt me also, and sent a man after me, who took me to his town house, where my sisters were waiting for me. From there we went to the Serai, or government building, where a Turkish official wrote down our names in an enormous ledger. After this formality we went to his summer villa in a suburban village, thinking we were saved.

For a few days we lived among friends, in luxurious surroundings, but these gave us no comfort, and on the contrary increased our agony. Nevart and Eugenia cried at night when we went to bed. Eugenia was barely seven, yet she realized much.

The fatal July first came and passed. And the death sentence against our people was carried out. After we had spent a week in the home of this lawyer he received an order to hand us back to the government. We were to be taken care of in one of the orphanages the government had magnanimously opened for Armenian children whose parents had been deported.

A gendarme took us to a vacant Armenian house — a large building — and we thought this was a trap, they would kill us here secretly, this was the end for us too.

"Don't be afraid," the gendarme said, "this whole building will be filled with Armenians."

And soon gendarmes brought a crowd of some forty Armenian girls, crying hysterically, and about fifteen boys my age, sullen and tight-lipped. This was a Catholic group. The Catholics had enjoyed the traditional protection of the French and Austrian ambassadors and were in close communal ties with the Franks. Many of them spoke French in their homes, and they had hoped they would be exempted, but were not.

A few days later gendarmes brought in another group of women and children, and we were overjoyed to find among them Aunt Azniv, Victoria, Vardanush, and Uncle Garnig's younger boys Michael and Simon and ten-year-old daughter Zephyr. Aunt Azniv told us Father and Mother had not been deported and were hiding in our house, which the Turks had somehow overlooked, perhaps because we lived in a Greek street, when on the morning of July first gendarmes, police and *chetas*, led by members of the Ittihad, had driven all the Armenians out of their homes and started them on their way to Mesopotamia. We were the only Armenian family in our street, all the others being Greeks.

"But if the Turks find them hiding?" Nevart gasped.

Aunt Azniv drew a deep breath and closing her eyes crossed herself. "Let us pray they will not be found. Dr. Metaxas may be able to save them, he may be able to take them to Monastir. God have mercy upon us!"

Other hopeful news was that by order of Remzi Sami Bey our two grandmothers were taken to a government hospital of which he was superintendent. But little did we know that they, too, were condemned to death, and were to die soon of poisoned coffee. It was, at any rate, a less cruel way of killing them.

"Do you know what has happened to Uncle Leon?" I asked Aunt Azniv. I was worried about him most of all.

"They arrested him and deported him by the sea route, I think. Oh, my dears, I don't know whom to mourn more, the dead or the living. I have no more tears left."

At sundown we saw our paternal grandmother seated at a window on the third story of the hospital, which was close by our orphanage. I cried, *"Neneh! Neneh!"* and waved my fez but she did not hear me. What was she thinking of, we wondered? She did not move, but sat there as if she were not our dear *Neneh* but her ghost. She sat watching the summer sun go down, a silent, helpless protest against humanity and God. We were sure that she refused to talk with Remzi Sami Bey, with any Turk on the hospital's staff. She was a headstrong woman. And when the sun had sunk behind the Promontory of Yoroz and it became dark she vanished from our view, like an apparition. We never saw her again.

We were like prisoners and were not allowed to go out. Our only visitors were the local leaders of the Ittihad, polished, well-groomed Turks, many of them Prussianized, whose sole concern seemed to be our comfort and well-being. They would taste our food, inquire after our health, were always willing to supply us with the things we needed. With the attractive girls — and there were several of them, smartly dressed mademoiselles — they acted like gallant cavaliers. One day one of their favorite girls requested a sewing machine. Soon porters brought in a dozen sewing machines together with what seemed to be the entire contents of an Armenian dry-goods store. The girls got busy making new towels and garments for all of us. I got a new pair of pants. The ones I was wearing were already torn from climbing trees in the garden. (A new pair of pants lasted me about a week.) It was impossible to believe that these men, so courteous and urbane, putting on such benevolent airs, were the executioners of our race.

We had been at this orphanage about two weeks when a Turk brought us a letter and a blanket from Father. The letter, sent from Gumushaneh, was addressed to Aunt Azniv. She read it over and over, puzzled by its contents. "Mother and I have just reached Gumushaneh comfortably," Father wrote. (I am quoting his letter from memory.) "We are being deported in a carriage. Do not worry about us, we have been promised absolute security. See that the children don't catch cold and watch their diet. Don't give them any fried food. I am sending you a blanket to make sure that the children don't catch cold."

It was Father's handwriting, there could be no doubt about it. We learned he had given himself and Mother up to the police after hiding three weeks. He had lost his mind. As gendarmes led them through the streets like two captured criminals Mother sobbed aloud, "Give my children back to me! Where are my children? Where have you taken them?" Greeks who heard her hysterical cries closed their windows and wept.

But we did not cry on reading Father's letter, and said nothing. There are sorrows too deep for words or tears.

Gumushaneh, a town sixty miles inland, famous for its pears and apples and deriving its name from its silver mines, had gained a new and terrible meaning as the station on the highway to the interior where the exiles from Trebizond disappeared. Our parents had reached Gumushaneh and apparently enjoyed certain privileges denied the others. They were given a carriage, had been able to communicate with us, but would they go much beyond Gumushaneh? We doubted. In fact, we had no hopes whatever of ever seeing them again.

This Turk, who looked kindly enough, presented himself as a friend of Father's and wanted to take us to his home. He assured us he could secure our release. But he did not look like a particularly influential or prosperous man, wore baggy breeches and not European clothes. We did not want to be separated from Vardanush and Uncle Garnig's three children. We would share their fate, whatever it might be. Aunt Azniv felt herself responsible for all of us. Moreover, we had an instinctive fear of living in a Turkish home. We could never renounce our nationality and faith and become Turks. We were resolved to die as Christians, if die we must.

A few days after the visit of this friendly Turk, while I was on a peach tree with a number of other boys, a gendarme popped into the garden and with a motion of his fixed bayonet ordered us all to get down. Fearfully, we obeyed. We can't even climb trees any more, I thought. He drove us out.

"Where are you taking us?" I asked him. I wanted to show my companions I was not afraid of a gendarme and could talk to him.

"*Surgun,*" he said. "Deportation."

"Let me run upstairs then and get my fez." I tried to sound gay and innocent, as if I did not realize what *surgun* meant.

"You can't go upstairs, *yasak der,*" he snarled.

We joined a crowd of terrified older girls, women and boys in the yard.

Aunt Azniv, Vardanush, Victoria, Michael and Simon stood trembling together, bayonets bristling over their heads. I did not see Nevart, Eugenia, and Zephyr. "Where are they?" I asked. They told me they were in the building with other girls. The door was locked but we could hear their loud cries.

The gendarmes took us to the Armenian prelacy. The streets seemed so strange after our imprisonment. Looking at our school building and playground, which were in the prelacy compound, I could see the spirits of my vanished schoolmates play strange ghostly games in a deathly silence.

Women, girls and boys from other sham orphanages were also brought to the prelacy, and we understood they would send us off in the morning.

That night, waiting for our death, I sat curled up in an armchair, afraid to breathe. The lamp on the table beside me glowed with a blood-red light. The sheer animal fear that had seized us was enough to drive anybody crazy. All of us were a little insane as we brooded over our immediate fate in a mad, tense silence, leaning against each other for support, yet so terribly alone.

I dozed off in my chair, and when I opened my eyes I saw the others huddled in the room, grave and silent in the blood-red light, torpid with unslept sleep. Nobody spoke. Nobody moved. It seemed that we were already dead and I was seeing nothing but ghosts. They were awake, their eyes were open, but they appeared petrified. I reached out and touched Aunt Azniv's arms, and was startled when she spoke.

When the blackness of the night melted outside the windowpanes and we saw through the gray light of dawn trees, walls, roofs, we got up and moved about, turned off the lamps in the rooms, exchanged a few words — all of which struck me as odd. This mere moving, talking, touching things, was a resumption of our past normal life, it was living again, and had a soothing effect on us.

Aunt Azniv managed to buy through a gendarme, by bribing him, a small tin box of English biscuits, paying for it one gold pound. The whole box was left to me. Nobody cared to eat. They had layers of chocolate and cream and fruity flavors in them, and it was almost worth dying to eat them, I thought.

"Nothing can destroy your appetite. Your stomach has the cat's seven souls," Aunt Azniv told me with a wan smile.

We were lined up in the yard — our school playground. Our names were read off an official list and our number counted again by a commissioner of police. Then like a funeral procession, surrounded by a cordon of gendarmes with fixed bayonets, we came out of the prelacy compound and walked slowly through the streets. Munching my biscuits I gazed up at the familiar buildings and sights around me, which now, at this hour of our final separation, were so poignantly dear that I choked. Though I was not hungry any more I thought I might as well eat all the biscuits in the box before I died.

We passed by the American consulate, and I looked longingly at the Stars and Stripes. Then the road went down to the beach, and continued its zigzag course along the shore. Our feet sank in the thick ash-gray dust and the air of that summer morning was like blasts of furnace heat blown in our faces. None of us carried a bundle, though presumably we, too, were on our way to Mesopotamia.

We passed Xenophon's camp, and I glanced at the ruined tower of Vank, the Armenian monastery on the hill above it, remembering happy days there. The highway went up the fearful narrow valley of the Mill River; the city and the sea were shut off from our view. Terror gripped our hearts. We had left Europe and civilization behind us and were in the bloody wilderness of Asia, it seemed.

After about an hour we were ordered to stop. The *bash chavush*, or top sergeant, of the blue-coated gendarmes who were escorting us to our death, stood up on a rock, announced that we were in danger of being attacked by bandits at any moment. He asked us to give him our money and valuables for safe keeping, hinting that a bakshish or bribe was necessary for our protection.

They lined us up along the road and robbed us one by one. Aunt Azniv had to give them all the money she had, ten or fifteen gold pounds and six piasters in silver and coppers. They took the gold and let her keep the small change. Fearing they might later take even those six piasters — thirty cents — she gave them to me.

The sun baked my bare head, and having eaten all the biscuits I was very thirsty. My cousin Vardanush wore high-heeled shoes imported from Paris, and her feet were already sore. One much perspiring heavy woman who shuffled along in house slippers, with her gray hair streaming down her back, slumped down on a rock.

"Get up!" a gendarme ordered her angrily.

"You might as well shoot me now," she said.

Those who could not walk for any reason were killed on the spot. The

gendarme stood by her while the rest of us trudged on. When the road
made a turn and we could not see them any more the valley resounded with
a rifle shot. A few minutes later the gendarme rejoined our convoy, a killer's
glitter in his beady eyes.

They let us rest for a while on a marshy ground. We were not allowed to
go near the river and had to drink the water of stagnant pools swarming
with tadpoles. I kept dipping my biscuit box in a slimy pond and passing it
around to the women and girls.

We had not gone far after this brief rest when I saw a woman's nude
body in the river, which was rather shallow here. Her long hair floated
down the current, her bloated white abdomen glistened in the sun. I
noticed that one of her breasts was cut off. Further up I saw another body,
this time a man's; then a human arm caught up in the roots of a tree. The
corpses became a common sight, but after I had counted fourteen of them,
Aunt Azniv scolded me and told me not to look at the river any more. I
had never seen bodies of grown people in the nude and gazed at them
with a morbid curiosity.

When, some minutes later, I looked at the river again I saw a long, long
band of frothy blood clinging to its banks. It is impossible to describe the
impression that ghastly scene made upon me, although I can see it now as if
it were before my eyes. The exposed roots of trees and shrubs coiled around
like blood-sucking, blood-loving red snakes. Now none of us spoke, we all
tramped on silently, on our faces the solemnity of death.

I prayed desperately, reciting in my mind the *Lord's Prayer* over and over,
saying the words, "and deliver us from evil," with a special pleading. I
thought God looked upon me with favor, there was an intimate, close
understanding between us two, and as long as I prayed nothing evil could
happen to me. I became lighthearted and confident, as one who has most
cheering news among despairing people but slyly keeps it to himself.

"Don't worry," I whispered to Aunt Azniv confidentially. "I am praying.
God will save us."

"Pray, my dear, pray, I am praying too," she sighed.

We dreaded the approaching night. Not that we spoke about it. Words
were not needed, we conversed in silence. When the sun set and a pall of
darkness fell over this valley of death the noise of the river grew much
louder. I wondered if we should ever see the sun again.

We reached a khan adjoining a flour mill, were given some muddy water to drink, and driven into the gloom of this oriental resthouse. It was pitch dark. We huddled on the bare floors like sheep. I had filled my biscuit box with water, and held it tight against me. We expected the gendarmes to kill us here and throw our bodies into the river, which seemed to flow directly beneath us with a hellish roar. The massacres usually took place at night. The river howled like ten thousand wild beasts hungry for our flesh, like ten thousand wild beasts whose muzzles dripped with blood.

The room occupied by the gendarmes was lighted dimly. We could hear them talking in low voices, going out and coming in. Their every movement aroused our suspicions, increased our alarm. We smelled cucumbers, and quiet reigned in the khan while they ate. No food for us. Then we heard the voices of new men, gruff voices. Were they *chetas*, the irregulars, criminals released from prisons, we feared most?

Suddenly we heard screams, moans, cries for mercy, beating of quick, light feet, and coarse male voices and the stamping of heavy boots in the other rooms.

"They have started it," Aunt Azniv said. She fumbled in her blouse, tore a seam, and took out the poison Father had given her. "Give me the water — quick!"

I handed her my biscuit box. It was still half full. She mixed the powder in the water. "We will drink this before they get to us."

She drank from the deadly solution, then passed it on to Vardanush, who did the same. Victoria and my cousins Michael and Simon followed. Finally it was my turn. My hands shook as I held the box. There wasn't much left in it, but I knew it was enough to kill me.

"Drink it!" Aunt Azniv said, seeing me hesitate. "Its action is painless, it will put you to sleep, and you won't ever wake up again."

I was terrified when I imagined myself still alive while they lay dead beside me. I did not want to die, but I did not want to appear a coward either — I who was brave...

Michael and Simon had not hesitated. I raised the box to my lips and drained it to its last drop, and then waited for the poison to overpower us gradually and to close our eyes forever.

The savage river now seemed to be leaping into the room to snatch away our bodies. Well, I thought, it would soon have us, all right. I could see us, stripped of our clothes, being thrown one by one into its foaming jaws. But I had the comforting thought that the river would carry me to the sea, and like a primordial mother the sea would rock me tenderly in its arms.

While we waited calmly for death, two gendarmes towered in the doorway of our room, one carrying a smoky little oil lamp. They eyed the women and girls with lustful, appraising glances, and suddenly one of them bent forward and grabbed a girl. She screamed and fought in vain to free herself from his arms. He dragged her out, the gendarme with the lamp silently following.

Nobody dared say a word. We all lay on the floor dead still.

The gendarmes were merely taking away by brute force the girls and women of their choice to violate them and were not killing the people in the other rooms, as we had thought. None of us, however, expressed any regret for having taken the poison. They would kill us later in the night, or the following day or night, or a few days or nights later. It was all the same. We were six living dead.

I watched for signs of the approaching death in me, but strangely enough felt nothing. And neither were the others affected by the poison, except Vardanush, who felt sick, leaned against Aunt Azniv, resting on her shoulder. Apparently the poison was of insufficient dose to kill six people. When Father gave it to Aunt Azniv he had no idea she would have to share it with five others.

Victoria crawled behind us so that the gendarmes would not see her. She would have been their prize catch. We sat on her. A few minutes later two other gendarmes came in, one, as before, holding a smoky lamp. When they reached our corner they held the lamp over Vardanush, who was in a semi-conscious condition.

"Is she sick?" they asked.

"Yes," Aunt Azniv replied.

Without saying another word they continued their inspection, and seizing a shapely girl carried her to the room where the other women were being violated.

This orgy lasted all night. They released their victims early in the morning, and the two girls from our room came back crying and hiding their faces from shame.

After another roll call we began our second day's journey to death. Vardanush was so weak, and so gaunt and pale, that Aunt Azniv and Victoria had to drag her along, and she tried to look bright and well. They walked in the center so that the gendarmes wouldn't notice her and shoot her.

At noon we were taken to a shady glen off the highway.

"Sit down and rest!" the gendarmes commanded.

We obeyed by sitting down, and looked for signs of a previous massacre, expecting to be fired upon by "bandits" in ambush, with our gendarmes at first pretending to defend us and then joining them in the slaughter. After about fifteen minutes of such rest we went back to the highway.

We had not met a single traveler since leaving Trebizond. The highway was closed to traffic so that people would not see us. We met only a crew of Greek soldiers working on the narrow-gauge military railway that connected the harbor of Trebizond with Jevizlik, some twenty miles inland. This miniature railway did not have locomotives and Greek soldiers pushed the cars, which were loaded with sacks of army tack. They wore their civilian clothes and looked at us with sorrowful eyes. It was good to see Christian faces again, faces of real human beings, faces that expressed human emotions! I hailed them in Greek.

"You are not allowed to talk to them!" a gendarme growled at me. He was very suspicious and wanted to know what I had told the Greek soldiers. "Be careful or I'll have you walk in front with the other boys," he warned me.

The boys walked in front of the convoy, unless they had sisters or close relatives among the women and girls. The gendarmes were especially harsh with us boys and watched us closely so that we wouldn't try to escape. I was always on the lookout for a chance to escape.

We arrived at Jevizlik late in the afternoon, and here they separated us boys from the women and girls, and we had to spend the night in separate khans. "New instructions" had come from the governor-general. We boys had to be distributed among the Moslems of this district, which meant we had to become Turks.

An official brought a few baskets of warm brown bread.

"Don't eat it, it's poisoned!" said several boys.

But we were so hungry and the bread smelled so good that after some hesitation we ate it. I had had the biscuits, but the others had not eaten anything for two and a half days. We crawled into the bunks of our khan. It was both for horses and men. A gendarme sat outside the gate with his rifle between his knees.

Michael and Simon fell quickly asleep, but I was too restless, I wanted to run away. By a kind of mental telepathy I communicated with a few other boys who had thoughts similar to mine, and we held a consultation in tense whispers, squatting on our haunches in the center of the earthen floor, covered with straw and horse manure.

"There is a hole in the back wall."

"Is it wide enough?"

"Yes."

"The gendarme won't hear us."

"But where can we go?"

"To the mountains," I said. "We can live on the mountains until the Russians come."

"But there are wolves and bears in the forests."

"And there are gendarmes and *chetas* down here, you can take your choice."

"Ssshh!"

We got up and peered out through the crack in the crude, thick wall. It was like day outside, so bright was the moonlight. The pebbles on the river bank shone like pieces of silver. The risk was too great. We would surely be seen if we approached the river, which we had to cross to go to the mountains, and the Turks could readily recognize us as Armenians by our European clothes. That lovely moonlight spoiled our plan. We climbed back to our bunks, preferring life in Turkish homes to certain death.

When I awoke in the morning most of the boys were up and about and everybody seemed to be in good humor. It was the sort of cheerfulness one experiences while convalescing from a serious illness, when the temperature drops to normal and one feels like living again.

We gathered before the khan waiting for the women and girls to pass by us on their way to Gumushaneh. During the excitement and hurry of our sudden separation I had not been able to return the six piasters to Aunt Azniv and I wanted to give that money back to her very badly. We saw them coming down the road escorted by fewer gendarmes than the day before. As they reached our khan I ran up to Aunt Azniv, although it was forbidden. Vardanush looked at me with glazed eyes without recognizing me. She was dying on her feet and Aunt Azniv and Victoria were dragging her along in the center of the convoy. I pushed the money into Aunt Azniv's hand.

"I don't want it," she said and tried to give it back to me. "Keep it, darling. You boys will need it."

"You need it more." I looked at her dear homely face. She was weeping without tears, because she had no more tears left.

"Oh, my God, what will happen to you boys!" she sighed. "Don't separate from Michael and Simon if you can."

A gendarme ordered me back to the khan. Well, I had at least given her the money. I knew I would never see them again, that they were marching to their death — yes, marching! There was a strange rhythmic rapidity about their gait, as if the extension of life granted us boys had relieved them of a big load and they could now face death cheerfully. I watched them go with that silent stupidity that affects people who are so overwhelmed with sorrows and losses that they become insensible.

CHAPTER 8

The Automobile in Jevizlik

We boys were put on exhibit before the government building, guarded by a few gendarmes, and shopkeepers from the town and peasants from the surrounding countryside loitered among us, eyeing us with the shrewd, appraising glances of sheep buyers. The Kaimakam, or sub-governor of Jevizlik, a portly middle-aged man in a gray European suit, with a gold watch chain hanging across his ample waist, stood on the stone steps of the building and looked at us with a bored expression. Evidently we were just another group of children to be disposed of according to the instructions of his superior, the governor-general of Trebizond. It was all a matter of official routine to him; he expressed no personal hatred toward us.

This was like a slave market of captive enemy children, except that we brought no price and any Moslem could come and take any boy he wanted. There were several women among our visitors, some wearing stiff black veils, others half veiled or unveiled. But veiled or unveiled, men or women, they all ignored me. I seemed to scare them off, though I tried to look gentle and docile.

A *cahveji* looking for an older boy to work in his coffee house picked Michael, who was eleven, serious, sensible. A frock-coated, hook-nosed *arzuhalji*, or petition writer, took Nurikhan, my best friend, because his father, as interpreter of the Russian consulate in Trebizond, had done this Turk a favor in the past. This worthy looked like a scholar and seemed the only civilized man in Jevizlik.

Simon was barely eight, with a perfect oval face, bright red cheeks and clever eyes. All the women stopped to admire him, and they all wanted to adopt him, but he wouldn't go without me.

"We are brothers," I would say, "and can't be separated."

I was angry with Michael for leaving him. That was no way for an older brother to act. I liked Simon, he was a daredevil. He could ride on the bare back of a horse, which was more than I could do. Michael, on the other hand, never played, had his nose always buried in a book. He could read French and Italian and knew fractions. He regarded me as a noisy, ignorant child.

My desire to have Simon stick by me was not entirely altruistic. I wanted to protect him and keep him Armenian, yes, but I also hoped to save myself through him… Since nobody wanted me alone, perhaps some kindly woman would take me along for his sake.

In the evening Simon and I returned to the khan with some twenty other unlucky boys. We were to be given another chance the following day, and were told that those of us who found no Moslem guardians by four o'clock in the afternoon were to be deported. But I knew we had reached the end of the road, there was no more deportation for us and they would simply take us out of town and kill us.

The next morning we were again put on exhibit. Our visitors now were mostly country folk. They had come to town to sell their produce and do some shopping, and paid us a passing call, some obviously out of curiosity, others with the hope of returning home with an Armenian child in the bargain.

A group of prosperous-looking peasant women raved over Simon, and one of them, only half veiled, was determined to adopt him. I told her we were brothers, I could not let him go without me, meaning that she ought to take me too. But she was not interested in me, she wanted only Simon. He would not go.

"You aren't brothers! You don't look alike!" she said in an angry voice, shaking a hennaed finger at me. "You had better let him come with us or I will have you punished as a liar."

"*Vallah-Billah*, we are brothers," I vowed, calling Allah as my witness.

"Is he really your brother?" she asked him.

He nodded "yes," but it was the kind of "yes" that meant "no." However, he still loyally stood by me.

"You devil!" these women seemed to tell me with their flashing eyes. "You will always remain an infidel and keep this lamb an infidel too."

I realized it would not do to push the matter too far, this might be his last chance. They threatened to take me over to the Kaimakam and demand that I be isolated from the other boys as a "dangerous" character.

"We are not brothers," I finally admitted. "We are only cousins." I told them where his real brother was, and let him go.

Nobody wanted me. Six or seven of us were still left, guarded by a single gendarme. My rejected companions waited silently for their fate. I wanted to shout to them, "Let's do something! They will kill us, don't you understand? They will kill us and throw our bodies into the river!" But I too was speechless. Each seemed to be ashamed of himself, especially a boy who was blind in one eye. Each had withdrawn into his own shell, tightly, like a snail pricked with a pin. We were the rejected, the leftover goods in this slave market. Nobody had wanted us, and only the river clamored for us.

I became panicky. Every minute was precious, I *had* to do something to save myself. They were not going to kill *me*.

I was determined to live. A mounted irregular rode up to the government building and looked at us with a sardonic grin. His *bashlik*, or headgear, was pulled down to his eyes at the most rakish and murderous angle. A typical Laz cutthroat, armed to his teeth.

He who is drowning clings to the snake, says an Armenian proverb. "For the love of Allah, adopt me!" I begged him. "They will deport me this afternoon if you don't."

He frowned darkly and stared at me. "Can you be a *cheta* like me?"

"Yes, effendim," I said, bringing my heels together and standing at attention.

My answer and military bearing pleased him. He measured me from head to foot.

"I like your eyes. I will take you." He dismounted, and I went to the Kaimakam's office with him, where the diligent secretary added my name to the list of those boys who had been Turkified.

"I can't take you to my village right now," this irregular told me. "I'll be gone for three weeks, but I have a friend who will take care of you." He opened his string purse and gave me a copper coin. "Run along and buy yourself some bread, and meet me over the bridge at sundown."

So I was free! The profession of my benefactor did not matter at the moment.

I went to a bakery and bought a big slice of brown bread. I found

Michael busy in a coffee house taking orders from the grave customers, asking them whether they wanted their coffee with or without sugar, *shekerli* or *sadeh*. With each tiny cup of coffee he balanced dexterously a glass of water on the tray, like an experienced waiter. Some passed their time playing backgammon, banging the men over the boards, inlaid with mother-of-pearl, with much force, and counting the dice in Persian: *"Du bara! Du besh! Shesh besh!"* Others smoked narghiles in dreamy tranquillity. The walls were decorated with gaudy, fly-specked lithographs of highly romanticized battle scenes from Turkish history.

Michael was fairly satisfied. The *cahveji* was treating him well, he told me. "But he doesn't want me to associate with Armenian boys any more. He wants me to forget my past. I am a Turk now, he says."

I next visited Nurikhan, who was again his cheerful self, cracking jokes. "The *arzuhalji* told me I don't have to become a Turk," he said joyously. "He is an educated man and took me just to save my life. But his wife won't let me in the house, the devil take her. She says I am thirteen, too old, and she has a fourteen-year-old daughter. Both pull down their veils when I enter the house. Husband and wife have been arguing about me; I would have to sleep in the office here. But it suits me fine. All I have to do is to carry a few buckets of water for the wife."

Nurikhan was the most fortunate among us. His eldest sister was the wife of the Swiss consul in Trebizond, who was keeping his other sisters and younger brother in the consulate. He was a long-legged, curly-haired Catholic boy, and claimed to be heir of an immense fortune, 30 or 40 million pounds, left by an Armenian merchant prince in India. Hence, the "Khan" in his name, which in Persian means prince.

Why did I have to be so unlucky? The prospect of spending the rest of my life in a Moslem village terrified me. I went to the bridge with a heavy heart. The irregular was waiting for me with his friend, a genuine barefoot beggar with a bread sack slung from his shoulder and carrying a stick.

"He will take care of you until I come back," the irregular said.

The beggar grinned. He filled me with a sickening revulsion. I could not stand near him, he emanated the sour, fetid odor of the beggar tribe.

"He will be a *cheta* when he grows up," my benefactor said, putting his hand on my shoulder.

With repeated orders that the beggar take good care of me, he mounted his horse and rode away, to rob and kill more Armenians.

The beggar was so deferential with me that it was comic. He seemed to be very proud of the fact that I should be entrusted to his care. He was blondish, about twenty-four, with two of his front teeth missing. We walked to his village up the highway. Filthy little ragamuffins playing in the thick dust on the road greeted him with loud jeers, calling him "Crazy Hassan."

"Who is that giaour dog? Where are you taking him?" they shouted, throwing stones at me. He raised his stick and went after them as they fled in all directions.

"Crazy Hassan! Crazy Hassan!" they yelled from behind bushes and walls. "Let us have him, son of a donkey, we want that infidel bastard." They shouted what they would do to me.

The obscene, degenerate language of these lecherous urchins showed the state of morality that prevailed in this filthy village. I shuddered.

We turned into a labyrinth of flat-roofed mud hovels and entered the beggar's hut, which was the most wretched of all. But he had two wives, wearing voluminous bloomers mended beyond recognition of the original material. They received me with tearful affection, and raising their eyes and arms heavenward wailed in a note of prophetic doom that Allah would punish the Turks for their crimes.

"Curses be on their heads!" they said, meaning the officials, the gendarmerie, all those who kept them in such poverty and perpetrated these crimes. We had common enemies.

Kneeling on the clay floor they asked me with wonder and pity in their voices and eyes:

"Your parents were rich, weren't they? You had everything in your home, didn't you? You are wearing such nice clothes and shoes. Oh, *yavrum*, my soul, now you have to live with poor people like us, we can't afford to buy even a box of matches!" They recited the long chronicle of their woes, and wept over me, a "rich city boy" who had fallen to their level. "*Vakh, vakh,* what harm had you done, my lamb, my soul!"

The hut was lighted fitfully by the resinous flare of a pine stick. We retired without eating supper, for they had nothing to eat. The bed was on a dais in a corner of the room, and they honored me — to my intense loathing and dread — by letting me sleep in it with the beggar, while the two women slept on a rush matting spread on the floor in the same room. The beggar did not bother to take off his rags or wash his feet, nor did the wives undress. I took off only my shoes. The threadbare quilt was sticky and stiff with the accumulated dirt and sweat of many years. I was very careful not to touch it with my lips. I lay as far away from him as possible, but his big feet sometimes touched mine. I knew how addicted the Turks were to homosexual practices, and I was jittery.

When I awoke the next morning I found myself alone in the hut. I got up, put on my shoes, and went out into the yard. The sun had risen high. The beggar must have gone to town for his daily beat, but I wondered where his wives were. I asked a young girl living next door and she said they were working as reapers in a wheat field, and told me how to go there.

I sauntered down the road, pretending to go to the wheat field. The inhabitants of this village apparently had no use for latrines. The ground under the walls of their hovels was littered with human feces. I was afraid I would lose my mind if I slept another night with the beggar, if his feet ever touched mine again, and as soon as I reached the highway I ran back to Jevizlik, in a hysterical condition.

I spent the day with my companions. As evening approached Nurikhan advised me to return to the beggar's home, otherwise, he said, I would be considered a runaway, and runaways were punished by death. I had to go back, though death would have been preferable. On the highway, not far from the government building, I met the Kaimakam, taking his evening stroll with a few other portly Turks.

"*Akshaminiz hair olsun!* May your evening be felicitous!" I greeted them. It was one of the polite phrases I had learned from my Turkish playmates, Shukri and Mahmut. They stopped and looked at me curiously.

"Kaimakam Bey," I said in a shaky voice, "I am pharmacist Karapet effendi's son, from Trebizond. A *cheta* adopted me yesterday and turned me over to a friend of his, a beggar living in that village, to keep me three weeks. But they are so poor they don't have even matches in their house. Please allow me to stay in Jevizlik until I can find another Turkish father."

Twiddling their tasseled amber beads, they listened to me gravely, and I felt, not without some sympathy. Both the irregular and the beggar were familiar characters to them, and they expressed surprise that a man of that cutthroat's reputation should have been good enough to adopt an Armenian boy. It seemed funny to them. The Kaimakam gave me permission to stay in Jevizlik, provided I found another guardian.

I slept that night with Nurikhan in the office of the petition writer. We had no lamp or candle, but he had already invented a new method of illumination, hazel nuts strung on a piece of wire. When the last kernel burnt out we knelt and prayed. Then he curled up on a bench and I on a table, and we fell asleep.

The next morning I found a respected merchant, Osman Agha, to adopt me. He had a grain store, and wore the tribal Laz costume. He walked with a swaggering gait, the muscles of his thighs bulging under the black cloth of his tight breeches, the loose balloon seat of which moved rhythmically left and right like the fat tail of a karakul sheep. He had a well-shaped head, dark brown hair, brown eyes, and strong white hands. He carried a silver dagger, and the cartridge pockets on his breast were trimmed with silver thread.

Osman Agha took me to a tailor's shop and ordered linen underwear and a Laz costume like his for me. He named me Jemal.

I could not bring myself to call him "father." I wanted to like him, he was saving my life, but I could not, I hated him. I was reserved and stiff in his presence. He was very pious and five times a day faithfully performed his prayers. On hearing the muezzin's chant he washed his face, his hands and arms up to his elbows, his feet up to his ankles, and prostrating himself on a small prayer rug, murmured verses from the *Koran*.

I thought he would let me stay with him in town, but in the evening he took me to his village. It was high up in the mountains, farther away from the sea. I wished I had stayed with the beggar, his village was at least closer to the sea and Europe. I thought I would never be able to escape from this distant mountain village; they would catch me before I reached the highway.

Osman Agha lived in a neat cottage. His wife, a tall woman, was nice to me. He had a husky, handsome son, Ali, a year or two older than I. Both mother and son were shy of me, for evidently I represented to them city life, the wonders and glamor of *Avropa*, Europe. My Laz costume was not to be ready for some time and I still wore my own clothes.

I slept alone in the front room, in a clean bed spread on a rush matting. Pulling the quilt over my head I crossed myself and prayed to God frantically not to forsake me in this wilderness.

The next morning Osman Agha returned to Jevizlik while I was still asleep. When I woke up there was nobody in the cottage, his wife and son were out too. I dressed in a hurry and went out into the yard, where I staged what I thought was a master stroke of diplomacy. I cried out, *"Ana, neredeh sun?* Mother, where are you?"* By calling her mother I wanted to show her and the neighbors who were sure to hear me that I had accepted her as such.

I could never have called Osman Agha father, but his wife was different, there was a motherly kindness about her.

The news of my arrival had spread through the village, and the neighbors knew who I was and whom I was calling. My call was relayed from one house to another, and Osman Agha's wife, who had been visiting some friends and no doubt telling them about me, came running along a hedge.

"I didn't want to wake you up, Jemal," she said, blushing. "We have had our breakfast, but I have kept your portion. Would you like a couple of fried eggs?" She looked highly pleased, and all the women and girls who peered out from windows and doors watching us smiled.

I wondered, though, how they would treat me if I told them I had not become a Turk, and even if she was a good woman I could never forget my own mother and accept her in her place.

While I was having breakfast, Ali entered the cottage with a huge fagot on his sturdy back and deposited it in a corner by the hearth.

"Be sure you take your brother Jemal along next time you go to the wood," his mother told him. "You must keep him company."

He looked guilty and bashfully nodded "yes." Then seizing a wooden water vessel dashed out. I concluded from his haste that he did not want me to carry water, he was glad to do all the work himself. When he finished his morning chores and was free to go places with me he took me around to meet his friends. We called on a young man who had served in the Turkish Navy, was a person of consequence in the village. Apparently he was expecting our visit because the womenfolk were out and his house seemed to have been tidied up in a hurry. They treated me as if I were a celebrity. This sailor was courteous and respectful. To prove his sophisticated background he told me he had lived not only in Trebizond, but also in Istanbul.

"Show him your uniform," Ali urged him, as further proof.

He opened a cabinet and proudly showed me his white sailor's uniform, washed clean. There were no other garments in the cabinet — it was too sacred a vestment apparently to be kept with other clothes. I liked him. He had lived in cities, he was a man of the sea. We could understand each other, we could be friends. Neither he nor Ali made any reference to my Armenian past. They treated me as a Turk, as one of themselves, only better. They never questioned me about my family, and the word Armenian or Christian was never mentioned during our conversation.

The village mullah came to see me — like the devil in a turban. After a consultation with Osman Agha's wife he told me, like a grinning old wolf, that he would have to circumcise me, slapping me on my back with his horrible witch doctor's hand.

"Don't be afraid," he said, "it won't hurt much."

Ali told me it was a bloody operation, but what really alarmed me was its religious significance. I thought that once I let the mullah circumcise me I could never become a Christian again, it would be the final, irrevocable act of renouncing my faith and nationality and family and Europe and civilization and everything else I cherished in my aching heart.

After brooding over it for two days, I decided I would rather die than be circumcised.

I told Osman Agha's wife that I was not used to living in a village and wanted to go back to Jevizlik. She saw that I was very unhappy, and sent for her husband. Osman Agha was angry with me for not wishing to stay in the village, and realized I would never become a Turk.

He hardly spoke a word on our way back to town, both of us being silently hostile. I felt it was no use pretending any more.

Our separation, however, took place without any quarrel or argument, without any apparent ill feeling between us; I just left him when we got back to town, and avoided him thereafter. He would see me pass by his store but would not call me in, as if we were total strangers and he had never known me. Now we were open enemies, the fiasco of father and son relationship between us was over, and I could feel his glowering hatred for me.

The other Armenian boys had somehow managed to adjust themselves to their new life and seemed to be quite content, but I was in open rebellion.

Jevizlik was now observing the Ramazan, which required strict fasting from dawn to sunset. The fast was broken by the discharge of a horse pistol from over the bridge. At nights a few of us boys would get together on the main street and talk in Armenian, and even indulge in some merry horseplay, for even we were infected by the nightly holiday spirit of Ramazan.

"If you don't forget that accursed language," a swaggering young Turk with a dagger threatened us, "we will cut your throats too."

Now that I had left Osman Agha I was very defiant. I spoke Armenian in a loud, challenging voice.

Nurikhan gave me shelter at nights. I lived mainly on blackberries and wild fruits I picked in the woods along the river. Once I looked in the mirror of an inn where one of my companions worked and was struck by my changed appearance. I looked like a wild boy, with an emaciated face.

One day during this period of my vagrancy I saw an automobile, an open sedan, parked before the government building. I thought it must be a German officer's, and I gazed at it in loving wonder. I wanted to feel it with my own hands to make sure that this messenger from Christian Europe was not an apparition and would not vanish into thin air if I touched it. There it was, a delegate from Civilization.

The luminous vision of the good world from which it came flashed in my mind, but it was so remote, like a world beyond the world. In a sudden burst of silent sobs I wanted to embrace that automobile and press it to my heart as a dear friend I had found in the wilderness. I wanted to throw myself at the feet of the German officer when he came out of the government building and beg him to protect me, to take me with him to the beautiful world by the sea. He was a Christian, he had come from there himself. I thought that surely he had had a happy childhood like mine, attended a kindergarten, gone to church on Sundays, read *Robinson Crusoe,* and that his mother had knitted socks. But with a pang I realized the futility of appealing to a German officer. He would simply be annoyed with me, he would push me away from him, he might even kick me into the dust of the road, after which I could expect no mercy from the Turks.

I walked away, heartbroken, lonelier than ever before, with a sense of being lost forever, doomed to a dark prison world of death and torture.

A few minutes later the automobile sped past me with a German officer at the wheel and... my former Turkish playmates Shukri and Mahmut seated beside him. They seemed to be taking a joy ride. Shukri was startled as he saw me and rose to call my name, but his vicious younger brother pulled him down, and the automobile drove away at full speed, laughing at me, ha ha! and blowing clouds of dust and benzine smoke into my face.

CHAPTER 9

The Sea! The Sea!

The ships were gay with multi-colored pennants fluttering in the breeze and blew in a basso profundo that could be heard for miles around as they reached the harbor. I imitated that sound again by blowing against the stretched-out skin between my thumb and forefinger. I remembered the ships I drew with my colored crayons, lying on the floor. Looking over a vine trellis, my elbows on a window sill, I used to gaze at the sea for hours, oblivious of the passing of time — and I saw again the French, Austrian, Russian, English, Italian ships, coming and going, and the sailboats that fairly flew over the crests of the waves. I knew the sea in all its moods and colors: rose-and-gold early in the morning — sky-blue at noon — bubbling with all the hues of the rainbow at sundown; now smooth like a mirror, now with myriads of white horses racing shoreward in a thunderous charge.

There were wonderful colored stones on the beach before the Potters' Ward. And boats were drawn up on the black sand, their curving keels exposed, looking monstrous out of water, like the black shells of giant prehistoric birds. The naked throng of boys on the Armenian Rock, led by "revolutionaries," fearless fellows, ready to fight with the noisy multitude on the Greek Rock, led by no less bold *palikaria*, for supremacy on the sea on Saturday afternoons, when schoolboys of both nations crowded on the beach. Most of the Armenian boys were dead now, had perished on this highway of death.

And even though the sea too had become a sea of death, it held the promise of my deliverance. For the waves that washed the shores of Trebizond washed also the shores of that glorious free world whence ships and the automobile, which I had seen, came. And now that I was reassured by the automobile that Civilization still existed, that there were still countries where rang the sweet anthem of Christian bells, where you could travel on a train, where the streets were lighted at night by electricity, and happy children read the story of Robinson Crusoe — I heard a Voice calling me. It was like the voice of God, and it said to me: "Follow me, I shall be your guide from now on."

Wandering around, with that Voice inside me, I discovered a hardware store. The two proprietors were Greeks. I did not know there were any Greeks here. I walked past this store several times, thinking they might not care to be seen talking with me, the Turks would become suspicious, but finally, taking a deep breath, I stepped in.

"*Kalimera,* good morning," I said.

"*Kalimera.*" They took me for a Greek, for I spoke Greek like a Greek, but I told them who I was and why I had left Osman Agha.

"You must be that boy!" one of them exclaimed under his breath.

"Has anybody been asking about me?" I said anxiously. "We have many Greek friends in Trebizond."

"I was in the government building this morning," the Greek merchant said in a whisper. "I saw Osman Agha in the Kaimakam's office and heard him making a complaint about you. The Kaimakam gave orders to have you taken out of town tonight——" he hesitated.

"And shot," I said, smiling.

They nodded their heads gravely and looked at me with pity in their eyes, wondering if I realized the danger I was in.

"Don't worry!" I chuckled. "They can't catch me."

I don't know how to explain my lighthearted manner. There was perhaps affected bravado in my indifference, though I wasn't exactly acting brave, heroic.

They were very cautious, didn't tell me to stay in Jevizlik, or advise me to escape. For where could I go? And the penalty for assisting an Armenian to escape was death. But when I told them Dr. Metaxas was our closest family friend, they took a personal interest in me. They told me his family was at Monastir, not far from their own village. Every Greek knew Dr. Metaxas. He was one of their great men.

To raise myself further in their esteem I said my brother was with his family, he hadn't been deported, Dr. Metaxas was keeping him in the monastery.

But I immediately realized my indiscretion. That was too great a secret to be divulged. "Please don't tell anybody," I begged them frantically. "Not even your folks at home." They assured me they would not.

They told me they would hide me in their home at night, asked me to meet them behind the trees on the other side of the bridge when it got dark. But I had to come back with them the next day. They couldn't keep me more than one night. I was grateful even for that.

"I'll go to Trebizond!" I said. "I will hide in vacant Armenian houses until the Russians come." I was sure Uncle Russia would be in Trebizond sooner or later. Monastir was only a few hours' walk from Jevizlik but I was afraid if I went there I would endanger my brother's life. The Turks might seize both of us.

I kept out of sight, and in the evening met these two Greeks behind the bridge. They closed their store unusually late so that nobody would see us leaving the town together. Their village was high up in the hills. Everybody except a young woman was in bed when we entered an attractive white cottage by an apple orchard. The air of this Greek village was so sweet to breathe! Here I was back again in the beautiful world.

After a good supper, which we ate in silence, a clean bed was spread for me on a rug and we all quickly retired. I didn't have to curl up, I could stretch out my legs.

They woke me up at dawn, when it was still dark. I had hoped they would ask me to stay in their home at least a few days until we could communicate with Dr. Metaxas, but they were so nervous and afraid they did not even let the members of their own family know I had slept in their house that night.

When we returned to town they gave me two piasters, cautioned me against a guardhouse on the highway where gendarmes examined the passports of travelers, and indicated they could do nothing else for me, I had to find my own salvation.

I felt so confident I decided to ask my cousin Michael to join me. Venturing into the market street I went straight to the coffee house. His master trusted him so completely he slept all day, now that it was Ramazan, and let Michael manage his store. The only customers I saw were a group of irregulars, bristling with Mauser rifles and cartridge belts. Michael was washing dishes in the back room. I signed him to come out, that I had something important to tell him.

He came out, timidly. "What is it, Jemal?" he asked me in Turkish, wiping his hands on his apron.

"Why do you call me Jemal and speak Turkish with me? Have you really become a Turk?" I said in Armenian, and loud enough for the irregulars to hear me, just to upset poor Michael a little more. They were watching us with their mean eyes, and he was very uncomfortable under their gaze. So was I; these men were killers.

Michael did not answer.

"Listen, I am running away tonight, going to Trebizond. Want to come with me?"

"Are you crazy?" he whispered in Armenian. "They don't let a fly escape them. When they catch you they won't shoot you, they will *cut off your head*. They caught two brothers at Hamski Koy and that's exactly what they did to them. I heard the *cheta* who butchered them like sheep tell people here about it. He said their bodies jumped around for five minutes after he cut off their heads. They didn't die immediately, their arms and legs kept moving."

"Well, they will kill me anyhow if I stay here. I just can't become a Turk, Michael. It's no use trying. Osman Agha complained to the Kaimakam and two Greeks heard him giving orders to shoot me. Last night I slept in their home in a Greek village."

Tears welled up in his eyes.

"They will catch you, Zavén," he mumbled.

I wanted to tell him about the Voice, I wanted to say, "Don't stay here, let us go back to the sea, to the beautiful world." But I could not. I didn't know how to word it.

Michael went back to his coffeepots and cups. I was more sorry for him than he was for me.

I stayed in the woods on the outskirts of the town, and in the evening slipped into the office of the petition writer. Taking my two piasters Nurikhan went out to buy bread and olives for me, as provisions for my journey. He took advantage of his legitimate shopping and returned with his pockets filled with enough filberts to last him a week.

"Where do you think I will be at this hour tomorrow night?" I asked him, as we cracked the nuts.

"In the river," he laughed, stringing a kernel on the wire. "Are you scared?"

"Me scared?" I said indignantly.

"You had better be this time! If they catch you it's this." He made a clicking sound with his tongue and ran his hand across his throat.

I decided to get a little sleep before starting at midnight. We knelt and prayed. With the reflection that now everything depended on God, I lay down and fell asleep.

I dreamed that one of the irregulars I had seen that morning in the coffee house seized me, and pressing his knee hard on my chest, drew out his knife to cut off my head. I woke up with a start just when he put the knife against my throat. Slipping off my table I stood trembling on the floor. But I had awakened from one nightmare to go through another, a real one.

From the moonlight in the room I concluded it must be around one o'clock, not too late. Nurikhan was still sound asleep.

"I am leaving!" I murmured into his ear, shaking him by his shoulder.

He mumbled something and turned over.

I shook him harder. "Yes, yes, I am awake!" he said, sitting up. He rubbed his eyes, yawned. "So you are leaving?" As if it were nothing.

We waited for the night watchman, an armed sentry, to pass. I thought if he stopped and questioned me I couldn't lie and tell him I wasn't leaving town if I carried food with me. On the open road I would be better off without my bread and olives. So I gave them to Nurikhan. He kissed the bread and broke into a jig dance. "Tomorrow is a holiday for me!"

When the sentry was well past our office Nurikhan carefully raised the window, which was four or five feet from the ground. "You had better jump before that son of a bitch turns back," he said, trying to sound casual. But now when I had to take the plunge, I hesitated. I realized the awful risk I was taking. Oh, my God, where was I going? Returning to Trebizond would be sheer suicide, just running into the arms of the police there. But if I went in the other direction, toward the interior and not the sea, I would have to go to bloody Hamski Koy and Gumushaneh. The whole country was a vast death trap for the escaped Armenian. There was no place for me in the world, but if I had to die, I wanted to die after seeing the sea once more.

What tormented me so much was not the thought of dying, but of dying all alone, with nobody I knew and loved near me. It was this utter solitude in death that terrified me most.

"Well, aren't you going to jump, you good-for-nothing?" Nurikhan said impatiently, holding up the window.

I crossed myself and jumped.

I didn't have a moment to lose. Keeping close to the shutters of the stores I scurried away on tiptoe, glancing back now and then to see if anybody was following me, if the sentry had turned back. All Jevizlik was asleep. There were no lights, no sounds. I slowed down when I reached the open road, walking very fast, but not running.

I was alarmed when I heard the loud rumble of an approaching cart behind me, but the driver turned out to be a Greek.

"Where are you going, Uncle?" I asked him in Greek.

He pulled up. "To Trebizond."

"I am going to Trebizond too. Will you give me a ride? I am tired. My foot hurts."

He eyed me suspiciously, knitting his beetle-brows. "Where are your folks? Why do they let a small boy like you travel alone at this hour of the night?"

I had to think fast. "My mother is in Trebizond. We live in the Potters' Ward. (An exclusively Greek quarter.) I took a bundle of clean underwear to my father who works in a labor battalion, and now I am going back."

"You walked all the way?"

"Yes, I had to."

He rubbed his chin, thinking. "All right, climb up."

I got up and sat down on the box beside him. He shook up the reins, and the cart, filled only with a light bedding of straw, rolled down the broad moonlit road with merry jolts.

"I won't charge you more than a mejidieh," he said.

A mejidieh (twenty piasters or one dollar) was a lot of money. I told him I had only a copper penny in my pocket.

"That's all right, your mother will pay," he said.

"But Uncle, we are very poor. My mother can't pay even one piaster."

He pulled up. "I can't give free rides. It takes money to feed my horses."

I pleaded with him in vain. He angrily ordered me out of his cart. I was afraid he suspected me of being an escaped Armenian boy, and not to aggravate him further I got off with many apologies. He drove on.

I was walking now across a moon-frosted land that was like the setting of an angel's dream. It stirred such a wordless rapture in me that I forgot the gendarmes, the irregulars, the Kaimakam. The fingers of the Pontic night had woven a golden loom in the sky.

And now I was not alone, the moon walked with me to keep me company. When I stopped, she too stopped, and when I broke into a short run she raced in seven-league boots, meanwhile grinning and making faces at me. Cheering too was my mischievous shadow on the road, which amused me with all kinds of monkey tricks. I seemed to have been changed into moon-stuff and shadow myself.

The river sounded like an organ in the cathedral of the night, and spouted fountains of heavenly pearls. But when I passed by painfully familiar sights on the road and remembered the night we took poison, the river suddenly changed, it howled savagely, and nude bodies seemed to shoot upward with the spray — whirl a macabre dance in the air — and topple back into the rushing waters. I would look up at the friendly moon, and by some magic the night would become again peaceful and comforting.

The stars fainted away one by one, the moon faded, but the world was no less lovely in the cool, gray beauties of dawn. A dismal old building, the guardhouse where gendarmes stopped travelers and examined their papers, loomed into view, its evil roof sharply etched against the pale, opalescent sky. My first impulse was to turn back and try to make a detour through the bushes and trees, but I thought it wiser to walk on boldly, for, being the only traveler on the highway, the gendarmes had surely seen me, I thought, and any nervousness or hesitation on my part would arouse their suspicions.

My legs threatened to collapse under me as I came close to the guardhouse, but strangely enough nobody stopped me, I saw no gendarmes. Apparently they were all asleep. I walked like a stealthy cat lest they hear my footsteps and wake up. When I was safely behind a mound I giggled like a fool, and hopped along merrily. I could have somersaulted down the road.

The sun emerged from the golden forge of dawn. I felt I was witnessing the creation of the world, for at dawn one comes face to face with the mysterious drama of cosmic beginnings. Sunbeams played along the highway, magnifying the stones and dust particles — over the chilled waters of the river — up and down the wooded slopes — as if a thousand searchlights had been turned over the earth for the sun to conquer. And the earth responded to the sun's warm embrace by smiling up at him with the white teeth of sweet corn, cultivated on steep gradients along the road.

I marched rapturously through this grand festival of the morning, forgetting Jevizlik and death. How good it was to be alive!

I felt as if I had just awakened from a strange, painful dream, as if I had not been deported at all, something had happened to me, I did not know exactly what; I had been lost, but now I had found my way and was hurrying home. I walked faster and faster for fear I would be late for school. My mother was waiting for me. The swallows twittered and flew around our house, our bedroom windows were aglow with the brilliance of the morning sun. Downstairs in the dining room the steaming samovar was whistling its gay old tunes and Aunt Azniv was toasting bread on the copper brazier. I smelled tea, cocoa, buttered toast. Father had already gone to the pharmacy; his large blue coffee cup was on the dining room table.

Mother kept looking down the street, waiting for me.

"Don't you worry about that rascal, he will turn up," Grandmother said.

Our cat entered the dining room mewing, with its tail raised high — when the ringing thud of horses' hoofs behind me roused me from my trance. Glancing back, I saw a squadron of Turkish cavalry cantering down the road, their long lances gleaming. Had the Kaimakam sent them after me? I was paralyzed with fear. But I regained my composure as I realized a single gendarme would have been enough to capture me, and these soldiers were not concerned with my flight. I stepped aside. The officer bent down from his horse and asked me:

"Little countryman, how far is Trebizond?"

"I don't understand Turkish," I replied in Greek, shaking my head.

They clattered away on their horses, while I stood and admired their lances. I did not give him the information he wanted because my Turkish was too good. Greek boys could not speak Turkish as I did; he would have become suspicious.

After these soldiers were gone the first traveler I met on the road was an old Greek peasant woman, trudging along with her donkey.

"*Kalimera,* grandma. Where are you going?"

Her wrinkled face brightened. She gasped for breath, and in a wheezing, squeaking voice said, "To Kirech-hana, son."

Kirech-hana! Why, our neighbors the Persideses were there! I remembered my mother saying once that they had moved to that village after the great bombardment by the Russian fleet. But I was not sure.

"Do you know a city family in Kirech-hana by the name of Persides?" I asked.

"I certainly do!"

"I am going to Kirech-hana too," I said indifferently. "Madam Persides is my aunt, she and my mother are sisters. She wants me to stay with her a few weeks until my mother gets well. My mother is sick in bed. We live in the Potters' Ward. We couldn't afford to go to a village this summer."

She looked at my feet, my dirty, torn clothes. "Where are you coming from?"

"From Jevizlik. My father works in a labor battalion there. My mother sent me to Jevizlik to take him some food. On my way back Turkish boys beat me, tore my clothes and took my cap."

I attached myself to her, and anxiously waited for the moment when we should leave the highway and turn into the side road to her village.

The sky gradually became mottled and shadows fell on the mountain sides. The clouds gathered thickly on the eastern horizon. The sun was now veiled by a cloud, now shone brightly in a patch of blue. The changing weather intensified the chill of the river-grave.

"It will rain," the old woman said, looking up with screwed-up eyes.

The clouds rolled out in huge masses and engaged in stupendous maneuvers. By and by they completely buried the sun. It became dark again, and the eastern horizon, flaming red earlier in the morning, turned into a scowling black.

Like the long red tongue of a snake a fierce zigzag light darted out from a black turret on the cloud battlements of the sky. The highway was illuminated with a tremulous yellow flash, followed by a cracking roll of thunder. The old woman crossed herself, exclaiming, "Holy Mother of God!" She prodded her donkey with her stick and we walked faster. In a few minutes a tornado of shower struck the highway, filling the air with a sharp fusty smell. The river began to boil and turn brown.

We were the only travelers on the road, but suddenly a horseman came galloping toward us through the blinding rain. He wore a long, black, hairy cape with stiff shoulders which gave him a satanic aspect. When he came to within a hundred feet of us my heart stopped: it was Osman Agha! I began to talk to the old woman, pretending not to have seen him at all, but he instantly recognized me as he shot past me like a black demon with bullet speed. He yelled something, tried to rein in his steaming horse and turn back.

At this critical moment we had just reached the side road to her village without my knowing it, and when we left the highway and began climbing a wooded hill, Osman Agha could not see us any more because of the dense growth of shrubs and trees. I kept up my conversation with the old woman as if I had not heard him yell, and she, good soul, was hard of hearing and suspected nothing. I did not dare glance back to see if he was following me, and walked with a cringing sensation, expecting to feel his death grip on my shoulder and hear him snarl into my ear with satanic satisfaction:

"I caught you!"

But he did not follow us. He must have wondered if he had seen the ghost of the perverse Armenian boy who was supposed to have been shot, or perhaps because of the driving rain he let me go. If he had met us further up the highway, or if the weather had been clear, he would have captured me and killed me on the spot, or taken me back to Jevizlik, which also meant death and the river grave.

The old woman took off her cowhide moccasins and thick gray woolen stockings, rolled her bloomers up to her knees, and following her example I took off my brown shoes and socks, for the road, a mere bridle path, became a torrent of mud. But I didn't mind this Pontic thunderstorm, indeed, it gave me an added sense of security. I loved the murmurous rush of the rain in the quiet wood through which we wended our way; I was enchanted by the eerie yellow-green flashes of lightning in the leafy hollows about us, which looked like the casements of fairy castles inhabited by the phantom green folk of woodlands. The mighty thunderclaps were now nothing but glorious salvos by the batteries of the heavenly artillery firing under the personal command of God to rout the forces of evil.

Constantly on the lookout for the sea, I saw it presently from the top of the hill.

"*Thalassa! Thalassa!* The sea! The sea!" I cried. The old woman smiled, not knowing the cause of my intense excitement.

I felt like hugging both her and the donkey, which had a miserable time toiling on under its load of grain, its nervous feet sinking deep in the mud and coming out with popping sounds. I saw everything about me in a new light. The world had changed back to its former magic colors. Jevizlik seemed a million miles away. I was back in the beautiful world.

I bounced back and forth through the wet grass unable to contain my joy. I climbed a wild apple tree, fairly hugging it. The apples were hard and green, but they had a fresh, pure, rainy taste — the taste of the beautiful world by the sea.

"Don't eat them, son, they will give you a stomach-ache," the old woman said.

I tucked a few fairly ripe ones in my blouse. "I will take them to my cousins." I did not want to go to Kirech-hana without a little gift for the Persides children.

We were now traveling through a country of rolling green hills. She pointed to a settlement of white buildings with red roofs in the distance, so pretty it might have been in a picture-book. "That's Kirech-hana," she said.

Instead of leaping with joy, however, I became very sad. Our Greek neighbors were living there, nothing had happened to them, they had not been deported, all of them were leading a normal life, under the same roof. But now I had no home, I was all alone in the world, a fugitive.

My past life with the Persides children unfolded before my eyes in dream-like scenes. I saw Delesila, the oldest daughter, on her wedding day. Weeks of exciting preparations. We children made paper candy bags embossed with the pageantry of ethereal young ladies and gentlemen in top hats, of broughams, lilies and roses. Delesila came out of the house lovelier than an angel in her white bridal gown with a long train, a wreath of orange blossoms on her head, her hand resting in the arm of the tall groom, a handsome young doctor who had recently returned from his studies abroad. She was like a luscious peach filled with the sweetness of her nineteen years, and as fair as he was dark. We went to church with the bridal party in a long procession of phaetons, the bride and groom riding in a shining black brougham drawn by two glossy-coated chestnut horses with docked tails. A banquet was given in the evening. The guests drank champagne and made speeches. We children ate downstairs in another room, and had much more fun than the grown-ups, playing bride and groom. My bride was the gentle, pale Anthula, Delesila's young sister, whom I loved dearly.

I saw the snow man we made that winter when it snowed so hard. It suddenly rose in my vision and grinned at me with its merry black eyes, a pipe in its mouth, leaning over a broom. The sea gulls, gleaming in the auroral splendor of the sun, gobbled up the bread crumbs we threw into the air, and thrilled us with the loud thrum and flap-flap of their wings. I saw vividly the sea gull Anthula caught without trying; it just alighted on her shoulder like the dove of the Holy Spirit. We caressed it and then let it fly away to join its screeching companions, because it would have been a sin to keep such a heavenly bird.

As on the highway early that morning, I became oblivious to my surroundings, and was back in happy scenes, playing with the Persides children, so that I was startled when I found myself in the village. The rain had changed to a light drizzle, there were no people outdoors. The smoke curling up from chimneys indicated pots of warm, nourishing food, cozy, comfortable homes, Christians leading a normal life. We stopped before a cottage. Its thick door was closed.

"Your aunt lives here," the old woman said, and never suspecting my identity, left me in the yard and padded down the road with her donkey.

I hesitated to go ahead and knock on the door. Water trickled down my face, I was soaked to the marrow of my bones, and covered with mud. I thought I would be an unwelcome guest. Mr. Persides was an austere man who never smiled, I had always been afraid of him. He bobbed his head up and down when he walked, and always looked as if he were coming to thrash me with his cane. Madam Persides, though, was a kind, motherly woman.

Presently the door opened and out thrust their pretty heads Anthula and her sister Penelope. They screamed as if they had seen a ghost, and shut the door. I heard an outburst of feminine voices. The door was opened again and Madam Persides came out with all her brood. I could tell by the expression on their faces that they wanted to verify whether it was me or my ghost, and I could not help smiling.

They took me in and asked me how I happened to be alive, how I had found my way to their house, but I could not speak, was tongue-tied, and stared stupidly at them. The girls smothered their sobs by putting handkerchiefs to their mouths. Finally I told them my story in a few spasmodic phrases.

They told me Remzi Sami Bey, our Turkish neighbor, had adopted my two sisters and was treating them like his own daughters. Our Greek laundress had seen them, they were well, but dressed like Turkish girls, and had Turkish names. I did not know what had happened to them after our separation. I told them I had seen Remzi Sami Bey's two sons, Shukri and Mahmut, in an automobile in Jevizlik, but they had deliberately ignored me.

They heated water and gave me a tub bath, fed me and put me to bed. I had walked twelve hours without a moment's rest and could have walked two or three days more by sheer nervous energy, but now, when I was no longer in immediate danger, I felt very tired, and fell asleep.

I must have slept for a week. When I woke up the children came in and joked about my being such a sleepy head. They told me a peasant widow living next door to them and who baked their bread had agreed to keep me in her home, Mr. Persides paying for my board and care.

"We are too well known, everybody in the village knows us," Anthula

said. "And we have Turkish friends who visit us. They will want to know
who you are."

"The Turks will hang papa if they find you in our house!" Penelope said.

I stayed nine months with that peasant family. Neighbors took me for a
Greek boy from another village. My Greek name was Yanko. But I wasn't
allowed to go out of our neighborhood lest some gendarme or passing
Turk recognize me as an Armenian. Sometimes I would secretly climb to
the top of a small wooded hill, from where the sea was clearly visible. The
sea was a vision, an infinitely beautiful mirage, but forever beyond my
reach, it seemed.

Toward the end of that desolate winter the Russian fleet, after a year's
absence, began a systematic bombardment of Trebizond, and Russian
planes roared over our hills, dropping bombs. Every Turk who had a gun
rushed out to take a shot at them from behind rocks and trees, but the planes
swooped down seemingly for the sheer fun of it, or circled round and round
like giant hawks, indifferent to the lively rifle fire of the Turks. As the
Russians advanced on Trebizond the Turks fled panic-stricken, burning
their houses. They were afraid of the Armenian soldiers in the Russian
Army. Before Remzi Sami Bey moved his family to Constantinople, and my
sisters too, they escaped from his house, brave girls, and eventually reached
Dr. Metaxas' home in the monastery of Sumelas, disguised as Greek peasant
girls. They had passed through the village where I was hiding, had even
spent a night there, but I did not see them. Thus we two brothers and two
sisters were alive, and if not free, at least with our Greek friends.

The Turks in our village were fleeing too. One bright April morning
shortly before Easter, we gathered on the village green and watched the
burning Turkish houses as if they were bonfires. Suddenly we saw Russian
soldiers running up the hill, their bayoneted rifles at the ready, led by an
officer with revolver in hand. They came straight at us as if we were the
enemy. We crossed ourselves to show them we were Christians, their friends,
and very happy indeed to see them!

They were about forty big blond fellows with small blue eyes who were
soon smiling at us like children. The village notables gathered to do them
homage. Even the stern, dignified Mr. Persides was a-flutter. A local worthy
who had lived in Russia for some time acted as interpreter. The officer
inquired in what direction the Turkish troops had retreated, and wanted to

pursue them, but the notables raised their hands. No! They could not let them go without serving a breakfast. They were our deliverers.

The Russians sat down and had a feast on the village green. The Persides girls waited on them. The notables clicked glasses with the officer and his men, made speeches of welcome.

"So these are the Russians!" I kept saying to myself. "So I had to live to see this day!" I was the happiest of all. I wanted to roll on the grass, shout, tear my clothes from joy. But oh, if only the Russians had come sooner to save also my parents and relatives!

This platoon was soon followed by whole regiments, a veritable Russian avalanche rolling across the hills. They were magnificent troops, well clothed, well armed, glowing with health and vigor. Their long, rod-like bayonets made them look even taller than they were. I followed them worshipfully, picking up the cartridges and empty shells they dropped on their way. I collected a bagful of them. I also raided Turkish houses, carrying away window sashes, doors, chairs, anything movable I could find.

On Easter Sunday, after mass, when a joyous priest sprinkled holy water on us with a sprig, we had meat, the widow having managed to buy a cow's head with her savings. For nine months, every day, we had had nothing but bean soup cooked with olive oil for dinner.

Two Russian Armenian soldiers came to our cottage and wanted to take me away with them. I belonged to the nation, they said. The nation would take care of me. Orphanages for children like me had been opened. Although I understood what they said I could hardly speak with them, having forgotten my native tongue. There were tears in their eyes. It was only after I assured them in a mixture of Greek, Turkish and Armenian that I was with good friends who had saved my life, that they consented to let me stay, and go to the city by myself. They wanted to be sure I wouldn't grow up as a Greek.

The next day I went to Trebizond with the widow. She carried a basket on her back containing two clay pitchers of milk and two clay jars of yoghurt, which she was going to sell; also half a loaf of corn bread and a bunch of green garlic for our lunch. It was just another trip to the city for her, but I was returning to a lost world where I had lived many thousand years ago.

We went down a tortuous road. When we approached the city the road hugged the western gorge or moat of the old Greco-Roman citadel which rose like the great throne of the once proud empress of the Black Sea. The appearance of these battlemented walls and towers gave me a sad, lonely feeling. A weird little stream swirled along at the stony bottom of the gorge; flowing, it seemed, through the catacombs of time.

On the precipitous sides of the moat, through a profusion of creeping lichens, grew wild fig trees, holding up their green fingers as if they were the hands of the ancient warriors slain under these walls. I sensed the battles that had raged around this citadel, and through the profound brooding silence of time seemed to hear the cries of the attackers and defenders, the roar of the barbarian swarm that swept along these eternal ramparts to the sea.

We descended a few steps to an old half-ruined chapel under a bridge. Crossing ourselves we kissed a miracle-working image of the Virgin. The holy myrtle grew lavishly in these ruins. Through the gap of a crumbling wall I caught a glimpse of the sunlit sea, which was now so thrillingly close to me that I could have almost touched it.

The outlying Turkish quarters were completely deserted, but in the business part of the city, which was also the Christian section, life was returning to normal. Stores were being renovated and painted in anticipation of a booming trade with the Russians. Enterprising Greeks were already replacing Turkish characters with Russian ones on the windows of their stores.

It was noon. The swallows were building their nests under the eaves and balconies, the air rang with the noise of their springtime homecoming. They flew around me, screeching their notes of welcome, as old friends of mine, grazing my shoulders. The air was sweet with the attar of roses and the delicate heavenly fragrance that oozed lazily from the purple flagons of the wistaria.

Crossing the town we went down to the Potters' Ward, where the Greek woman had relatives. Sky and sea were of the same deep pure blue, joined on the horizon.

We stayed there for a while. She had some business to attend to, and female tongues started wagging in the good old Greek fashion. I slipped out of the yard and dashed down impatiently to the sea. I tore off my clothes and dove in, laughing to myself but sobbing too.

CHAPTER 10

The House Where I Was Born

I was on the lookout for an Armenian when we went back to the business district from the Potters' Ward, and my heart leaped with joy when I saw one in a dry goods store across the street from the French School, measuring cloth at the counter. He wore the black shirt and tie of the Armenian Revolutionary Federation, and looked like Uncle Leon.

"That man is an Armenian!" I said to the Greek widow. "Let me go in and talk to him."

"*Barev*, hello," I said to him, entering the store.

"*Barev*, boy. What's your name? Whose son are you?"

I gazed at him with wonder and affection, and the words he spoke sounded so strange to me. It was the language of my dream world, the sweetest ever spoken, and at once the most sorrowful and beautiful. I told him who I was. He turned out to be a close friend of Uncle Leon's, and told me my mother's cousin Barnak, who had been on the mountains with a band of peasants, was in town.

The widow was waiting for me out in the street. I told her I had found a relative and would not return to the village with her. So we separated, agreeing to meet again at five-thirty near the shoe store where her two sons were employed as apprentices. She intended to spend the rest of the day in the city.

I was curious to know how this young man, whose name was Arakel, happened to be living. And answering my halting questions, he told me about himself.

"I was in the mountains with my elder brother. We weren't in Barnak's band. We two had to fight our own battles. We were lucky to recover most of our stock when we came back to town, and now, as you can see, I have put my rifle away and taken up the old measuring rod again." He was tall and slender like Uncle Leon, and talked like him too. I did not know yet that he was also actor, poet and musician — like most revolutionaries both a fighter and intellectual. I was to become his pupil later, and learn from him the folk songs of Armenia.

"They finished us off this time," he said. "We believed them, and see what they did to us." He clenched his teeth and shook his handsome head. "They drowned poor Leon, drowned him alive, with a big stone tied to his neck. Don't you ever forget it, my dear." He seemed to be talking to himself as well as to me. "There aren't twenty Armenians left in this town. They extinguished our smoke by the German method. These donkeys too have learned to be efficient and scientific. Lining up ten men, one behind the other, with their arms and hands tied with ropes, and shooting them through with one bullet, to save ammunition, after making them dig their own graves." He quoted a Turkish proverb: "'The Turk goes rabbit hunting in a carriage.' Yes, my dear, the Turk makes the rabbits come to him, he is so wily. We are a stupid people, stupid! We never learned our lesson."

I was dying to see our house, and told my new friend I wanted to go out for a walk. He asked me to be back in his store before closing time in the evening. Barnak would be with him then, and he would take care of me, I needn't worry.

As I walked toward our house, it seemed to me I was going home from school. It was noon, and I could see Mother in the kitchen straining spaghetti and Victoria setting the table in the dining room. I had walked along this street so many times on my way to school and back. I knew every stone and crack, every rose bush, wistaria and telegraph pole. My heart pounded as I saw them again. Glancing up at the blue sky I experienced the same thrill I had felt when the return of warm weather promised another summer vacation in the country.

Turning left on the main street I began to run as soon as I was out of the business district proper. I ran faster and faster, and meanwhile prayed, pleading with God to perform a miracle and let me find my mother at home, in the kitchen, as I saw her so clearly in my mind. I tried to assure myself she would be there, I would find everything at home as usual, I was merely going home from school for lunch. The buildings, walls, flowers, telegraph poles were all there, all the same. Nothing had changed. Only the Russians were here now, and we were free and safe. I ran madly into our side street — and stopped. I saw it overgrown with weeds. They came up to my waist. Doors and windows were shut, our street was silent and still, like a street of the dead. Our Greek neighbors had all gone to villages, and apparently I was the first one to return.

I walked to our house at the end of the street slowly, with dragging feet. The weeds before our house were the tallest of all, they reached up to my shoulders. Our door was left ajar, the only one open. I stood before it for several minutes, afraid to go in and not find my mother in the kitchen. At last, with a feeling of extreme reverence, my heart beating fast, I entered our house.

I felt as if I had entered a large tomb. Standing in the flagged entrance hall I looked around. It was bare, bare like the walls of a mausoleum. The dining room door, the living room door, the kitchen door, the drawing room door, all of which opened on this spacious hallway, had a vacant, fixed, bony stare, like eye sockets from which the living eyes had been gouged out. I could see that all the rooms were empty and dead.

I stepped into the first door to my right. Nothing was left in it, even the linoleum had been stripped off the floor. On rainy days Onnik and I used to spin our tops here, I thought, and Mother used to chase me around the table to spank me with her slipper, but could never catch me. And it was here, on the dining room table, that Onnik and I made our kites in red, blue, yellow squares and triangles, with long swishing tails of paper strips. And here, too, Onnik practiced his violin lessons, and a map of Greece hung on the wall, at which the Persides girls would often come in to look.

I went to the living room, where we had a larger map, that of Italy, hanging on the wall. For a long time I had taken it for the picture of a giant's hairy leg, and only after I studied geography in school did I realize that it represented Italy, with the "hairs" being the names of numerous cities. Father liked maps, brought a new one home from time to time. I remembered the maps of Turkey I drew, using a different color for each vilayet or province; that an island is land surrounded by water, a lake water surrounded by land; that the earth is round, not flat, and moved around the sun.

Here, in this living room Father used to write hundreds of French letters to his customers on winter nights. Respectable customers paid only once a year, after receiving an itemized bill in French. When Father made a mistake he would throw the paper on the floor, and I would instantly pounce upon it, to add it to my collection. And I remembered the night Father beat me.

If he would only beat me again! Grandmother sat there, by the stove, on a thin mattress under which Father kept his papers. I remembered the soldier's uniform he gave me on New Year's Eve, when he distributed the gifts. I had seen Mother sew it, but did not suspect anything until I opened the large box tied with a ribbon. Greek boys came to our door with a lantern and sang *Ai-Vasil,* St. Basil's hymn. Father gave a silver mejidieh to the leader, and we filled their pockets with almonds, candy, St. John's bread, oranges, apples, dried figs and apricots.

Mother sat there, by the windows, when she sewed on her Singer machine. And Nevart, Onnik and I would fight for elbow space at the table on which we copied our lessons, Nevart using purple ink.

I fled to our drawing room, and immediately heard Father's loud voice, playing baccarat — *"Quarrrrraaaaaannttte! Brrrrrrrrr!* This will clean you up, my friends, you are sunk, this won't leave a seed in your pockets — *Quarrrrraaaaaaaaanntte,* I say!" And the round walnut table under the crystal chandelier shook as he brought his hand down on it with all his force, and turning up his card for all to see, waved it under their noses, with another long *brrrrrrrrrr!* — to lose again.

"Bis! Bis! Repetez! Repetez!" I heard Brother Vertanes saying, clapping his hands. Eugenia's doll was usually on the sofa there, a chubby, bright-cheeked thing with long eyelashes like hers and a broken arm, closing and reopening its eyes as I laid it down on its back or made it sit up. I could see Eugenia coming into the room, playing "bride," kissing the hands of our guests one by one, her eyes cast down with true bridal modesty. And on the wall there, stuck in a Japanese bamboo panel, with pictures of parasoled, slant-eyed women, were photographs and French cards, and the postcard of Napoleon on his horse Aunt Azniv had sent me from Beirut.

I ran out of the drawing room to the kitchen. It occupied almost half of our house, and was so high it was impossible to keep it warm in the winter. No, Mother was not there. But I could see her boiling a caldron of figs for our annual supply of fig preserve, and we children, teaspoons and saucers in our hands, smacking our lips in anticipation of another helping of the hot, delicious purple foam that formed on the surface of the simmering caldron.

I went down a flight of stone steps to the dark, damp basement, where we stored our charcoal and chopped wood. In vain I groped for a piece of charcoal or wood to press it to my heart. It too was empty. I ran up to our storeroom attic, where we kept our pickles and olives, white cheese in brine and "country cheese" in goat skin, apples, walnuts, filberts, dried fruits, boxes of macaroni and soap, sacks of flour and rice, wooden containers packed with salted butter, big bottles of olive oil, heavy conical loaves of sugar wrapped in stiff blue paper which we broke into small pieces with a hammer and an old knife minus its handle, a discarded spinning-wheel, Grandfather's narghile, Eugenia's high baby chair, the cradle in which Victoria had rocked me to sleep — my earliest memory. I looked in vain even for an empty jar or our mouse trap. Everything had disappeared.

I hurried upstairs, to the bedrooms, the balcony, the bathroom, in my frantic search for something to keep as a memento of our house, but I found nothing. I lingered at the door of Mother's bedroom, and caressed the glass knob, thinking, Mother's hands have touched it. Then I clawed the walls, wanted to strike my head against them in my anguish and rage. The bare, empty rooms looked at me with their sad, fixed, bony stare, in tombstone silence.

Finally I went into our backyard. Even our chicken coop was gone. I remembered how I used to "drill" our roosters and hens in military formations, and insisted they understood and obeyed my French commands. The sparrows Onnik and I used to catch here with a sieve trap! Watching them from the living room, our noses flattened against the cold window-panes, as we held the string of the trap. The sparrows knew our tricks and were very suspicious. They hopped around the sieve, tilted over a stick to which the string was attached, tempted by the bread crumbs and grain we had scattered under it. They would cock their heads, listening, observing, wondering whether they should take a chance. Then one foolish sparrow would recklessly enter the trap, we would pull the string, and the sieve would fall over it with a thud. But our paternal grandmother would not let us keep the sparrows we caught; we had to let them go free. "God punishes boys who harm the sparrows," she said.

"Miaow! Miaow!" I heard a familiar sound, and looking up, saw our cat crawling along the tile-topped wall that separated our backyard from the garden of a Turkish house in the rear.

"Kitty! Kitty!" I called.

He jumped down and came to purr between my legs, his back stiffly arched, looking up at me with a painfully human expression on his dear whiskered face. "Where have you been all this time?" the cat seemed to ask me. "Where are the others? Aren't they ever coming back? Why did you all go away and leave me alone? I have missed you so."

"And I have missed you, too," I said, taking him up in my arms. He used to be the king of our storeroom attic, and all the little rice-and-cheese-loving mice were in terror of him. Generations of them had fallen into his claws. He liked to play with them, toss them around. But now there were no more provisions for him to guard, and he had grown gaunt from hunger and grief.

I did not want to leave our house again, I wanted to stay there forever with our cat — but I did not know what was the matter with my throat, I could not breathe. I had no place to keep our cat — and I was afraid if I stayed another minute I would choke to death. As, alarmed, I put the cat down and ran through the kitchen back to the entrance hall, he followed me, clung to my legs, miaowing fiercely. I managed to dodge him, though, and shutting the door behind me, staggered out into the weeds of the street, gasping for breath, like a person escaping from a house on fire. I ran away from our house, with the cat crying after me behind the shut door, shaken by a deep, violent weeping that does not break into tears.

Away from our house, I could breathe again. But now the sky, the buildings, the flowers and telegraph poles were not the same any more.

I noticed another Armenian store open, a china shop. I went in and greeted the owner's son, who knew me. He introduced me to a girl, saying they had just married.

"How old are you?" I said, surprised.

"Seventeen. She is sixteen. We were engaged before the war."

Both had lost their parents and families, but had found each other, and the Turks had somehow left the valuable stock of his father's store intact. They were busy cleaning and sorting it out.

"I went to our house," I said, "but I couldn't find anything."

The girl sighed. "Our house is a complete shambles."

"They have torn down practically every Armenian house to find hidden treasures," her youthful husband said. "But the Turkish police have dumped a lot of furniture from Armenian homes in our new church, in the prelacy compound, where our school is. Why don't you go there?"

I envied them. They were starting life all over, together. He tried to act very grown up and business-like. "There is more of this stuff at home," he said enthusiastically. "I have three girls working there for me. I can use you too. I will pay you."

Here was a chance for me to buy the Greek widow a gift before she went back to the village, and I eagerly accepted his offer. He sent me to his house, which happened to be right across the street from the new church. So first of all I decided to see what I could find there. As I entered the compound I remembered my happy school days — the first bombardment by the Russian fleet when we were having our Turkish lesson about the frog that talked too much — the horror of our last night in the prelacy rooms, before I, too, was deported with Aunt Azniv, Victoria and my cousins.

An Armenian doorkeeper would not let me into the church. He made me so angry! As soon as he left the gate for a few minutes, I slipped in. The great building, in construction for many years and not completed yet, over which our community had proudly spent much money so that we would have the largest and finest Christian church in town, was filled with a mountain of furniture — heavy pieces like bedsteads, bathtubs, bureaus, sofas. It would have taken me hours to find anything belonging to us. I ran along the aisles, glancing quickly left and right, afraid the doorkeeper would come in after me. Soon I dove into a big pile of photographs heaped on the floor. After a minute's breathless search on my hands and knees I found our family picture, also Uncle Leon's and Brother Vertanes's in a Turkish officer's uniform. I dashed out of the church before the doorkeeper got back and didn't stop until I was clear around the block.

Was that little boy in the starched white turned-down collar and flowing cravat, holding a hoop, really myself? I could hardly believe it as I gazed upon my likeness at the age of seven, many thousands of years ago. I stood beside Mother, who was seated, her elbow resting on a decorative table, on the edge of which sat Eugenia, doll-like with a comb and ribbon in her hair. On my other side sat my paternal grandmother, her wrinkled hands in her lap, wearing her long fur-lined coat, the muslin kerchief drawn tight over her head. Victoria, in a lacy white dress and white bow in her hair, stood behind me. Onnik, in long black stockings while I always wore short socks winter or summer, was leaning against Grandmother, with a dreamy, thoughtful expression in his eyes — I was wide-eyed. Next to him stood Nevart, in a white dress, a white bow in her hair. And as if to show the length of her hair, part of it streamed down in front over her right shoulder. Unfortunately Father and Aunt Azniv were not in this portrait. Father did not like to be photographed, to take time off from his pharmacy to pose for a picture. And Aunt Azniv was still on her pilgrimage to Jerusalem when we had this taken.

I wept bitterly over these photographs, without tears. I was stronger then. At last I had found something linking me with my dream-like past. At last I had definite proof in my hands, to convince myself that I had not been always alone, not always an orphan, that I was not just imagining I, too, once had a mother and family, which I had begun to doubt.

I worked a few hours with the three girls. We had to clean, dust off, sort out and rearrange two roomfuls of china and glassware. The faces of the girls were prematurely aged, and though I asked them no embarrassing questions, I suspected they had been forced to satisfy the lust of their Turkish masters. All three were dressed in black and sang mournful songs. They were sisterly toward me.

I was disappointed to learn I wasn't to be paid for a day or two, our youthful employer being short of cash. So I went to meet the Greek widow with coffee cups and saucers tucked away in my pockets and blouse — small, delicate cups for Turkish coffee. My conscience bothered me for stealing them, but not much, because I thought the Turks might have taken them themselves, not left him anything, as they had left me nothing, he was very lucky to recover his father's stock. At any rate, we were fortunate to be alive, and he wouldn't miss a few cups and saucers, I said to myself.

The widow was waiting for me near the shoe store, basket on back. She appreciated my gift, not knowing it was stolen goods.

"It's very nice of you, Yanko," she said, as she wrapped them up carefully in her shawl and put them in her basket. "I can certainly use them. The price of sugar will go down now that the Russians are here, and even poor folks like us can drink a little coffee on holidays. Ye-es, when you grow up you will be a rich man. Don't forget us."

"Never," I declared. I did not know how to thank her for saving my life, even though I had not been happy in her home. "Some day, I will come to visit you," I said. I imagined myself returning to Kirech-hana loaded with gifts: building a city-like house for her, a new school for the village, and treating everybody to a feast.

After we parted I went back to the dry goods store, where I met Barnak. He had been a legend to me. I had seen him only once or twice before the war and did not know him well.

"Are you still climbing trees?" he asked, with a twinkle in his eye. He knew all about my tree climbing, Uncle Leon and Grandmother had told him.

I questioned him about his famous band which included the entire population of an Armenian village, men, women and children. Even the women and children had fought. And strangely enough, one of their leaders was a Turk who had rebelled against his own race and joined his Armenian neighbors.

"If at least Uncle Leon were living!" I said. I missed him most next to my mother.

Barnak looked at his photograph and frowned. "I sent him word to come and join us," he said.

"He didn't want to leave Grandmother alone, and he was afraid the Turks would torture her if he escaped."

"They didn't spare her."

He took me to a newly opened boarding house near our pharmacy, at which I cast a furtive glance, and seeing that it wasn't a pharmacy any more, I looked away.

"You can stay here for the present, but you need home care," Barnak said. "This is not the right place for you. Do you know that you have relatives in Batum?" I did not; I was glad to hear that. "Mariam Hanum, your mother's and my aunt, lives there with her son and daughter. I think you had better go to Batum. I will write to her."

I slept in a makeshift bed that night. The next day I met Nurikhan on the street, who also had saved my life by giving me shelter during my dreadful days in Jevizlik.

"You alive!" he exclaimed, taken aback.

I was so glad to see him!

"I thought they had caught you and dispatched you to the other world, you good-for-nothing," he added, laughing, and I laughed with him. "We heard in Jevizlik they had caught an escaped Armenian boy and we thought it was you."

The Turks were still in Jevizlik. He didn't know what had happened to our companions there, for he had escaped four or five months after me, his sisters in the Swiss consulate had kept him, although he had had some very close calls while in hiding. Gendarmes raided houses for deserters. He, too, was soon going to relatives in Russia; he told me proudly his cousins had a tobacco plantation near Ekaterinodar, where the Cossacks lived.

CHAPTER 11

My Russian Cap

The Russian ship was wary of the German submarines prowling in the Black Sea and hugged the rugged coastline of Lazistan. Dolphins raced with us as we passed small Turkish towns — clusters of glittering white buildings with red roofs. I had never been on a ship before, and I was going to my great-aunt in Batum, with a group of Armenian war orphans.

At sundown we entered a mined bay crowded with Russian army transports and destroyers. The ship surged through a sea of molten glass, and moved right up to the edge of a cobblestoned pier, instead of anchoring half a mile or so off the shore, as ships did in the harbor of my home town, Trebizond. Presently the streets of Batum bloomed with electric lamps. I had never seen electric lights before, and was enchanted.

We needed no rowboats for going ashore; all I had to do was just walk down the gang-plank. As I stood on Russian soil I felt so secure, and somehow at home, though I found myself in a different world altogether. This was Christianity and Civilization, this was a land of laughter, goodness, and music. Carrying my little bundle, I went and sat down on a green iron bench, looking around, thrilled by everything I saw. Gay crowds were promenading on the esplanade, girls singing and sailors playing balalaikas. The girls were chubby and barelegged, and wore light summer clothes with colorful kerchiefs tied round their blonde heads. They flirted with the sailors, and now and then I heard a chorus of feminine shrieks.

"So I am in Russia, so this is Batum!" I kept saying to myself.

A woman and two boys approached me. "Did you come on this ship, son?" she asked me in Armenian.

I said "yes," wondering if she was my great-aunt, whom I had never seen, and admiring the Russian school caps the two boys wore. They also spoke to me, in halting Armenian, pronouncing the words like Russians. She was not my great-aunt, but a friend of my mother's. She asked me if my parents were living.

"The Turks killed them," I said. "They were deported and killed. I was deported too; they gave me a Turkish name and tried to make me a Moslem, but I ran away."

"Oh, your mother Zvart was so beautiful!" she sighed, drying her eyes with a handkerchief. "She was here once with your Uncle Leon. And what a splendid young man he was! What happened to him, do you know?"

"They drowned Uncle Leon in the sea," I said, trying hard not to cry. "He was a revolutionary."

She told me my great-aunt, Mariam Hanum, was at Borzhom, a summer resort, and wouldn't be back for a month. She didn't look very prosperous, and I didn't want her to think I expected her to keep me until Mariam Hanum returned. "I'll go to the orphanage with the other boys," I said, though I shuddered at the very sound of the word orphanage.

They assured me it was a good place, and the two boys said enviously that the orphans swam every day. She wanted me to stay with her for the night, and I went to a cobbled court with them, where they lived in an old tumbledown cottage. Neighbors came to see me, questioned me about their relatives in Trebizond, and some of them cried, which made me very uncomfortable.

The next day she brought me a pair of new shoes, which I needed badly, and took me around visiting people who knew my mother.

"Zvart's son, would you believe it?" she would tell them.

I heard a story about my mother which made quite an impression on me. While she was in Batum, Tsar Nicholas II visited the city, and everybody admired the beauty of a young princess in the imperial party. My mother was sorry she missed the parade and didn't see this lady. Friends told her she looked just like her. Since my mother resembled a Russian princess I felt almost like a Russian, and one related to the imperial family...

The two boys took me on a sightseeing tour and taught me a few Russian words. Then I went to the orphanage on an excursion train — my first train ride. It was located in the village of Kobuleti, the second station on the railway to Tiflis, and like a fashionable suburb of Batum. The orphans lived in a handsome villa fronting the beach. They were deeply tanned, barefoot boys with their hair sheared off. Here, I learned to swim, and gained weight, after months of hunger. A neighboring farm supplied us with bucketfuls of rich, foamy milk. We stole fruits from the surrounding orchards, and I stuffed myself with purple mulberries, tangerines, Japanese persimmons, big yellow plums. We were on the beach all day, my skin peeled off completely, and I emerged as a genuine member of the dusky orphanage tribe.

And so I was not anxious to go back to Batum when my great-aunt returned from her vacation and her daughter came to take me from the orphanage. We were in the middle of summer. Still, I was proud to be claimed by an attractive, well-dressed young woman. She smiled as she saw me, and I realized I looked funny. She seemed disappointed. "You have taken after your father," she said. I knew I was homely.

Mariam Hanum received me kindly. She lived in a small house with her daughter and son Sarkis, a gloomy young man. She was a gentle woman with a pale face and blue eyes. I went to the bazaar with her every morning carrying her shopping bag. The bazaar was a cobblestoned square with many booths, divided into various sections: the fruit and vegetable market, the fish market, the meat and poultry market, and so on. There were great mounds of watermelons and cucumbers, huge barrels of sauerkraut for borsch, and some booths sold nothing but barbecued sucking pigs, the Georgian's idea of heaven on earth. I had never seen pigs before, for the Turks did not eat pork and pigs were not allowed in Turkey.

I played with Russian boys, who all wore Russian school caps with their Russian shirts and belts. And I who had worn a fez in Turkey but was now in Russia wanted nothing so much as a Russian cap. I wore a white summer cap which was too big for me and belonged to Sarkis. I thought everybody who saw it knew it wasn't mine. There wasn't another boy in Batum who wore such a cap. Sarkis had bought it in Paris, and it was a nice cap for a grown-up man who had been to France to wear, but it wasn't a Russian cap.

I learned to speak Russian, and hummed to myself Russian songs, which I liked very much, especially "Volga, Volga, Mother Volga," from the song of Stenka Razin, the great Cossack bandit who helped the poor. I went to all the military parades, drank kvass, the sour Russian beer, cracked sunflower seeds like any genuine Russian boy. I was being rapidly Russianized, except for my cap.

Every day was like a holiday in Batum, the largest and most attractive city on the Caucasian coast of the Black Sea, a happy vacation land for the

Russians. Many of them who came from places like Omsk, Moscow, and Astrakhan had never eaten oranges and persimmons before, and had never seen mountains. They loved the boulevard on the beach, with its Australian palms and bamboos. The boulevard was the most popular rendezvous. A Cossack band played in a pavilion. Nursemaids pushed baby carriages along the graveled walks, on sand piles plump children with flaxen hair dug with their spades. A casino served kvass, ice cream, Caucasian mineral waters. Under large umbrellas that dotted the beach like great poppies people read books, magazines, newspapers. Statuesque Russian blondes lay on the hot sand all day long, and even at nights, when the beach was flooded with a tropic moonlight. They had strong, shapely, nut-brown bodies with shocks of wheat-colored hair, and their cute little noses were turned upward. Their lush thighs quivered as they walked on the clean white pebbles.

During the vesper services in the Russian cathedral I could hear, no matter in what part of the city I happened to be, the ringing of its many bells — an air-borne concert of thunderous bronze and delicate silver chimes, the sweet vibrations of the little bells sounding as if produced by the beating of angels' wings, while the big fat bells boomed like cannon. This church had soaring domes of indigo blue, onion shaped, topped with double-barred golden crosses, and old Turkish guns gaped around its landscaped grounds. Magnificent and a bit barbaric, it represented all the might of Holy Russia near the Turkish border.

And then there were the great express trains that came from all parts of Russia via Baku and Tiflis. I would go to the station and watch the locomotives with their enormous steaming wheels and hissing pistons. The oil was pumped from Baku to Batum through an underground pipe-line a thousand kilometers long, and in the oil harbor flat-bottomed boats crawled like giant turtles, making a chug-chug-chug sound.

On Sundays we visited a family who lived in a *dacha*, or country house, and I fell in love with the daughter of this family. Her name was Shushik, or Little Lily, and she was as white as a lily, too. She attended the girls' gymnasium, and captivated me with her dashing manners and laughing, sensuous voice. She had many admirers, gymnasium students who clicked their heels when they kissed her hand. She was unaware of my secret passion for her and treated me with contempt and pity because I was an orphan from Turkey. I was so miserable in her presence that I hardly dared speak to her.

She had a chum, Araxi, also a gymnasium student, whom I loved in a different, spiritual way, for hers was a fragile, sensitive, ethereal beauty, and she had moist, soft eyes. Her mother was an actress. These girls were like two young fairy princesses, though both were distantly related to me. They habitually spoke Russian.

One day I boasted to them I could read French. "Oh really?" Shushik said, surprised, and a little sarcastic.

"Let's see if he can read our French textbook," Araxi said.

I read: *"J'ai, tu as, il a, nous avons, vous avez, ils ont."*

They were impressed. Here I was, an orphan, and only eleven years old, reading French. I felt better, but I was still very self-conscious in their presence and would have given anything for a Russian cap.

One day I found one in the bazaar, trampled upon by the passers-by, but a real Russian cap such as all the schoolboys wore in Batum. I trembled with joy as I picked it up: it seemed as if God had dropped it for me from heaven. It was greasy and soiled and had one or two burnt holes in it, but I thought I could clean and repair it. I put it on my head, and it fitted me almost perfectly. I ran home with it and hid it in the bottom drawer of a bureau, hoping nobody would find it there. I imagined wearing it in the boulevard, during parades, while playing with Russian schoolboys. I could carry it in my blouse while leaving or entering our courtyard, for I didn't want to seem ungrateful to my relatives for not wanting to wear the white cap they had given me.

But the very next day Sarkis, whose discarded cap I was wearing, found my Russian cap. He lifted it up with two fingers as if it were a dead rat, and looked at it curiously with his gloomy black eyes.

"Who brought in this filthy thing?" he asked Mariam Hanum, and she replied that I must have found it somewhere. I was playing in the yard at the moment, but I could see and hear what they said. Sarkis came out on the porch holding my Russian cap, and with a look of intense disgust threw it into the rubbish can. He was an odd young man, always well dressed and well barbered, but not working, morose and taciturn. I was careful not to irritate him in any way and was always eager to show him my appreciation of his cap, but this was more than I could bear. I ran and took my Russian cap out of the rubbish can and dusted it off. He didn't say anything, but I could tell by the angry look he gave me that he meant to say, "Don't you dare bring it in again!"

"Where did you get that cap? Throw it away," Mariam Hanum said to me, after witnessing this tense little drama between us.

But I would not, I could not, throw it away. It meant too much to me. I was choking with an emotion that was more than fury and humiliation.

I ran away with my Russian cap and wandered through the streets for hours. I debated in my mind what I should do, and decided to go back to the orphanage. So I began walking toward Kobuleti, which was ten or twelve kilometers from Batum.

It was getting dark by the time I reached the industrial suburb near the oil harbor. The sky was cloudy, and a few big, cool drops of rain splashed against my face. I walked faster and faster across railroad tracks, past freight cars and tank cars, warehouses, colossal storage tanks, refineries, tin works. I had never been through this part of the city before, and it fascinated me and terrified me at the same time. I felt very lonely, lost, was seized by a strange fear. The ground under my feet shook with the noises of distant places, of Baku and Derbent on the mysterious shores of the Caspian, with the sounds of other worlds, and the immense wall of the Caucasian mountains looming before me became more and more menacing. The trees took fantastic shapes in the twilight, muggy darkness; the air was thick with steely goblins clacking and screaming in a grotesque carnival, pounding their fists against I knew not what, and showing their deadly iron teeth.

I got so scared I turned back. And moreover, I felt guilty. My great-aunt had been good to me, and even Sarkis, whom I didn't like, was after all my mother's cousin. I thought of the scandal my return to the orphanage would cause. People would say I was a spoiled, ungrateful brat, or would blame Mariam Hanum. This is a family quarrel that should remain in the family, I said to myself.

But it broke my heart to throw away my Russian cap. I dropped it into the sea, watched it float, then turned around and walked back, feeling again very much an orphan.

"Where have you been?" Mariam Hanum asked me, glancing at my shoes, which looked like a tramp's. "Come on, wash yourself and have your dinner."

They had eaten already, and fortunately Sarkis was out. I smelled the warm, rich fragrance of eggplants and tomatoes stuffed with spiced ground meat. I stood before her with bowed head, partly from shame, and partly to hide my tears.

"You silly boy," she said. "It was just a piece of rag."

I was silent. How could I tell her what that Russian cap meant to me, even though it was a rag? I wasn't a child any more. My desire to wear a Russian cap wasn't just a childish whim, and it wasn't because I looked so comic and pathetic in a man's cap. No, I could not explain it to anyone. It had to do with a magic Russian city beyond the horizon, on the other side of the mountains, and my sole hope in the most desperate and sorrowful moments of my life on the highway of death, during the massacre. It had to do with my wordless rapture in being alive and free and Christian again, for recovering the good world I had lost and which I loved passionately with every fiber in my little body. It had to do with songs and balalaikas, electric lights, trains, a certain Russian princess. It had to do with God, Europe, Civilization, and everything.

CHAPTER 12

Reunion

One day, after I had been in Batum six months, a young man returning from Trebizond brought me a letter from Onnik. Yes, once upon a time I had a brother but I could hardly believe he actually existed and was back in our home town.

"After the Russians occupied Trebizond the Turks deported Dr. Metaxas and his family to Ardasa, and we went with them, but now, glory be to God, we are free and in good health, and have been in Trebizond two months," I read. "Come back as soon as you can because the Mekhitarist School will reopen and I have already registered you as a pupil. The school will later send us to Venice, to the Mourad-Raphael College." A bank note was enclosed, with which Onnik wanted me to buy him a wrist watch.

I read and reread this letter to Mariam Hanum and others in our courtyard, and told my Russian playmates I was going to Italy. I no longer felt so inferior to Shushik and Araxi.

"I might study also in Paris and London," I said to my playmates casually. I imagined myself returning to Batum and *ignoring* Shushik and Araxi at a ball. They would try to attract my attention, but I would be surrounded by other girls.

I went back to Trebizond on a Russian ship.

We sailed at night, without lights. An eerie voyage, with no moon. A few small stars twinkled faintly like dying glowworms in a black-velvet sky. There was a heavy swell, and through the rush and thunder of the sea Russian destroyers emerged like gaunt gray wolfhounds, poking their noses in the air, as they patrolled this treacherous coast against German submarines.

I slept on the deck. When I awoke in the morning the sea had calmed, and the stark, sharp mountains of Surmeneh shot into the flaming sky like gigantic geysers of rose-colored lights. And soon I was entranced by the white radiance of Trebizond, at its most dazzling from the sea on a sunny October morning.

The Russians had converted an old Roman pier into a modern landing-place. I could see signs of progress everywhere. Dredges were deepening the shoal areas in the bay. Small locomotives, puffing white smoke and whistling merrily pulled long lines of those little boxcars which starving gangs of Greek soldiers used to push up to Jevizlik. And as in Batum, the harbor was mined and full of ships. A sailor pointed out the hulk of a steamer a German submarine had sunk, before being driven away by the Russian shore batteries.

Getting off the ship I swung my little bundle on my back and walked up the harbor street, which now bore a Russian name, to my joy. Store windows were emblazoned with Russian characters, newsboys sold Russian papers, peddlers shouted their wares in Russian. The traffic on the harbor street was blocked not by sheep from Erzurum, as in former days, but by an endless procession of army trucks, their drivers sucking oranges. The Kuban and Don Cossacks rode on big horses almost twice the size of ours and the Siberian Cossacks on shaggy, curly-coated ponies, carrying lances. Gun carriages rattled along, drawn by mighty teams of Belgian artillery horses with huge hairy hoofs that clopped down like enormous clogs. It was no longer the old Turkish Trebizond, but a Russianized, booming city pulsating with the rhythm of a new life.

I met Onnik at the door of Dr. Metaxas' house just as he was going out — a dream figure from a lost world miraculously become immediate and real. We almost bumped into each other, and were speechless for a while. There was a growth of pale golden down on his face, and he looked very mature (he was almost fourteen now), in his blue suit with long trousers, while I still wore short pants.

"You are already taller than I am," he said. "How you have grown!"

I gave him the wrist watch. He had earned money by working in a tobacco shop. Hearing my voice Nevart and Eugenia came rushing down the stairs. They fell tearfully on my neck.

"I am crying from joy," Nevart said. "Let us thank God," she raised her eyes and crossed herself, "all four of us are alive and have been reunited. So many families have completely disappeared!"

And indeed compared to them we were fortunate.

Nevart had not changed much, but Eugenia was no longer the little mite I used to know. She had grown prettier, too. They said I looked healthy and tough, my back was so broad.

"You have become a regular roughneck," Nevart laughed through her tears.

Before I met the doctor, I greeted Madam Electra, his wife, Haji Mana, his mother, and a formidable array of other Greek ladies visiting them in the drawing room.

"He is not like us, the roughneck," Nevart told them half apologetic and half proud, "but he would not be alive today if he were."

"He does not look like any of you," commented Madam Electra, not very approvingly, I thought.

"I remember him when he was born," Haji Mana said. "He was a brown, skinny, ugly thing, not like Alexandro, who was a pink and plump baby." Alexandro was Onnik's Greek name. Nevart was Niobe now, and they pronounced Eugenia's name as in Greek.

"Well, you haven't your brother's looks, but you try to be smarter," Haji Mana told me. She added in an undertone, as an aside for the visiting ladies, "That's a big order." Onnik modestly blushed. "You should have heard, my dears, Alexandro reading the gospels and singing our church hymns in the monastery. The monks themselves could not read them better." Then turning to me again: "You go to school, my boy, study hard, become a good and honorable man, and maybe," she winked, "I will give you Georgette as wife."

Georgette, the doctor's second daughter, was a little charmer with perfect classic features.

My brother and sisters had become an integral part of the doctor's family and impressed me as more Greek than Armenian, while by now I had shed the Greek character I myself had acquired before going to Batum.

After this formal introduction we four left the drawing room and went into the garden. We had so much to talk about. I asked my sisters if Shukri and Mahmut told them they had seen me in Jevizlik.

"Yes, they did," Nevart said. "We cried so much Selma Hanum sent a gendarme to Jevizlik with a special order to bring you back. She wanted to keep you with us. The gendarme searched but could not find you. Later we heard through our Greek laundress you had escaped and were in Kirech-hana.

"Mahmut would tell me you were fishing at the bottom of the sea," Eugenia said.

"Oh, well, he was just a child," Nevart said. "He never said such things in the presence of his mother."

When the gendarmes came to the sham orphanage and separated us, the remaining girls were shown to crowds of Turks, who came and picked the ones they liked. The older girls were chosen for marriage and the younger ones for adoption. Selma Hanum, who apparently knew where they were, adopted my sisters. She had moved back to the city with her family. Nevart and Eugenia insisted they were treated well, that Remzi Sami Bey and his wife had been really kind to them.

Remzi Sami Bey had poisoned our grandmothers in his hospital, with other leaders of the Ittihad he had directed the deportation and massacre. And yet, he had tried to be like a father to my sisters, had even engaged a piano teacher for Nevart. He was good to them as long as they pretended to have become Turks.

"We were very comfortable, but we did not want to stay with them because we could never give up our nationality and religion," Nevart said. "When the Russians occupied Erzurum and advanced on Trebizond Remzi Sami Bey prepared to move his family to Constantinople, and we were going with them. One morning the Turks went to the harbor to celebrate the arrival of a Turkish warship. Eugenia and I were on our way to the harbor with our Turkish maid when whom should we meet but Dr. Metaxas? I was dressed like a Turkish girl but my face was not veiled and he recognized me. We stopped and talked with him in Greek, so the maid could not understand what we said. 'Don't go to Constantinople,' he told us, 'but run away and communicate with me from the nearest Greek house. I will find a way of sending you to Monastir.'

"At noon we returned home, and I was setting the table when I suddenly thought we had better escape right now because with the exception of the maid everybody was out, and the Turks were still celebrating at the harbor."

"I was so afraid when Nevart told me 'let's run away,'" Eugenia said.

"She didn't want to," Nevart continued, "but I finally coaxed her to, and putting on our charshafs we hurried out of the house while the maid was busy in the kitchen, and nobody saw us when we went and knocked on the door of a Greek house. We told them we had just escaped from Remzi Sami Bey's house and needed their protection. They refused to take us in. 'We are afraid,' they said, 'we have no menfolk.' But as soon as I gave Dr. Metaxas' name and told them he would send us to Monastir they consented to take us in.

"The doctor came and told us to stay in that house a few days until he could arrange for our transfer to Monastir, but we had to spend three weeks there, so close to Remzi Sami Bey's house, in constant danger of being caught! Remzi Sami Bey had policemen and women spies hunting for us everywhere. He was very angry. He suspected Dr. Metaxas because the maid told him I had spoken to a Greek doctor on our way to the beach. The police searched the doctor's house and took him before Remzi Sami Bey for a severe questioning. He wanted to know the doctor's every movement from the moment he saw us.

"'You are keeping Karapet's daughters!' he shouted in his face. 'I will hang you if you don't deliver them to me.'

"The doctor insisted he knew nothing of our whereabouts. His leg had been paining him for some time, and, feigning lameness, he said he had been lying in bed and had enough troubles of his own without looking for more.

"They searched for us several days. When Remzi Sami Bey lost all hope of finding us he said bitterly: 'Ungrateful girls!'"

They reached Monastir disguised as Greek peasants, with Eugenia carrying a basket on her back with a few snails in it, as if they had come to town to sell snails and now were going back to their village. After three days on rough country roads, traveling alone and surviving a terrible snowstorm, they had reached the monastery more dead than alive. I had never expected them to be so resourceful and courageous.

"A monk opened the monastery gate," Eugenia said, "and we went up a long stone stairway up a great rock. It made us dizzy. The monk thought we were beggars!"

"And were seeking shelter from the snowstorm," Nevart added.

Besides saving the lives of my brother and sisters Dr. Metaxas kept in a cave forty wounded Armenian men. Eventually the monks had to slaughter their mules to feed these wounded men. Onnik described them — their swollen faces and savage appearance in the cave, where they lived month after month without ever seeing sunlight.

"Oh, they scared us so!" Eugenia exclaimed.

"When we went to the cave some of them would stare at us like insane men," Onnik said. "When gendarmes came to the monastery we also hid in the cave."

Neither my brother nor sisters spoke about their most painful inner experiences, which, like mine, could not be told. In fact I could not tell them anything about myself, nor did they question me. They knew I had escaped from Jevizlik, and that was enough. By a sort of silent agreement we took care not to mention our parents, and other relatives whom we dearly loved. Their names, or anything to remind us directly of them, were barred from our conversation. If one of us, for instance, had said "Mother" inadvertently, we would have bawled, all four of us. Our deepest sorrows lay buried in our hearts, wounds that would never heal, and we tried to forget them in the joy of our reunion. Onnik and I were resuming our interrupted schooling, and we looked hopefully to the future.

CHAPTER 13

Disciple of the Abbot Mekhitar

In the air was the rich, mellow sweetness of autumn, and the pavements were purple with fallen wistaria flowers. The swallows had not departed yet to southern climes, reluctant to leave our town, though the sharp summits of our mountains were already white with snow.

Onnik and I were on our way to school, our shoes brightly polished, carrying new books which had a clean gummy smell. We met a group of young Greek girls also going to school, and I called out to one of them, "Hello, fatty!" and sang to her merrily from a Greek song:

> Come here, come here, I love you,
> I have something to tell you.

I pounced on her and gave her a naughty hug. She screamed, cursed me, tried to scratch my face, while I laughed shamelessly.

"Nasty boy!" her companions said, but one of them giggled.

After I released my victim she trotted away with her schoolmates, all of them slapping their posteriors, while I shouted after them, "I'll hug you again tomorrow morning, fatty!"

Ever since my return from Batum I had been trying to show Onnik how "grown-up" I was and what a devil of a fellow.

Presently we saw a man whose gait was so "funny" to us that we shook with laughter. Everything became excruciatingly "funny." The slightest grimace by Onnik, a man's walk, the way a horse switched its tail, anything whatsoever made me laugh as in those happy days before the massacre and our separation, when we used to sit in our pharmacy and, watching the passers-by, or a fly, or the grocer across the street, laugh like a couple of fools.

"Don't look at me!" I shrieked, bending over in an uncontrollable fit of laughter as I leaned against a wall, holding my sides.

"I am not looking at you," Onnik said, "but at that donkey over th-th-th-there!"

And while we were convulsed with this mad, silly laughter a picture flashed through my mind — Turks killing my mother. Onnik continued making faces and saying "funny" things, but they were not "funny" any more, and I did not want to tell him why I suddenly became so thoughtful and serious.

At the Maydan we joined Nurikhan and Vahan. Both had returned from Russia like me to attend the reopened Mekhitarist School. Seated in a row over their saddles and baskets the Turkish hamals in the Maydan were talking and joking while waiting for customers, exactly as when Trebizond was a Turkish town.

"Dogs! Sons of donkeys!" we muttered angrily as we passed by them.

The reappearance of the hamals enraged us because these human vans had been employed by the Turkish police in cleaning out the Armenian houses and stores, and no doubt at least some of them had participated in the plunder.

In the shade of a large plane tree before a coffee house bearded old Turks were smoking narghiles and sipping their morning coffee with that imperturbable tranquillity of the East. Many Turks had gradually drifted back to the city, for the Russians not only did not molest them, but were often good to them. And we didn't like that.

Our school was two short blocks from the Maydan. I read proudly the Italian sign over its gate:

"Collegio Armeno dei Mechitaristi."

Aram was already in the school yard. A model pupil, he was always first to arrive. Retired to a corner under a magnolia tree he was busy drawing.

"Hello, rabbit!" We called him rabbit because he looked like one when he ran. He was born in London and could speak English, his father was the secretary of the American consulate, but we looked down on him because he was not an orphan, had not been deported, because of his father's official position. He had not suffered like us, he had no daring deeds to his credit, but he too had a claim to distinction: the white flag which the American consul had flown when he surrendered Trebizond to the Russian Army was Aram's bedsheet, which made him in his estimation an historic character.

"What's that you are drawing, rabbit?"

"Oh, nothing." Mysteriously.

"Let's see what it is."

"No!" He put it away in a book and would not let any of us see it, which made us even more curious. It could not be the picture of a nude girl, for Aram was not the type to draw such naughty pictures. After a brief scuffle I snatched the book away from him and looked at his drawing.

"It's nothing but a railroad car," I said. "I saw a lot of them in Batum."

"It's not a railroad car." He was indignant.

"What is it, then?"

"It's an electric tram."

Electric tram! I had seen real trains, but no electric trams. To gain our favor Aram took us into his confidence and said he had invented a new type of electric tram which he would manufacture when he grew up. He explained various improvements in the design and operation of electric trams he had made, which I could not understand, but he would not reveal the most important and revolutionary part of his invention. That was a great secret and he was going to get an English patent for it. He hinted he might need some partners when he founded a company to exploit his invention, and as we wanted to share in the fabulous profits, we became more respectful with him.

There were about twenty-five orphan pupils in our school varying in age from seven to fourteen, and divided into three classes, higher, intermediate, and lower. Even though I was in the higher class I still played soldier with the small boys. We mounted our stick horses, I whipped out my toy pistol, and crying "*Avanti!*" led my band of braves on glorious forays.

The bell rang, we put away our stick horses, and silently marched to our respective classrooms. There were six of us in the upper class — Nurikhan, Arsen, Vahan, Aram, Onnik and myself, I being the youngest "big boy."

The dean of our school was also the new Catholic Armenian prelate of the city, whom at his request we called simply Vardapet, or Doctor, and not Holy Father or Your Supreme Grace. Our first lesson of the day was Armenian, which he taught himself. We sprang to our feet when he entered the classroom — a black satin skull cap covering his baldish head, and walking with quick, short steps like a woman wearing a narrow skirt. He was a little man, not much taller than I.

"You may be seated."

We sat down.

Our lesson that day was a poem, *The Moon of Armenian Cemeteries,* by Father Leo Alishan, Mekhitarist. Our Armenian reader was a wonderful book. It was not only an anthology of Armenian literature, but contained in translation specimens from the works of many foreign authors — Oscar Wilde, Maurice Maeterlinck, Pierre Loti, Hippolyte Taine, Leconte de Lisle, Leonid Andreyev, Pushkin, Tolstoy, Ludwig Uhland, and under the heading "American Literature," a poem by one Larry Hough. (If I have spelled it right.) Its full-page colored reproductions of famous paintings interested me even more than the absorbing text — Aivazovski's *The Shipwreck,* Balestrieri's *Beethoven and His Music,* and especially a picture called *War,* showing a nude lancer riding on the bare back of a white horse in a vast battlefield strewn with heaps of nude corpses. Looking at this tremendous army of uncoffined dead I thought *Massacre* would have been a more appropriate title for it; those corpses reminded me of the nude bodies of deported Armenians I had seen in the Mill River.

The poem was full of words and archaic expressions whose meaning I did not know, yet I understood it perfectly with a sort of instinctive inner knowledge. It revealed the grandeur of ancient Armenia. In a sacred mystic land lambent in the moon, I could see mighty saints, Christian warriors with abundant locks and giant limbs, lying dead but deathless amid a vast litter of shields, lances and arrows. And over that sad, sweet and silent land hung the moon of Shavarshan like the lamp of God suspended from a long silver chain.

Through the words of this poem the eternal spirit of my forefathers who had died fighting for the Cross was distilled into my soul, stirring strange new emotions in me, and the image of ancient Armenia blazed in my mind as a lunar landscape of lovely ruins.

I gazed at the picture of Father Leo Alishan in our reader, a patriarchal man with gentle and noble eyes, and it impressed me even more than his poem. Vardapet, being one of his former students, read the poem as if uttering a rapturous prayer, and even though Alishan was not sainted by the Catholic Church, he was a saint to him, and in his opinion, the greatest genius in our modern literature. He told us anecdotes about Alishan, how he spent all the money he earned through his books — monumental volumes on the history, geography, flora and fauna of Armenia — on the poor, and considered even a pair of new slippers for himself a worldly luxury. He was as simple and unassuming as a child and liked to appear ignorant, Vardapet said. He told us how in his youth Alishan had visited many of Europe's famous poets with Lord Byron, who lived then in the Mekhitarist monastery and studied Armenian. All this made a great impression on me.

We had no classes in the afternoon, it being Saturday. After a frugal luncheon in the refectory we played for a while in the yard. But there was much smoldering grief in our hearts, and suddenly five of us got together and decided to beat up a Turkish hamal. In the back of our school yard a ruined Armenian house constantly reminded us what the Turks had done to our homes.

Vardapet and the other teachers were out. We lured a husky young hamal to this house by telling him we had a load of broken furniture for him to carry. When he realized what we were up to, he turned pale and backed toward the door, but we blocked his way, and suddenly his fez with the turban-kerchief flew off under a blow.

"Let me go!" he cried with tears in his eyes. "I haven't done anything wrong against Armenians, *vallah-billah* I haven't!"

As he bent down to pick up his fez we fell on him like five hungry tigers and rained terrific blows on his head. He was strong enough to carry a piano on his back, but he was so scared he made no attempt to defend himself. We pummeled him mercilessly, and in our frenzy of racial revenge seized pieces of a brass bedstead lying on the floor and brought them down over his head, back, shoulders. His head was soaked in blood, the hot animal smell of which sickened me.

His cries grew weaker and weaker and he was sinking at our feet when he slipped into a big hole on the floor and fell to the basement under our savage kicks. We threw his saddle after him and told him to go tell the other hamals what we did to him.

The Turkish community made a formal protest to the Russian military governor asking for damages and our arrest and punishment. We had inflicted such wounds on his head and body that the hamal was under medical care. And we would have been arrested if friendly officials had not hushed the matter up. But Vardapet expelled us from the school.

For the next two or three days we roamed in the streets and on the beach, smoking cigarettes, spitting like gamins, acting tough, and resolved to live only for revenge. We had no business going to school after what the Turks had done to us. Nurikhan told us exciting stories full of duels, caves, mysterious persons and happenings, which his fervid imagination reeled off hour after hour, though he insisted they were true, he had read them in books.

This free, gaminish life was much more to my liking, but friends intervened, and Vardapet consented to take us back provided we begged his pardon *on our knees*. At first we rejected that humiliating condition, but were prevailed upon to comply with it, since after all he was a prelate and in a way our collective father. He considered us stubborn and willful and was determined "to break our will," the two cardinal principles of our school discipline being *silence* and *obedience*. Beating up a Turkish hamal was, among other things, an act of rebellion on our part, and rebellion was the most serious offense, punishable by instant expulsion.

For the sake of going to Venice we returned to school and went upstairs to Vardapet's office to beg his pardon. The door was closed. Nurikhan gently tapped on it, while we nudged one another, shook our fists and legs, snickered and tittered.

"*Entrez!*" came Vardapet's voice.

We opened the door, went in, and knelt in a row before him. He was seated at his desk, immaculate in his black Benediction cassock, and seemingly in deep meditation. He did not look at us, his large brown eyes were cast down on some papers before him. On the wall behind his desk hung a crucifix and under it was a portrait of the Abbot Mekhitar. There were a few other pictures in the room — the Island of San Lazzaro in Venice, the Virgin and the Child, the photograph of a funeral ceremony in Trebizond, showing Vardapet burying the bones of the Mekhitarist vardapets the Turks had murdered.

We waited for him to speak, but he was silent, thinking. Then he leaned on his desk, carried his priestly white fingers to his glossy brow, closing his eyes, and said in a voice charged with emotion:

"Revenge is the most sinful of all human passions."

After another interval of silence, as if collecting his thoughts further, he opened his eyes and looked at us. "My dear sons, the Turks have cut down the ancient tree of our nation," he said. "You must avenge yourselves, most assuredly. It is your greatest patriotic duty, your sacred life work. But you must avenge yourselves as Christians and Mekhitarist gentlemen by rising to great heights of achievement and bringing such honor to your school and nation, and being so dear to God, that the whole civilized world will point to you and say:

"'These are the new branches of that sturdy old tree the Turks felled, but could not destroy its roots. It has grown and blossomed again.'

"Our Lord forgave his enemies and said they know not what they are doing. The task I am imposing upon you will call forth the manliest qualities you possess, requires the greatest courage and application."

He indicated we could get up. We rose to our feet and kissed his hand.

"You may wonder," Vardapet said, smiling, and in an entirely different, cheerful tone, "why I wanted you to kneel down before me. Some day you will thank me for it. Napoleon said: 'In order to command well one must first learn to obey.'"

In a few weeks I changed completely, was no longer the same boy. I now possessed an inner world of my own, a secret world, which was like an island in tropic seas, also a whole universe in itself, and I became, so to speak, two persons in one, my usual outward self, and my secret inward self.

I discovered the vast treasure-trove of books, was stirred by a tempest of thoughts, sought the answers to a million questions. I looked upon every book, every scrap of printed matter with a gluttonous eye, wanted to devour everything that was ever printed, unlock all the secrets of mankind. I planned to live alone on my island, like Robinson Crusoe, and read and meditate there continuously for seven years, after which I would return to the world a wise man.

Learning of Benjamin Franklin's diary from Vardapet I immediately started one of my own, writing down a list of virtues to be observed daily in a special copybook I made for the purpose, and every night during our study period in school — for by now we had become boarding pupils — I put plus or minus signs opposite these virtues, grading myself severely. I pretended to be copying my lessons while I busied myself with this moral bookkeeping.

At this time the Russian revolution struck Trebizond like a hurricane. Like clouds of locusts the Russian soldiers deserted the front and swarmed along the roads and on every ship, going home, *domóy*. Drinking vodka, cursing, singing, playing accordions and balalaikas, firing their rifles into the air, they rushed homeward for I knew not what. But I perceived there was something rotten in the state of Russia, and the revolution presented the other side of the medal, what I hadn't seen during my six months in Batum.

In a few months the Russians were gone. The hamals went to join the Turkish Army, which was just on the other side of the Promontory of Yoroz. The Turks had only the Armenians and some Georgians to fight now.

Armenians and Georgians were organizing national armies of their own. For the Turks the Russian revolution was Allah's greatest gift.

A Georgian prince was in charge of the shipping between Trebizond and Batum. We had to flee before the Turks came back to the city. There was no one to oppose them. Vardapet invited the prince to dinner, knowing well the psychology of the Georgians: eat, drink and be merry. Almost every other Georgian was a "prince." Waiters and cab drivers were "princes." But this man looked like a dapper aristocrat — a true Prince Charming, in appearance and manner. He came to our school with his staff, wearing the uniform of a Russian officer, a white lambskin cap on his head, and a small gold sword at his side.

They ate in Vardapet's office upstairs, gorging themselves on roast duck, pilav, macaroni, apricot stew, yoghurt, *paklava* — thin sheets of pastry stuffed with walnuts and honey. And they drank bottles of Kakhetia wine. (We were already starving.) Vardapet was in his best diplomatic form, humoring and flattering them. At a signal from him we boys went in and sang a Georgian drinking song he had taught us. If there is anything a Georgian likes more than wine, it's one of his native drinking songs. The prince and his staff were delighted. He got up and embraced a few of the small boys. Then one of my classmates stepped forward, at another signal from Vardapet, and recited a French poem on Armenia, explaining, in French, that it was by Jean Aicard, of the French Academy. This was one of the most diplomatic compliments Vardapet paid them, for gentlemen were supposed to know French. They may not have understood a word of it, but they applauded nevertheless.

The prince gave the necessary orders, and two days later we sailed to Batum on a military transport ship. Meanwhile, my sisters went to Novorossisk with Dr. Metaxas and his family, in a Laz sailboat. Many Greeks stayed in Trebizond, but the doctor did not dare face Remzi Sami Bey again.

Batum, the gay city of balalaikas, was now mournful and desolate. Soviet Russia had been forced by Germany to cede to Turkey the Batum-Kars-Ardahan area of the Caucasus, as well as the whole of Turkish Armenia the Russians had conquered. But the Georgians and Armenians, claiming this territory as their own, refused to recognize the treaty Soviet Russia had signed. The Georgians undertook to defend Batum, and the Armenians Kars, Ardahan and Baku. Baku was not in Armenia, the Azeris claimed it as their capital, but Armenians of every faction were determined not to let the Turks and Germans take Baku. They suppressed Mohammedan uprisings in that city, and kept the Germans and Turks out of Baku for ten months.

After recapturing Trebizond the Turkish Army under Enver Pasha, the butcher of our race, marched on Batum. The small Georgian garrison of the town fled in disorder. We escaped to Tiflis. The rejuvenated Turkish Army continued advancing, rapidly in some sections, slowly in others, temporarily halted here and there. The Georgians managed to save their skin by putting their country under German protection.

It was said five thousand German troops were on their way to Tiflis. We had to escape again. There was only one gate open before us and other Armenian refugees: Soviet Russia. Vardapet went to the Kuban ahead of us to find means for re-establishing our fugitive school in some safe town there. We followed him by walking across the Caucasus Mountains to Vladikavkaz.

After three days on the Georgian Military Road we reached the Cross Pass, where I felt as if I had flown away from the earth. As we stopped and gazed around in awed silence, I could hear a heavenly music of pipes and drums, guitars and violins, played by deathless musicians in this Caucasian Valhalla. The mountains moved along with us, warriors with white pointed beards carrying silver shields and lances, in white top boots, dancing a grand aerial *lezghinka* in sparkling vacancies of holy blue.

Mohammedan Ingush cutthroats on horseback blocked the road near Mt. Kazbek, would not let us pass. They were in an ugly mood. But they fled at the approach of a Soviet staff car from Vladikavkaz. On arriving in that city we were struck by another enemy — typhoid fever — and scattered in hospitals and homes. I recovered in a Red Army hospital in Krasnodar, where we witnessed the violent street fighting between the Reds and Whites. But my mind was in Yerevan, the heroic famine- and typhoid-stricken capital of the new-born Armenian Republic, and with the forty thousand Armenians slain in the streets of fallen Baku. Armenians were retaliating by massacring Turks and Tartars. It was blood, blood everywhere. I wrote in my diary:

I must learn the cause of wars, massacres and revolutions, of poverty and injustice, to show men how to live in peace and abundance. I must know the secret which the great teachers of mankind, the great philosophers, saints and scientists, have sought in vain. And people would say, pointing to me, "He is a disciple of the Abbot Mekhitar, a poor Armenian monk."

CHAPTER 14

The Society of Self-Gods

Our new proctor (*surveillant*) looked like a Bolshevik commissar. He was a husky, blondish young man, with keen, bold eyes, free and rough in his movements. He wore a brown leather jacket and army top boots, and his canvas bag was filled, we learned, with manuscripts. After wandering through southern Russia for six months our school was re-established in Yeisk, on the Sea of Azov in the Kuban.

We watched him curiously from behind a window, as he walked in the garden, seemingly absorbed in lofty thoughts.

"He is a poet," Paul said with a smile. "Vardapet sent him from Krasnodar."

"What's his name?" we asked.

"Bagrat Yergat (Iron Bagrat). He is from Malatia; escaped to the Russian lines during the massacre with the help of Dersim Kurds."

"He looks like a Kurd himself," one of us said, and we all laughed.

Paul, a medical student, was Vardapet's brother. The war in Europe was over and Vardapet had gone to Italy to arrange for the transfer of our school to Venice.

"You had better go and break him in," the boys urged me.

As I went to the garden and introduced myself to him, "Let's walk down this way," he said. "Tell me about yourself and the school. How many are you here, what are your interests, what have you been studying? Vardapet showed me your school magazine."

"Most of us are from Trebizond, and orphans," I said. "There are a few new boys from Kars, Bitlis, Krasnodar. Four of us are in the upper class; the others are in the intermediate and lower classes. A few left, a few died of typhoid fever, I had it bad, too, and our present number is thirty-two. We lead a very quiet life. Vardapet doesn't want us to be contaminated by the outside world." He smiled with me. "Yeisk is a dreary town. There is nothing here but windmills and geese. The winter was so cold the Sea of Azov was frozen. We continue living a monastic life. The Mekhitarist discipline hasn't changed in the past two hundred years. Chapel twice a day. Silence in the dining room and dormitory. We are wasting our time until we go to Venice."

"Wasting your time in a garden like this, and when it's spring?" He filled his lungs with the rain-washed air. The leaves sparkled with rain drops. Birds were feasting on cherry trees.

"I wish we had some good books to read," I said.

"You have the greatest book before you — the book of Nature." He stopped and broke off a cherry twig. "This contains all the secrets and miracles of Nature and of life. I would rather have a garden like this than all the books in Europe."

He pulled out a manuscript from the pocket of his leather jacket. "I just wrote it." He stuck out his chest, and began to read it in mighty, triumphant tones. It was a long philosophic poem in blank verse. I couldn't understand it, but it sounded just like printed poems. I was very much impressed. He was a genius!

"How do you like it?" he asked, after he finished it.

"It's marvelous," I declared, looking at him with awe and wonder.

He asked me what my ambition in life was.

"To be a good man," I said.

He smirked. "What do you mean by a good man? Do you know what good means? Can you define it?"

"That is good which is... which is... morally praiseworthy, and, pleasing to God," I stammered.

"Morally praiseworthy! Pleasing to God! What is God? Those are silly Christian superstitions."

"Are you a Bolshevik?" I said, shocked.

"Of course not."

"Then why do you speak like that about God?"

"Because there is no God. God is a myth."

He was an atheist! But I felt flattered that he should talk with me as if I weren't a boy of fourteen wearing his first long pants, but grown up, intellectually mature. "If God did not create man, then who created him?" I demanded. "Can anything come into existence of itself, out of nothing?"

"The ultimate principle of life is still something of a mystery, but religion has nothing to do with its solution. Science only can give us the right answer. The story of the world's creation in the Bible is just a fairy tale. Read geology, read Darwinism."

"But man has a soul," I insisted. "He is not just another animal, another fossil."

"There is no such thing as soul. The soul is merely a quality of the body, and just as material."

"The body dies, but the soul does not."

Bagrat Yergat threw away the cherry twig and picked up a stick, with which he drew in the gravel. "The body can be immortal," he said thoughtfully. "I don't expect to die. I know I shall live forever. I refuse to recognize the existence of either death or disease. I caught typhoid fever too, but I never went to bed, and I continued with my daily exercises. Forget your moral ideas and concentrate not on the perfection of your soul, but on the perfection of your body. Look at me. See how I have developed my muscles."

He flexed his arm, and I felt his muscles enviously. He was built like a circus champion. "I will teach you how to develop muscles like mine," he promised. I was skin and bones.

"Christianity has tried to destroy the body, being the very negation of life," he went on. "Religion is a product of sick minds. Goodness, charity, love, pity, are for slaves, the rabble. Only the strong are good. Consider the etymology of our word *bari*, good. It's derived from *ari*, brave, noble. Christianity has been the greatest curse of our race. Priests are Mephistophelean deceivers. Vardapet is the cleverest one I have met. A typical Jesuit. But I fooled him!" he chuckled. "He engaged me as soon as he saw my published poems. I came here to open up your eyes. You are still living in the Middle Ages. I am not a Christian. If I want to cross a river and there is no bridge, I would not hesitate to construct one with the bodies of my fellow men."

Bagrat Yergat turned my world upside down. Had I been deceived all my life? I reeled on the edge of a precipice: the world as I knew it became a chaotic phantasm. He terrified me and repelled me, but at the same time, strangely enough, attracted me. His ideas, so diametrically opposed to mine, to everything I had been taught and believed in, had an odd fascination.

I reported to my companions the conversation I had with him and they were even more impressed than I.

He took us to the beach in the afternoon, and we four remaining seniors walked with him like his four disciples. He swam halfway across the bay of Yeisk and came back in great style. He had a Herculean physique.

A pretty Russian girl with painted cheeks and mouth was promenading on the beach, twirling a parasol. She tried to attract his attention with coquettish glances, but he remained indifferent. To me she was like a butterfly, the spirit of the Russian spring.

"Why don't you wink at her?" I asked him. "Don't you see she likes you?"

"Love is a weakness, a disease. To love a woman is to be possessed by her, and all possessions are like chains to the free man." And soon he was discoursing again on the importance of being strong and hard.

Bagrat Yergat became our hero. We four "big boys" got up with him an hour before the rising bell and exercised furiously out of doors, aping his every movement. He had developed a system of calisthenics to perfect every muscle in the body, beginning with the eyes and ending with the toes — followed by a cold sponge bath under a tree. Then we strolled with him in the garden as he read poetry. He would ask us to compare his poems with those of Homer, Goethe, Dante, Victor Hugo. The sun shining on his bare chest, he sang of himself in his heroic metaphysical verses, proclaimed the coming rule of the immortal man. These outbursts of oracular utterances carried us to Olympian heights. We felt like Greek philosophers strolling in the garden of the Academy.

One day he revealed his mission among us. "Being master of his own destiny, and not the creation of some supernatural power, man can be a god," he told us. "I represent a secret world-wide organization which was started in Germany and is spreading to all parts of the world — the Society of Self-Gods. You can be members of it if you wish. From the slave, inferior group, you can step into this higher group of self-gods. As we are opposed to all existing governments and religions, we have to operate secretly."

Nietzsche had the first intimations of the principles of self-deism by his doctrine of the superman, he explained. By constant self-perfection, physical and mental, by the cultivation of all the truly aristocratic virtues of iron will, ruthlessness, hatred of the mob, brute strength, we could become immortal, he asserted. There is no reason why living matter should ever die. Human tissues, when put in special mediums, never lose their vitality. This has been proven by German and American scientists, he said. Death is wholly unnecessary.

It seemed logical enough.

He proposed that we go to Constantinople with him. In Venice we would have to suffer four more years of chapel and prayers. Religious education now became intolerable to us.

And so we four seniors staged a mock revolt. One morning when Bagrat Yergat rang the first period bell, we paid no attention to it. The small boys fell in line, but we stood aside, talking and laughing. He rang the bell again. We ignored it.

"Very well," he said, clenching his teeth. "I will have to report you to Paul for insubordination."

"Go ahead and report us," we said, and sang with merry voices:

> *Frère Jacques, Frère Jacques,*
> *Dormez-vous, dormez-vous?*
> *Sonnez les matines, sonnez les matines,*
> *Ding-dang-dong, ding-dang-dong!*

He took the small boys in, and a few minutes later appeared in the doorway, winked at us, and said aloud:

"Paul wants to see you in Vardapet's office — you stupid sophists!"

Singing and shouting as if we were drunk — and indeed we were intoxicated by the joy of our rebellion after three years of monastic discipline — we went upstairs to the office. Paul was seated at his brother's desk, a thick Russian book of anatomy before him, trying to look very grown up and important. He was only twenty, and preparing to study medicine at Padua.

"What's the meaning of all this hullabaloo?" he said. "If you have a complaint to make, why don't you make it to me? Fine example you have set before the small boys!"

We were confused, we did not know how to begin, what to say. We liked Paul. He was our friend, he had done much for us. The situation called for some oratory. "We have broken the medieval chains that bound our minds and propose to live as masters of our own destiny!" I shouted like a Bolshevik sailor making a speech. "This is the twentieth century, not the tenth! Down with religion! Long live science!"

Arsen, the oldest senior now that Nurikhan was gone, almost seventeen and already needing a shave, brought down his fist on Paul's desk. "Give us two hundred rubles and our certificates with good grades, and make it quick.

We've had enough of this false education!"

Arsen never got good grades, he was a poor student. But now he was a roaring lion.

Vahan spoke up. "We have discovered the truth and refuse to believe any more lies! The age of Mephistophelean deception is past." He blushed. He always blushed. His legs and arms were getting too long for him, and there were pimples on his face. He was fifteen, and had formerly attended a French school.

"In this age of enlightenment and reason—" my brother began hotly, but Paul cut him short.

"Have you boys gone crazy?" He leaned back in his chair and studied us with screwed-up eyes.

"We have come to our senses," I said.

"We are leaving school and going to another city," Onnik said.

"What city? Where?" Paul asked, running his hand through his sleek dark hair.

"We can't tell you," I said.

"It's strictly our own affair," Arsen said, looking as if he were ready to tear the world to pieces. He was feeling good. No more classes.

"Don't you want to go to Venice?" Paul asked.

"No!" we shouted together.

Paul shook his head. He rose from his desk, thrust a hand in his pocket, and began pacing up and down the room. He was a tall, dapper, handsome graduate of a Real-gymnasium, with a fine baritone voice. Though his brother was a Catholic priest he himself was worldly, liked gypsy music and wine. We knew that he had been carrying on secretly with a few Russian girls. He did not argue with us about God, but tried to convince us, in vain, that we were ruining our future, that we did not realize we were the most fortunate boys in Russia. He reminded us that the Mekhitarist Congregation was going to finance our education in the best universities of Italy or France, we could become doctors, lawyers, engineers. In three months we would be in Venice and have plenty to eat, while millions were starving in Russia.

We refused to listen. We had made up our minds. In the end he gave us some money and our certificates — with generous grades. We thought we needed them for entering other schools. He was puzzled and hurt. We could tell by his expression that he suspected Bagrat Yergat was the instigator of our rebellion, but he said nothing about it.

Some of the small boys cried when we left; we had grown up together. We told them we would try to communicate with them later. Our immediate destination was Rostov, where Bagrat Yergat was to join us after Vardapet's return, when he would resign his position on some pretext or other. We dumped a few belongings in a trunk owned by Vahan, and boarded a train for Rostov. We were on our way to feast at the banquet of Life, forever. We were now self-gods, immortal.

In Rostov we lived in an unfurnished room, sleeping on the bare floor and going hungry, having spent the little money Paul had given us. Vahan proposed to sell his trunk, the only thing of value we had, worth perhaps five rubles. He had a sentimental attachment for it as it had contained his father's botanical collection, which he had helped gather in Trebizond before the massacre.

But who was to sell it? Selling anything was beneath our dignity. All three ganged up against me and said I should sell it, as if I had no pride. It made me so angry. Arsen contemptuously reminded me of the socialistic poem I liked to recite, "Make way, we are coming, we dirty workers!" Now was the time for me to prove my proletarian sympathies.

"You ought to be shot by the council of workers and peasants," I said.

"All right, shoot us, but let us eat first," they said.

I lugged the trunk to the bazaar. Phalanxes of shawled Cossack women stood before their carts and yelled the merits of their tomatoes and cucumbers, watermelons and muskmelons. I wondered how I could make myself heard in that babel of lusty voices when a brilliant idea occurred to me: to pass the trunk off as American-made. It wasn't a Russian trunk. I knew at the word "Americansky" everybody would stop and listen to me.

"American trunk, very cheap, for only twenty rubles, American trunk, citizens!" I shouted at the top of my voice.

In a few minutes a crowd was pressing around me, eyeing, touching, examining the trunk, while I kept up my rapid-fire sales talk, meanwhile hissing at them in my mind: "You don't know who I am, you slaves! I am a self-god, I shall never die."

"It isn't worth buying," an elderly man said to the crowd. "It's German."

"Is it made of paper that you say it's German?" I cried. "Citizens, please feel it with your own hands, see how durably it is made of genuine American materials. You cannot find another trunk like this in Russia. It was manufactured in New York, an American officer gave it to me. I am a student, I speak English. Does anybody here know English? 'Vat ees dees?' I said in my Berlitz English, first four lessons. 'Eet ees a book, a pen, a vindo, a door. I have, you have, he, she, eet has, we have, you have, they have. I am, you are, he, she, eet ees, we are, you are, they are. All right, goddam!'" Which left no doubt in their minds that I spoke fluent English and the trunk was American, not German. Actually, it was Turkish.

A Cossack woman bought it for her daughter. She was engaged to marry and needed it for her trousseau. This girl with her sun-browned face, flashing white teeth and magnificent bosom, seemed to have sprung up out of the Russian wheat country. She was a darling wench. After much vociferous bargaining, we compromised on eleven rubles. I returned to our room with my arms full of bread, cheese, tomatoes, cucumbers, and a heavenly muskmelon.

After a few days we were hungry again, and were obliged to carry baggage at the station. I even sold papers in the streets. Self-gods, working as porters — it was awful!

We were discouraged. But as soon as Bagrat Yergat came to Rostov a few weeks later, our spirits rose. He had some money with him. After singing our praises in Venice and arranging for our transportation to Italy, Vardapet had returned to Yeisk to find us gone, his prize exhibits.

Our chapter of the Society of Self-Gods had its first formal conference, with Bagrat Yergat presiding. We passed resolutions, appointed committees, including a terroristic committee of two, consisting of Arsen and myself.

"The rules of our organization require the death penalty against anyone who stands in our way or betrays us," Bagrat Yergat said. "Assassination is a perfectly justifiable weapon in our hands. And there is no escape for the traitor. We have chapters even in America."

I stood up and said I would kill anybody whose death we decreed. Yet, there was a wild terror in my heart. We had been led into a trap. We were starting on a criminal career. He should have told us about this assassination business in Yeisk.

"Nobody knows my real name," he said. "I have many aliases. If I chose to disappear tomorrow, nobody can find me."

And really, we knew nothing about him and his past. He was a *mystery*. From time to time he made vague allusions to his father, but in general he spoke as if he had never had any parents, was not born of mortal man. He repudiated all family and national ties, and his sole allegiance was to the Society of Self-Gods. We lost the power of independent thinking and became puppets in his hands. He had hypnotized us. I did not know what diabolic Germans were behind him, but I was certain that eventually he would concentrate all the power of the organization in his hands. The wise and prudent thing for me to do was to keep on good terms with him until I could risk an open rupture.

The final battle would be between us two, I thought, and I visualized myself coming to grips with him in a titanic struggle fought on earth and in the air, like the immemorial combat between Ahuramazda and Ahriman, the spirit of good and the spirit of evil. But I would defeat him. I thought that the ultimate triumph of the good — the fate of the world! — depended on me. Outwardly, I was still his follower, but inwardly I was making plans for capturing the fortress from within, destroying the Society of Self-Gods.

We rose promptly at five-thirty in the morning, ran half naked to a wood in the outskirts of Rostov for our morning exercise. We were sun worshippers: Bagrat Yergat read poems to the sun. After a frugal breakfast of bread, cucumbers and tomatoes, with an occasional melon, we studied Darwin's *Descent of Man* and the *Origin of Species,* and criticized, according to the dialectics of self-deism, a scholarly thick volume on the history of the Armenian Orthodox Church, exposing its myths and fallacies. These courses were tough for Arsen. He tried to keep pace with us, but we were going very fast, devouring whole epochs of human knowledge in a few days. I did also much independent reading — Hegel's *Philosophy of History,* Faust, Schopenhauer, Samuel Smiles's *Self-Help.* This last, which would have aroused Bagrat Yergat's contempt if he had known its contents, became my new guide in life. I copied its moral aphorisms and maxims, and found much encouragement in the lives of Goethe, Newton, Sir Walter Scott, Faraday, Buffon and other great men, comparing myself with them when they were my age.

We posted announcements in the streets offering our services as tutors of French, Italian, modern and classical Greek, German, Armenian, the natural sciences, the mathematical sciences, the social sciences, philosophy, Froebelian pedagogics, Swedish calisthenics, violin and singing. A colossal bluffer, Bagrat Yergat liked high-sounding phrases. This tremendous Teaching Bureau of ours was his idea. He insisted that we write in the announcements "mathematical sciences," and not merely arithmetic. None of us had even taken algebra.

We secured two pupils, both of whom were turned over to me. The parents of a young girl of twelve wanted somebody to coach her in arithmetic. I couldn't solve the simplest problem. But I awed her by my speech and confident manner, posing as a very demon of mathematics. She was so shy, so retiring, that she didn't dare correct my mistakes.

My other pupil was an older girl, about my age. Her name was Anahid. I taught her French. Her buxom mother would leave us alone in a room, closing the door, so that we would not be disturbed. My knees sometimes touched Anahid's under the table, and when she moved her head loose strands of her hair would brush against my cheek — exquisite, titillating contacts. I wanted to kiss her, but I had never kissed a girl and didn't know how to go about it. Vardapet had told us even looking at a woman's legs was a sin. We were the chastest boys in Russia.

Anahid belonged to a girls' club. One of her companions, a tomboyish poetess, fell in love with Onnik. She wrote him passionate notes with the freedom of Russian girls, and asked for a rendezvous at a certain spot on the bank of the Don, begging him to take his violin along so that she could drink in his "divine music."

Bagrat Yergat called an extraordinary conference to decide our collective attitude toward Onnik's feminine admirer. She threatened our unity, our asceticism. We gave Onnik permission to have a rendezvous with this literary hussy, provided he behaved like a self-god. And we made this concession because she wrote well, had a style.

Onnik took his violin and went. But what happened on the bank of the Don, in a lovers' lane, he would not tell us. And we did not ask him.

But even I began to cut a romantic figure. Anahid was spoiling me. Her club invited both Onnik and me to an excursion. We went to the Armenian monastery, a literary shrine. The poets and patriots Michael Nalbandian and Raphael Patkanian were buried there. We had a picnic lunch and played various games.

In the evening, on our way back to Rostov, I found myself walking alone with Anahid. The other girls, singing, had wandered down the road. She wore a wreath of wild flowers on her head, and looked like the elfin spirit of that ravishing summer night. We took a short cut through a wheat field. She pointed to the moon. *"La lune, n'est-ce-pas?"* she said.

"Oui, c'est la belle lune de la Russie."

She darted off like a young deer, challenging me to catch her. I did — after racing halfway across the field. There was a sudden loud thrum of wings as a quail flew up from under her feet. She screamed and fell against me.

"Coward!" I said, catching her in my arms. But my foot slipped and we both fell, rolling over in the prickly wheat.

"Thank you," she said as I raised her up. But as she kind of clung to me still, I recklessly embraced her, pressing her tight, tight. I thought she would slap me, but to my amazement she let me hug her as hard and as long as I wished. Not a word of protest. Remembering, however, that love is a weakness, unworthy of a self-god, I released her, pushing her away from me. I didn't try to kiss her.

"You are dangerous," I said.

"Am I?" She looked hurt. She smoothed down her skirt, arranged her hair, replaced the wreath on her head, and we resumed our walk through the wheat field, too embarrassed to talk for a while.

We expelled Arsen for breaking the sacred rule of morning exercise, and his increasing lack of enthusiasm for self-deism. He had never been popular with us, and we knew from the beginning that he would fail in the intellectual perfection self-deism required. Bagrat Yergat excommunicated him. For the first time I liked Arsen: he had actually defied the Society of Self-Gods. We heaped abuse and ridicule on his head, and though he was the strongest boy in our school, he took it all silently. This was the beginning of Bagrat Yergat's downfall.

The money we needed for going to Constantinople we raised from among our countrymen in Rostov. Now that our treasury was quite full we sent Onnik to Yeisk to "save" those promising juniors whom Bagrat Yergat had converted after we quit school. Onnik was charged with that delicate, risky mission. Feigning remorse, and kissing Vardapet's hand, he put himself in his good graces again, was readmitted to the school. Vardapet hoped that the rest of us would soon follow Onnik's example. He knew Bagrat Yergat was the cause of the whole trouble, feared him so much that he carried a loaded revolver with him. After a few days, Onnik escaped with seven juniors, and our chapter in Rostov was augmented by seven new members of the Society of Self-Gods.

I did not know how my companions really felt about self-deism. We refrained from discussing it among ourselves. But I was suffering mental tortures, in desperate need of allies. If I showed my true colors, Bagrat Yergat might condemn me to death. There was no telling what he might do; I was afraid. Even if I escaped to America, he could still pursue me through the American branches of this sinister world-wide organization. I thought I would be trapped no matter where I went.

But gradually we three seniors began to doubt the existence of an organization like the Society of Self-Gods, and suspected Bagrat Yergat was fooling us. We formed a conspiratorial group against him. Having found allies — the juniors didn't count, they blindly followed us three older boys — I was no longer afraid of him.

But we had to stick together, for we had secured a collective passport for leaving Russia, and it was in his possession. We let him act as our leader for that purpose. He had his human side, was sometimes a lot of fun. He would dash off a poem on the spur of the moment no matter where he happened to be — in the street, in a government office, a store, and then read it aloud to anybody who would listen. He dedicated a poem to passport officials, another to ticket officials, several to a mysterious girl who would sit at a window in the floor over our room. She became his poetic dream girl. There was no sex in it.

After three crazy months in Rostov we went to Novorossisk. With its flat shores and shallow bays the Sea of Azov was purely Russian, but the Black Sea was our sea. In the air was the nostalgic odor of Trebizond, of the towering pine lands of Pontus. We saw again mountains. The western tip of the Caucasian Range begins here.

We saw Vardapet, Paul and the remainder of the small boys board a ship for Venice. I wished I could go with them. I had by now realized our mistake, but I was too proud to acknowledge it to Vardapet.

Nevart and Eugenia were still in Novorossisk with Dr. Metaxas. They were so clean, nice and wholesome that Onnik and I felt like tramps when we visited them. Dr. Metaxas had sent his family to Athens, and intended to go there himself later. We told them various lies and assured them we could get a good education in Constantinople.

We sailed on a Russian tanker, had a rough voyage. Bagrat Yergat, sensing our hostility, kept to himself. We separated on reaching Constantinople, without finding out who he really was.

We were sent by the Armenian authorities to a newly opened orphanage school in the monastery of Armash, near Izmid, in western Bythinia. On our way, walking through the wooded Bythinian hills, we passed by old Nicaea, of the Nicene Creed. Here, under this same sky, the Fathers of the Church had thought they had found the secret of immortal life in the sorrowful Christ. But wasn't that too an illusion? I was sad, bitterly sad. I wished it were possible to elevate man to the perfection and immortality of a self-god. And though I knew Bagrat Yergat had deceived us, I would have given anything if what he had told us were true.

The tragedy of man struggling against his fate! Our revolt against God was nothing but another aspect of that futile, universal struggle. But faith in God, as the Fathers of the Church had, also sprang from the same revolt against man's fate. What was the difference between belief and unbelief? I could see none.

It seemed to me that man stood against the sky and beat in vain on the invisible door of his prison, caught within the walls of his doom. Bagrat Yergat and I were fellow prisoners, brothers in fate, knocking in vain on the door. He, too, would turn to dust, no matter what he thought. He rose to the stature of a hero in my mind — or rather, an heroic clown, defying death, longing for the same immortality those old saintly philosophers of the Church had died dreaming of under this same sky.

I glanced at my companions and read the same thoughts, the same bitter disillusion, the same great longing and question on their faces, as we trudged on silently, the dry leaves of oaks and elms crackling under our feet.

CHAPTER 15

A Pilgrimage to Ararat

The monastery of Armash was situated in the hills around the Marmara, on the Anatolian side of that little sea. After two years in Russia I was keenly aware of the charm and beauty of this land, where the air, as in Trebizond, was sweet with the aroma of antiquity.

It gave one a sense of the migrations of ancient tribes — the Armeno-Phrygians crossing the Bosporus from Thrace and moving eastward through Bythinia, conquering, assimilating the hawk-nosed Hittites, the splendor of whose empire rivaled that of Babylonia and Egypt... Jason sailing to Trebizond with his Argonauts in quest of the Golden Fleece... The motley armies of Xerxes swarming through these hills to the Hellespont... The chariots of Mithridates the Great, King of Pontus, and the mail-clad cavalry of Tigranes the Great, King of Kings of Armenia, charging the Roman legions of Pompey the Great... The righteous Fathers of the Church traveling on foot or on mules and donkeys along these same winding trails to attend the Council of Nicaea.

Beneath the bloody cruelties perpetrated by succeeding sultans and political cliques in Stambul was the ancient noble earth itself.

Most of the vardapets of the Mother Church outside Russia were educated at Armash. But the professors and students of this famous seminary had been deported and all the goods and properties of the monastery confiscated. Its large farm, neglected for some years, was now cultivated by us orphan boys with much enthusiasm. We had classes in the morning and practical field work in the afternoon, and were being trained for service in Armenia. Our resurrected homeland needed trained agriculturists more than doctors of theology.

Our American director came from Constantinople for a brief visit and inspection. He did not stay, for the position he held turned out to be, to our chagrin, a complimentary one. We welcomed him by singing *My Country 'Tis of Thee*, wearing our new boy-scout uniforms. All of us were boy scouts.

The peasants of Armash had been deported, but many of them had returned to their homes, and the village was again fairly well populated. For various reasons the Turkish Government had been more lenient with Armenians in and near Constantinople. These peasants were again tilling their fields and tending their flocks. On Sunday afternoons the young people of both sexes danced on the green to the music of small native fiddles or bagpipes and drum. They danced in a circle, round and round, forward and backward, very gracefully, the men gallantly martial, the women promptly responsive with a swirl of silken skirts and a rhythmic pounding of red velvet shoes with silver buckles, their wine-colored or blue velvet jackets too tight for their sumptuous breasts. They had resumed their normal life. And like us they too wanted to go to Armenia, to be free citizens of our two-year-old republic at the foot of Mount Ararat. Their ancestors had lived in Bythinia for centuries, but the call of Hayastan, as Armenians call their country, was stronger.

There were a few Turkish officials in this purely Armenian village: a mudir or mayor, a police officer, a postmaster, an imam wearing the green turban of a descendant of the Prophet. They were easy-going, harmless men, and had nothing to do but drink coffee, play backgammon, and read their Turkish papers. Armash was under the jurisdiction of the Sultan's government — a new pro-Allied Sultan, and there was a repentant new Turkish administration in Constantinople, composed of politicians of the old school. The Ittihad leaders had fled the country. The Grand Vizier Talaat Pasha had gone to Berlin, where an Armenian student was soon to assassinate him.

My preoccupation with Armenia's fate became a monomania; I thought about it day and night. While working in the fields of the monastery, dressing and undressing, washing and eating — there wasn't much to eat, we were always hungry — I spoke in my mind before the Supreme Allied Council in Paris and at the sessions of the League of Nations in Geneva.

Completely ignoring the real master of Turkey the Allies concluded the peace Treaty of Sèvres with the effete government of the Sultan, one of its signatories being the Armenian Republic, represented by the poet Avetis

Aharonian. By this treaty, the Imperial Ottoman Government, recognizing Armenia as a free and independent State, agreed to abide by the decision of the President of the United States of America, who was to draw the exact boundary line between the Ottoman Empire and the Republic of Armenia in the disputed provinces of Van, Bitlis, Erzurum and Trebizond.

The Greeks had claims on Trebizond, but Venizelos had agreed to let Armenia have it. Among the Greeks there was now a movement for a Hellenic Republic of Pontus, which the Turks were trying to suppress by mass executions and wholesale butcheries. Hundreds of Greek villages were being destroyed by the *cheta* bands of one Topal Osman, or Lame Osman, a ruffian who had become the Tamerlane of the Pontus Greeks. The methods employed during the Armenian massacres were being repeated to wipe out the Greeks of the Black Sea coast, partly in revenge for the Greek occupation of Smyrna.

There was meanwhile much skirmishing along the Marmara between Turkish forces of the two opposing factions, the Sultan's reluctant troops, led by doughty — if not gouty — Circassian pashas gradually retreating before the vigorous attacks of Kemalist guerrilla bands.

We guarded the monastery compound at all hours of the night, and for a few months lived like a besieged garrison. A secret shipment of rifles and ammunition from Constantinople enabled our instructors to organize the village for self-defense. Several students had served in the Turkish Army or had attended Turkish military schools. We were going to fight if attacked. Our acting director, Mr. Torgomian, from Paris, would give us instructions, rifle in hand, and every boy was entrusted with a special task. It was all very exciting.

One day a young Circassian came to the monastery, claimed to be from the Caucasus, said he had no place to live and asked for our hospitality. We took him in, but suspecting him to be an Azerbaijan Turk and a Kemalist spy I was appointed to watch his every step because of my knowledge of Russian and things Caucasian. I befriended him. I was almost certain he was a spy trying to find out how strong we were and what arms we possessed, yet I could not help liking him. He had an engaging smile, was courteous, very handsome. After staying with us two or three weeks he suddenly disappeared as mysteriously as he had come.

When the British withdrew from Izmid our position at Armash became "untenable." After eight months we were obliged to leave the fields we cultivated with so much care, our lovely beans and tomatoes and onions and potatoes when they were almost ready to be harvested, and return to Constantinople, where we had at least the satisfaction of living for a few months in the Turkish military school at Beylerbey, requisitioned by the British authorities and turned over to us. It was next to Beylerbey Palace where the Sultan Abdul Hamid had been confined after he had been deposed.

My young sister Eugenia had come to Constantinople from Novorossisk with an Armenian woman "to go to school." She was placed in an orphanage while we were at Armash, and attended the American Girls' School in Scutari. She was a delicate girl, and had never known the hunger and privations of orphanage life.

"I am first in my class," she said proudly when Onnik and I visited her with aching hearts. "I have learned to read and write English — isn't it wonderful?" She had changed, was pale, looked undernourished.

I begged her not to study hard. "It is far better that you be last in your class but be strong and healthy."

"Don't you want me to be educated?" She looked hurt.

"Of course we want you to be educated," I replied, "but be a little indifferent like other girls; take things easy, don't try to surpass them all."

The doctor had told her she was anaemic, had "weak" lungs, and had forbidden her to sing in the choir. She loved to sing, and had learned a few American songs.

After "peace" was signed, the Armenian National Relief arranged for the transfer of our agricultural school to Armenia. We were to be the first group of repatriates. Onnik wanted to remain in Constantinople because of Eugenia; he had also begun to take free violin lessons from a prominent teacher and did not wish to discontinue them. He moved to another orphanage.

Going to Armenia was like going to war. Onnik, Eugenia and I had our picture taken; I might never see them again. Turks, Tartars, and even Soviet Russian troops were attacking our new-born republic from all sides, and its population was dying of famine and epidemic diseases.

About two hundred and fifty strong, we sailed to Batum on a French steamer, wearing our boy-scout uniforms. The entire Anatolian coast of the Black Sea was by now in Kemalist hands, and we were in hostile waters as soon as we came out of the Bosporus.

At the small coastal town Turkish boys came to sell us grapes, plums and pears in medieval high-prowed rowboats, black camels of the sea.

We anchored off Trebizond on the morning of the third day.

"Gentlemen, we are already in the historic waters of Armenia!" Mr. Torgomian declared in his best oratorical manner. The sea now looked different, became our sea. I wondered what Nurikhan was doing — if he was alive. We had corresponded after our separation in Russia, but I had not heard from him for a few months. Gazing at my home town from the deck of the ship I wondered what had happened to all the Greeks I knew there. The anchorage was desolate. Not another ship was in sight.

The next morning we docked in Batum, the harbor of which was full of activity. A different world altogether. The customs inspectors, stolid Georgians, went through our baggage methodically, unimpressed by our uniforms and other paraphernalia. Batum had been under British military occupation for two years, but the British troops had recently withdrawn. Georgians now were in control of this modern port, and they lost no opportunity to assert their authority and dignity as officials of Free Georgia.

With shouts of *"Vive la France!"* we bid farewell to the friendly captain and crew of our ship. Unfurling our enormous Armenian flag — horizontal stripes of red, blue and orange — we marched to the Armenian consulate, led by our drum and bugle corps. The consul made a speech of welcome, and took us to the Georgian governor to give him a taste of Armenian patriotism and the spirit of our youth abroad. The governor was a hairy, bearded man of noble appearance, a combination of prince and shepherd, with the dreamy eyes of a poet — a fine specimen of his race. He made a speech in Georgian, and upon its conclusion, we yelled "Hip, Hip, hurrah! Georgia! Georgia! Georgia!"

The relations between Armenia and Georgia were not particularly cordial in spite of their common historic past and religious and cultural ties, because of boundary disputes.

The next day we went to Tiflis. The Georgian coat of arms, St. George slaying the dragon, was painted on every passenger car as if Georgia itself had built these trains. No Russian letters were to be seen anywhere. This country was no longer Russian. A complete change had taken place in two years.

We staged another parade in Tiflis and "our ambassador" — what wonderful words! — gave us a banquet in the city's best restaurant on Golovinski Prospekt, which was now called Rustaveli Avenue after the name of Georgia's great medieval poet. The waitresses were society girls. The ambassador, a grave, homely, owl-faced man, welcomed us in the name of "our government" in quiet, measured words:

At this moment the guns are roaring on the heights of Sarikamish. Armenia is at war with Turkey. The eastern army of Mustafa Kemal has invaded our fatherland. In this perilous hour the democracy of Armenia is left alone, caught between the Turkish armies on one side, the Red armies of Soviet Russia on the other. They want to remove us from their path and join forces, for unfortunately the new communist leaders of Russia believe the fiction that Turkey has become a revolutionary Soviet state, while little famished Armenia has been transformed into a camp for the capitalist imperialist powers for enslaving the revolutionary workers of "socialist" Turkey. The Bolsheviks think Armenia is another Poland. We have no hope of getting help from anywhere and must defend our country and independence with our own forces. I am confident that we will be victorious in our struggle against the bloody Turkish pashas.

This new war was news to us.

We were told Kars could hold out for at least six months. The Armenian Army, even though it numbered only about thirty thousand men, and was ill-fed and ill-clothed, was considered quite capable of coping with anything the Turks had to offer. We had heard and read much about our army's victories at Sardarabad, Nakhichevan, Olti, Zankezur, Karabagh.

On our way to the Armenian border we read the latest issues of the Armenian papers in Tiflis, all with flaming red headlines, some even printed in red ink, and discussed the war and its possibilities.

"Our troops have withdrawn from Sarikamish for strategic reasons, boys. When we counter-attack, we will make one big swoop down to Erzurum."

"The Hassans and Mehmets have no idea what's coming to them."

"Do you mean to say, boys, we have big cannons and armored trains?"

"Certainly, what did you think? Our artillery is the best. Our peasants in Lori captured with their bare hands three out of Georgia's four armored trains two years ago."

"I wish Antranik hadn't gone to America. He should have been here now."

"Brother, what is this? We are fighting everybody, Russians, Georgians, Azerbaijanians, Turks, Tartars, Kurds."

"And beating them all."

"Boys, this Kiazim Karabekir Pasha who is commanding the Turkish eastern army is the best general the Turks have. Don't underestimate him.

He is a highly trained man. I met him in our military school."

"General Nazarbekian can outmaneuver him any time."

The train stopped at the Armenian border, which was only about forty miles from Tiflis. We got off and gave three more rousing cheers to Georgia, but to tell the truth, they were more loud than sincere.

"We are in beautiful Lori," Mr. Torgomian said ecstatically. "The Armenian Switzerland, rich in copper mines."

We looked with swelling hearts at the wooded hills, the trees and rocks, the weeds and wild flowers about us. They were not like the hills, trees and flowers of other lands but ours in a profoundly intimate and hallowed way, consecrated with the blood and tears, the songs and joy of Hayastan.

In an exultant and worshipful mood we gathered at a pastoral glen near the station of Sanahin.

"Here upon this sacred soil we stand as free Armenian citizens," Mr. Torgomian said. "Every inch of this soil contains the dust of our ancestors' bones. In that village over the hill, the historic Odzun, lies King Sumpad. And look at that white bridge: what a splendid monument of our ancient architecture! Gentlemen, generations of Armenians have died dreaming of this moment, to stand on Armenian soil, under Armenian skies, as free men. Let us therefore," and his ringing oratorical voice cracked, "kneel and kiss the sacred soil of Hayastan."

We all knelt and kissed it devoutly. It was a supreme moment in our lives.

After this ceremony, we scrambled up the hill to Odzun. We were met by the village elders, who wore large, conical wool caps and smoked long, thin pipes, and talked with them reverently. They lived in underground burrows exactly like those described by Xenophon in *Anabasis*, that immortal story of his journey to Trebizond with the Ten Thousand. Mr. Torgomian explained that this fondness of our peasants for underground dwellings, which I was seeing for the first time, was due to the severe Armenian winters. The peasants responded to our "Greetings, countrymen" with "Greetings, a thousand blessings!" They all added "a thousand blessings," and did not merely say "Greetings." I thought it charming. In my mind I chose the exact location of the agricultural school I was going to establish here. The Georgians had fought for the possession of this, the best part of Caucasian Armenia, even though not a single Georgian lived in the whole of Lori. It was purely, sacredly Armenian soil.

The peasants showed us the village church, built in the ninth or tenth century, and the tomb of King Sumpad. A thousand years had passed since King Sumpad fought and died for his people and the Cross. But what moved me most was a little scene I witnessed while roaming in the green hills with a few boys. We saw a young shepherd, ten or eleven years old, wearing the conical wool cap and cowhide moccasins of the men of Lori, cross himself and kneel before a rock. He did not see us. Taking something out of his pocket and putting it before the rock, he crossed himself again, rose to his feet and drove away his few sheep. We went over and saw that this outdoor shrine consisted of an old tombstone carved in the characteristic Armenian style, with an intricate lacing of designs around the edges and a large cross in the center. There was a collection of small coins and paper money before it, to which that ragged shepherd boy had added his own offering.

We waited at Sanahin station for the Armenian train that was to take us to Yerevan. It finally arrived, and the sound of its whistle in the picturesque gorge was the sweetest, most glorious music we had ever heard.

"Look, boys, Armenian letters on the cars!"

They were all boxcars, for Armenia had no passenger cars, Georgia and Azerbaijan having appropriated them all after the Russian revolution, but those Armenian letters, "Repaired at Alexandropol," made them more endearing than any passenger car could possibly be. We decorated the locomotive with green branches, and hoisted on one side of it our Armenian flag, on the other our scout flag. The engineer smiled. To him it was just a locomotive, but to us — oh, how could we tell him what it meant to us? With two or three blasts of its merry whistle the train pulled out of the station while we sang *Our Fatherland*.

What did it matter that our locomotive burned wood because Azerbaijan, the ally of Turkey, would not sell us any oil? What did it matter that we had no large cities, no impressive public edifices, no passenger trains, no ships, no factories? What did it matter that our country was small and poor, shut off from the outside world, crowded with orphans and refugees? It was the nucleus of the greater Armenia that would surely rise to take its rightful place in the family of nations. We had no Batum and Tiflis, no Baku and oil wells, but we had Aragadz and Ararat.

"There is Aragadz!"

"Aragadz! Aragadz!" repeated several voices.

It was early the next morning. I jumped up and rubbing my eyes looked out of the car door to see Aragadz. The four-peaked colossus of the Little

Caucasus rose heavenward from a sea-like plain, tearing at the flaming clouds with its bloody fangs, like a pack of four ferocious wolves leaping high in the sky. This terrific scene of the Armenian dawn impressed me like the mighty stage of God on which the drama of the world's creation and man's early history was still being enacted with Biblical lightning and thunder.

> Aragadz is a high mountain,
> Vai le-le le-leh
> Jan, le-le le-leh!

We sang as our slow train rolled across savannahs of seared grass, once the granary of Armenia, now a desert. Presently we saw the sublime Ararat. At first only the cloud-like summit of the great Ararat came into view, then the Little Ararat stepped up beautifully beside her lord, both peaks having a common base. They looked like a royal couple reigning truly by the grace of God, with a kingdom of amber and rubies spread at their feet.

Alexandropol. The second city of our republic. A fortress six or seven thousand feet above sea level, on a gloomy, treeless plain. Though it was a sunny day in late summer, the air was so chilly here we shivered. It's always cold at Alexandropol, refugees at the station told us. The youthful governor of Alexandropol made a fiery speech of welcome, pointing to Ararat. He was from Sassoun, and his heart pulsated with the same sentiments that had brought us to Hayastan. The mountaineers of Sassoun had fought their way to the Caucasus during the massacres, and this young intellectual was one of their leaders. They had settled in villages around Mount Aragadz, and a special cavalry regiment had been raised from among them for the Armenian national army. They were our best fighters.

The largest orphanage in the world was at Alexandropol. Thirty thousand children were under the care of the Near East Relief, and American flags flew over the former Russian army barracks housing those homeless waifs left in the wake of the Turkish invasion two years before. And the Turks were coming again.

It is impossible to describe the devastation wrought by the Turkish troops. The hordes of Tamerlane would have been more merciful. All the station buildings were wrecked, stripped of their furniture, doors, window sills, and the ocherous landscape of the Araratian plateau was smudged by the

charred remains of villages. Churches had been robbed of their valuables
and transformed into stables for army horses or latrines for the warring
Anatolian peasantry. In many villages the Turks had seized the entire female
population for a mass raping, not even sparing young girls of six or seven,
nor old women. Verily, the Turks had been through this country! I
remembered these lines from a Turkish poem:

> Grass doesn't grow again
> Where the hoofs of the Turk's horse strike.

I thought of the fierce wars of Urartu... Rusas I and Rusas II... the mad
kings of Assyria with their long curly beards... Queen Semiramis, the
passionate and cruel... Darius and Xerxes... the Battle of Manzikert in
1071... the fall of Ani... the Assyrians and Persians, the Scythians and
Sumerians, the Romans and Greeks, the Parthians and Arabs, the Seljuks
and Tartars, the Osmanlis and Russians, Genghis Khan, Tamerlane, Shah
Abbas, Enver Pasha — they had all passed across this land, leaving behind
them rivers of blood. By what evil chance our ancestors entering Asia Minor
from northern Greece chose to settle down at this crossroads of the world,
this lofty bridge between Asia and Europe, the East and the West, the North
and the South? The tragedy of our geographical situation! Battleground of
all the tribes and empires — that was the history of Armenia.

Ani station. Ani itself was on the other side of the Akhurian river, a
tributary of the Arax, the mother river of Armenia. We could not see the
ruins of our old capital, once celebrated as the Jewel of the East, the City of
Forty Keys and One Thousand and One Churches. It was the Armenian
architect Tirdat, the builder of the royal cathedral of Ani, who repaired the
dome of St. Sophia in Constantinople when it collapsed during an
earthquake in the tenth century. In those days Armenian architects were
recognized as the supreme masters of their craft. Ani was now a heap of
ruins, uninhabited, but the magnificence of its past glowed in our hearts.

Yerevan was like an oasis in the desert. Here Ararat loomed before us in all
its immensity but actually it was still thirty or forty miles away. We saw again
trees and greenery. In contrast to Alexandropol the sun in this garden town
was almost tropical in its warmth. The vineyards were loaded with grapes.

"Remember, gentlemen," Mr. Torgomian said, "Noah planted his vineyard
right here at the foot of Mount Ararat when he got out of the Ark."

"And he lay in the shade of that tree over there when he got drunk and passed out," a boy added.

"Old man Noah was a tippler, all right," Mr. Torgomian said. "Who wouldn't be, when you have wine made from our glorious Armenian grapes?"

Yerevan, to our chagrin, was a small provincial city compared to metropolitan Tiflis, but the presence of Ararat and the delicious seedless grapes that melted like drops of honey in our mouths compensated for its lack of imposing buildings and streets. There was a drowsy stillness in the air. Life in these gardens crisscrossed by irrigation ditches could be very pleasant if there were no war and famine. We were close enough to Persia to feel in the atmosphere something of the Persian mode of life with rose gardens and nightingales. Yerevan had been the seat of a Persian sirdar and though for a hundred years it was under Russian domination, much of its old Persian character had remained.

We were quartered in one of the barracks of the military school which the government had opened for training new officers for the Armenian army. All the cadets had gone to the front and the buildings and grounds of this institution were now used for drilling new recruits — peasants in wool hats and cowhide moccasins, with a few young men in Russian student overcoats.

For the first time we heard army commands in Armenian, and were thrilled. But alas, as in the case of the Turkish recruits in Trebizond, I saw no happy, joyous faces among them. They seemed to be drilling because they had to and not because they liked it and were proud to serve in the Armenian Army, ready to die for the nation's liberty.

Something was lacking in these soldiers, they were spiritless. They seemed to hate their arms — British Ross rifles — to stick their bayonets into the straw dummies. Their "Hurrah!" on making a bayonet charge sounded more like a wail of anguish than a war cry.

I ate an apple and one of the soldiers picked up the core I threw away, and swallowed it greedily. Oh, my God, our soldiers were hungry! I recalled Napoleon's statement: an army marches on its stomach, and was plunged into gloomy thoughts. How could we stop the Turkish Army with hungry men?

But hunger was not the only reason for their glum, dour expressions. The officers called them "Donkey's head!" "Stupid creatures!" and such uncomplimentary names. Products of Russian military colleges with their social and martial traditions, these Russianized officers were using the methods employed in the old Tsarist army. No wonder communist propaganda had made so much headway among our troops.

There had been an unsuccessful communist uprising in Armenia, the news of which had alarmed us in Constantinople. A Sovietized Armenia would have immediately turned the might of the British empire against us and deprived Armenia of America's help and friendship. I saw several sad Armenian faces behind the barred windows of a dismal prison overlooking the yard where the recruits drilled. They were communists, and we considered Armenian communists traitors to the nation, yet the sight of this prison made a most painful impression on me.

Nurikhan turned up at Yerevan, looking like a hobo.

"For two months I have been breathing the free air of independent Hayastan," he said, cynically.

He was disillusioned, like many Armenians who had come to Yerevan to see the miracle of independent Hayastan with their own eyes. He wanted to go back to Tiflis, where his sisters were now living, and then to his mother in Constantinople, whom he had not seen since their separation in Trebizond during the massacre.

The government intended to re-establish our agricultural school in the provincial town of Nor Bayazet, but the situation in the country was so critical and its immediate future so uncertain, that that plan was postponed from week to week. The war came very close to Yerevan when the Turks attacked also from the direction of Mount Ararat and tried to cross the Arax river; we could hear the guns thundering from morning to night.

I was only fifteen, too young for military service, but I was anxious to help our country in this life-and-death struggle with Turkey, and secured an appointment as "adjutant" to the Chief-of-Staff and the Minister of War, replacing an officer who was sent to the front. The Chief-of-Staff was a lieutenant-colonel. He had a fine carriage and beautiful dark eyes, and would have looked good in a ballroom in Tiflis. He explained my duties to me in his broken Armenian: I was to receive and announce visitors who had appointments with him or the Minister of War, whose office joined his; carry messages and other official papers, and most important, judging from the tone of his voice, I was to prepare his morning cocoa and serve it to him in a silver glass holder promptly at eleven o'clock. He showed me how to make it on a primus stove.

This elegant Chief-of-Staff was a very methodical man. He came to his office sharply at ten o'clock in the morning and left at three in the afternoon.

He did not order lunch, was satisfied with his American cocoa. He could not read and write Armenian, and conducted all his correspondence in Russian. I was willing to forgive him that; he was brought up in Russia, educated in Russian schools, and being a trained soldier, a technician, our people needed him. What disturbed me was his complete lack of national consciousness. The map in his office was not of Armenia, but of the Crimea, where General Wrangel was still holding out against the Bolsheviks. Time and again I saw him standing before that map, lost in deep meditation. He had marked with a blue string the positions of the White and Red troops on the Crimean front, and seemed to be totally indifferent to the position of the Turkish and Armenian troops. His mind obviously was in the Crimea with General Wrangel. We needed a great soldier as our Chief-of-Staff, but there was nothing great about this man.

The Minister of War was a peasant leader from Sassoun and as such "one of ours." On the morning I first reported for duty, I took his hat and raincoat as soon as he came in and reverently hung them from a rack in his office. I noticed that his battered hat was minus its lining, and his raincoat was a shabby one, which predisposed me further in his favor. At noon I brought him his borsch and black bread, exactly the same amount and quality as received by the humblest private; I hoped he would not eat his lunch and leave it to me, but he always ate it. However, he did not impress me as the right person to occupy such a responsible position. Our republic was not fighting Kurdish guerrillas but a regular war of international importance against crack Turkish divisions commanded by a first-rate general. He did not seem to have anything to do, and neither, for that matter, was the Chief--of-Staff particularly busy. I could not understand it. I thought they should be in their offices at least ten hours a day, giving orders, making urgent telephone calls, dispatching important messages, but because of their strange inactivity I myself had very little to do.

I would look at their faces to find out how things were going for us at the front. The Minister of War had a poker face and it was impossible to know what he was thinking, and he hardly ever spoke. The most silent man I had ever met. His face betrayed no emotion of any kind. And there were absolutely no signs of worry or emotional strain on the handsome face of the Chief-of-Staff.

The Commander-in-Chief, General Nazarbekian, about whom I had read so much, was a towering man with white hair, and tired, heavy-lidded eyes, wearing his uniform of a Russian general with the blue cross of St. George hanging from his neck. There was something of hoary Ararat about him, but like the Chief-of-Staff he spoke and corresponded in Russian. Every morning, before he came to his office, I would examine his large military map on the wall — at least he had a map of Armenia — and study the tragic progress of the war. I wondered, did he suffer spiritual agonies as he set the blue string on it back every day, ceding to the Turks another slice of territory consecrated by the bones of our ancestors and the blood of our peasant soldiers? That string always moved back, never forward. I could not help thinking that he discharged his duties as commander-in-chief as would any Russian general appointed to his post. He was too old, and should have retired long ago. We needed a man who would personally lead our troops at the front, encourage them, goad them to heroic effort.

I suffered one disillusionment after another. Our army, as I saw it, was incompetent or in utterly indifferent hands. We just did not have the right men, we did not have real Armenians at the head of our troops. I could not distract myself by reading, for which I had plenty of time. I would read a page or two from Turgenev's *Fathers and Children,* and Shakespeare's *Othello* (in Armenian translations) mechanically, without understanding what I read, and then pause and listen to the sound of the guns on the Arax.

Kars fell. The Turkish occupation of this key fortress meant the collapse of our front, but the Chief-of-Staff did not seem to be affected by the debacle at all: he came to his office promptly at ten o'clock, drank his cocoa promptly at eleven o'clock, and left promptly at three o'clock. Things continued as usual in the Ministry of War; the same old indifferent expressions on the faces of generals and colonels.

It was practically a hopeless struggle from the very beginning, but I thought with the right leadership we could have kept Kars either by a successful resistance or through the intervention of Soviet Russia, which professed friendship for our people: all we had to do was to adopt a pro-Soviet policy. Politically we were a naive and inexperienced nation.

Believing that it was a Bolshevik army attacking Kars with the purpose of handing it over to Soviet Russia, our troops, whose morale left much to be desired, were unwilling to fight their Turkish "comrades." It was the general belief among Armenians in the Kars region that the revolutionary army of Red Turkey was attacking under the red flag of socialism, for the Turkish flag is all red, with the exception of a white crescent and star in the center.

For three days these Turkish comrades robbed, raped and butchered the Armenians of Kars, not even sparing those who showed their communist membership cards. Hundreds of prisoners were stripped of their clothing and sent to Erzurum to work in labor gangs, and practically every one of them died of hunger and cold. Meanwhile there was a mass movement of Turkish men, women and children to Kars to settle in the vacant homes of massacred or exiled Armenians, and thus another part of historic Armenia was completely Turkified.

The Turks had won the war, and further resistance was futile. Armenia sued for peace. The Grand National Assembly of Ankara, speaking through its "People's Commissar for Foreign Affairs," demanded, and got, half of the territory of our republic, and almost all the arms, ammunition, mules and rolling stock Armenia had.

And while negotiations for a suicidal peace treaty were going on at Alexandropol, the government sent us to Nor Bayazet, to resume our agricultural studies.

CHAPTER 16

Dream's End

The storm started suddenly, without any warning. The weather was sunny and warm when we left Yerevan, and its vineyards were loaded with grapes. But in the mountains, on our way to Nor Bayazet, we found ourselves in a frozen world of pure-white domes. And soon a blinding snow, hard and sharp like broken glass, was driven in our faces by roaring gales blowing from Mount Ararat. Ararat was in a furious mood — for our indifferent army command and political mistakes, I thought — and had let loose upon Armenia all its evil devas and dragon-voiced airy monsters to show its displeasure.

It was a terrible but lovely storm, though.

"It's our own snow and wind!" I shouted to Arshag, who was groping blindly by my side. He nodded his head.

As night fell and the storm ceased we saw wolves and foxes scuttling about in the gray darkness, their eyes blazing like live coals. They were not like the wolves and foxes of other lands, but our very own, and almost like brothers to us.

I wasn't afraid of them. Armenia now gleamed like a many-domed cathedral of purest marble in the moonlight. We crossed ourselves as we caught sight of the cross of the old monastery on a small island in Lake Sevan.

It became so cold that our breath froze on our lips, making breathing difficult, but we didn't mind it. We reached a village singing *Our Fatherland, There Was No Moon, By the Banks of Mother Arax*. The inhabitants of the village lived in their prehistoric burrows clustered around a church, but they were real Armenians. We smelled the acrid odor of burning cowdung. Arshag held his nose with his fingers.

"What, don't you like it?" I asked him, breathing in deeply that historic fragrance of our land.

"No, I like it, of course, of course," he said, taking his fingers away from his nose.

"It's the traditional holy smell of Armenia," I said.

We were in good spirits, but desperately hungry.

"Who wants sizzling hot kebab with pilav and fresh white bread?" somebody yelled.

"Oh, shut up!"

"Boys, I could eat a whole roast sheep stuffed with rice."

"I'll be satisfied with a pot of meat and potatoes roasted in the bakery, with tomatoes, garlic and parsley."

"For God's sake, stop it! I'm falling to the ground."

"Do you see that star?" I said to Arshag. "It's the star of St. Gregory the Illuminator. Just imagine, you are standing under it. The Illuminator is looking down on you."

And following my example, Arshag gazed up rapturously at the constellation named after the founder of our Church in the fourth century. Great golden stars glittered in the purple sky — *Armenian* stars! This heavenly splendor of the Araratian winter was worth fifty snowstorms to see.

We dug up the mayor of the village and presented to him an official letter signed by the president of our Republic, ordering the civil and military authorities in the country to give us all assistance possible as honored wards of the State.

"So you boys are from Istanbul!" the mayor, a hefty peasant who pretended to read the letter we handed him, exclaimed. "Greetings, a thousand blessings!"

He was impressed, especially by our clothes and shoes. He couldn't get over the fact that we were from Istanbul and had left all the comforts of the outside world to come to poor, war-torn Armenia.

The news of our arrival and the fame of our clothes and shoes spread quickly through the village. And since there was no inn, not even a school building in this village, the peasants had to shelter us for the night in their homes. The mayor hinted that if we could spare some of our clothing for them we should have no difficulty in finding food and lodging for the night.

Divided into small groups, we went knocking on doors. I acted as the spokesman of our particular group, which besides Arshag included a few other boys. As I knew the Russian-Armenian dialect they let me do the talking. The peasants were hospitable enough, but there were hardly two hundred of these miserable hovels in the village, and whole families lived in one or two rooms, often with their horses and cows, if they had any left. Nevertheless, each family agreed to take in one or two of us. Finally only Arshag and I were left from our group. We knocked on another door. A pretty girl opened it.

"Oh, you are from Istanbul!" she gasped with a breathless charm before I opened my mouth.

"May I speak to the man in the house?" I said. "We are looking for a place to sleep tonight."

"Yes, I know," she said, smiling. "But we have no menfolk."

"Who are they, Satenik? What do they want?" a woman's voice called from the inside.

"They are Armenian boys from Istanbul, two of them," the girl replied. She said she would be back in a minute or two, and went in, leaving us at the door.

"Isn't she lovely?" I said to Arshag. "Typical Armenian virgin, like a gazelle with sweet wild eyes, fresh from the mountains."

"She sure is," Arshag said. "Did you notice her breasts? Just the kind I like."

"Don't talk like that! She is an Armenian girl," I said angrily.

Arshag clapped his mouth with his hand. He was two classes below me, and four years older. He had served in the Turkish Army, and his knowledge of our literature and history was sadly limited.

I helped him with his lessons, he in turn acted as my "bodyguard." He could have taken the shirt off my back and sold it to me, though. He was always buying and selling things, could outsmart ten merchants by acting dumb. He was foxy all right! And vain about his appearance. He wore a fancy jersey with blue and white stripes under his coat.

The girl came back, after consulting the authoritative woman inside, and even in the dim light I could see that the bloom of our fields was on her cheeks, all the wild flowers of Armenia. She said in a dignified and apologetic tone:

"I am very sorry, but we haven't room for both of you. Our house is very small, and we have no extra bedding. My mother-in-law says we can take in only one."

"Your mother-in-law? You are married?" I said, surprised.

She looked barely sixteen, and was the picture of the chaste, untouched maid of our folk songs and heroic tales, perhaps just ready to be kissed behind some hayloft or garden wall by a stalwart country lad, but surely unkissed yet.

"Yes, I am married," she said, lowering her eyes. "My husband is a soldier. I don't know where he is now. He was on the Kars front. We were married only a month when he went away."

It might have taken us an hour to find a place for both of us, so I told Arshag to stay there. The girl told me to try a house further down the lane. Separating from my companion I went and knocked on the door of this other hut and was admitted by its patriarchal owner. He was the head of a large family, and on his face I could read the whole history of our country.

Smoking a long, thin pipe, he asked me many questions about Constantinople, of which he still thought in terms of the old Sultans. He was curious to know what was going on in the outside world, in the great European capitals, and was convinced the Russians were coming back to Armenia, with plenty of flour from the Kuban, oil from Baku, sugar from Kharkov.

While we talked, a sorrowful woman, his daughter-in-law, was busy with her spinning-wheel. On the new Armenian rubles, printed abroad, the picture of Ararat was on one side, and of a woman with a spinning-wheel on the other. The spinning-wheel was the symbol of the Armenian home, and our home, with its Christian purity and grace, the secret of our racial survival.

To avoid all embarrassment I opened my knapsack and offered to sell them my extra shirt for food. Clothing was what these peasants needed most. I didn't care to tell them I was an orphan and not a rich boy from Istanbul, as they took me for. My host put down his pipe and felt the shirt between his gnarled fingers, admiring its material and tailoring. Then he passed it around, and it was admired by everybody in the room.

"How much do you want for it?" he asked.

"Give me what you can," I said.

Glances and murmurs were exchanged, the shirt was examined again, and my host made me an offer: two pounds of bread, a pound of white cheese, a pound of butter, and a bowl of honey, with a supper thrown in if I hadn't had supper.

"Fine!" I said, and we shook hands.

Turks had never been in this part of Armenia, and it was comparatively prosperous. The peasants had stored away some provisions for the winter. But only clothing like ours could buy food from them.

The woman at the spinning-wheel got up and served me a good meal

— fried eggs, cheese, bread baked in large, thin sheets in their *tonir,* or oven dug in the center of the earthen floor, and tea of mountain herbs sweetened with honey.

Before they retired, she made a separate bed for me right by this well-like oven, the choice spot in their house. I lay awake for hours. How could I sleep when I could hear the cavalry of St. Vartan descending from the slopes of Mount Ararat to meet the swarming Zoroastroan hosts and the elephant corps of the Persian King of Kings? Our immortal Vartan, with the holy priest Ghevond Yerets — Leontius the Elder — holding aloft a large silver cross, was leading his Christian army to battle. Was it the wind outside, or the sound of galloping hoofs and the neighing of horses, the clanging of shields and lances, the mass confession and recitation of prayers on the night before the Battle of Avarair?

And I could see Queen Satenik's capture by King Ardashes. After paying all the gold, leather and red dye which her father, the King of the Alans, demanded, according to their custom, Ardashes mounted his blackest steed and rode headlong into the river, on the opposite bank of which Princess Satenik was waiting for him with her attendants. The Armenian King crossed the river like a swift-winged eagle, shaking his red leather line with the golden ring, and threw it around the heaving waist of the young princess, and causing much pain to her tender waist carried her off to his camp.

The grand pageant at the royal temple at Ardashad. The King and his bride, whom he had captured as in war, rode side by side. Troops, nobles, servants and a multitude of happy people followed them to the temple, where the wedding ceremony was performed. To the father of the gods, the almighty Aramazt, were sacrificed snow-white bulls with gilt horns, snow-white horses, snow-white sheep and snow-white birds. The pagan priest poured the sacrificial wine on the sacred fire burning at the altar, and the flames shot up into the air. Satenik let loose snow-white pigeons and scattered roses over the golden image of Anahid, and threw handfuls of pearls to the people.

The rustic room where I lay by the underground oven was transformed into a marble hall in the palace of the King. All the nobles of Armenia and many kings and princes from neighboring states arrived for the wedding banquet. The nobles wore red trousers and earrings, and from their gold-mounted belts hung their long swords, their most prized possessions.

"Greetings, Sire," they said to Ardashes, embracing and kissing him.

"Welcome, my dear friend," Ardashes replied to each one.

Then they bowed before Queen Satenik.

The golden-domed banquet hall was brilliantly lighted with oil lamps, and its air perfumed with incense. With many mutual courtesies the guests sat in the throne-like chairs assigned to them, the ladies admiring the bouquets of roses, lilies, jasmines and violets, which decorated the long tables. They spoke both in Armenian and Greek, discussing the latest plays and books from Athens, the latest political news from Rome. Hannibal, sitting near the head of the King's table as his counsellor and engineer, described the battle tactics of the Romans.

The first course brought in by uniformed waiters was hot steaming soup, served in golden dishes. Then came the game, roasted deer and boar in huge silver trays, slaughtered by Ardashes and Hannibal on their hunting trip the day before. The roasted deer and boar were followed by trout from Lake Sevan, pheasants and wild ducks, and a variety of eggs.

After they had finished eating, boys in white uniforms brought in little barrels of wine and placed one before each guest, and the wassail began. The King and Queen stood up holding their drinking horns, and all the guests followed their example.

"Let us drink first in honor of the great Aramazt, the creator of heaven and earth, the almighty!" the King said in his deep voice.

And they all drank in honor of the chief god of pagan Armenia.

As they sat down, a group of gay minstrels trooped in, strumming their lyres and singing the hymn of the Armenian battle-god Vahagn:

> Heaven and earth were in travail,
> Was in travail the purple sea.
> The sea gave birth to a red reed
> And from that reed came forth smoke
> And from that reed came forth flame
> And out of the flame ran a lad.
> His hair was of fire,
> His beard was of flame,
> And his eyes were like suns.

The minstrels were followed by an orchestra composed of drummers, flute players, harp players, and trumpeters, who played wild, passionate love music, and dancing girls began their slow, sinuous dance. Then two clowns stumbled in and entertained the diners with their risqué jokes and tomfooleries. Everybody got drunk, the dancing girls sat on the knees of the nobles, and even Queen Satenik was recklessly gay.

Early the next morning we boys gathered in the village square and resumed our journey. Lake Sevan glowed like blue sacrificial fire in an immense marble basin. I felt like a towering prince in red trousers, with a golden sword, returned to Armenia after a lapse of two thousand years.

The knapsacks on our backs were heavier than the day before. The boys had traded clothing for food, as I had done. I noticed, however, that Arshag's knapsack didn't look fuller, and he wasn't wearing his jersey with the blue and white stripes. I figured it was worth at least twice the amount of bread, cheese, butter and honey I had received for my shirt.

"What did you get for your jersey?" I asked him.

He was reluctant to tell me.

"You fox," I said, "come on, tell me what you got for it. A Caucasian pistol?"

He shook his head.

"For heaven's sake, Arshag, why are you so mysterious about it?"

He gave a half-laugh. "Satenik, the girl who opened the door, the one with the nice front, took a fancy to it."

"And so you gave it to her! Bravo, Arshag! Now you are getting to be a good Armenian."

He was embarrassed by my patriotic praise.

"Don't be so modest," I said. "You've done a good deed as a boy scout." And I added jokingly, "She should have given you a kiss for it."

"She gave me more than a kiss," he muttered, blushing.

"WHAT! You are joking."

"No, I am not," he said, with a little crooked smile.

We walked on in silence for a while. I was sure we were thinking the same thoughts, as I noticed the look in Arshag's eyes. Something in our hearts which could not be put in words had been shattered, and it was quite some time before either of us spoke again.

CHAPTER 17

Turkey Gets Ararat;
Armenia the Picture

The thermometer in the square of Nor Bayazet registered thirty-two below zero.

"Good morning, comrade!" a soldier shouted to a man from across the icy square. I noticed a piece of red cloth tied to a button on his new army overcoat.

"How are you, comrade?" the other returned in a jolly voice. He, too, had a piece of red cloth on his breast.

People were laughing and joking in the streets and calling one another "comrade." A crowd was gathered before the town bulletin board reading something. I went over to see what it was. A brief typewritten government announcement proclaimed Armenia to be an independent Socialist Soviet Republic allied with the fraternal Russian Federated Socialist Soviet Republic.

The Armenian Government had signed an agreement with Soviet Russia and withdrawn from power. Armenia had to choose between Soviet Russia and Kemalist Turkey, which under the circumstances was tantamount to choosing between life and death. What disturbed me was the attitude of the natives toward this sudden change in regime: they were too glad about it.

A small detachment of Red Russian cavalry rode into Nor Bayazet. Its young blond commander, flanked by the equally young members of the local Soviet, addressed the people from the balcony of our school, the largest building in the town. At the end of his speech, he yelled, "Down with the lackeys of imperialism! Long live the Third International! Long live the dictatorship of the proletariat! Long live the brotherhood of the toiling masses of the East! Long live the fraternal republic of Socialist Soviet

Azerbaijan! Long live Socialist Soviet Armenia!" The Armenian speakers who followed him repeated these stock phrases at the end of their orations. Copies of an Armenian newspaper, *The Communist,* were distributed free. The men grabbed them eagerly, even those who could not read. For the next several days I saw people rolling cigarettes in bits of *The Communist,* which explained in part the enthusiasm with which that organ of the Armenian Communist party was received.

The drab walls of the town bloomed with propaganda posters, pictures of Karl Marx, Lenin, flamboyant caricatures of the hated capitalists. One showed a fat Russian priest receiving gifts of poultry and baskets of eggs from starving peasants. There were giant workers with hammers, towering Red soldiers pointing their fixed bayonets at terrified fat bankers.

The local Soviet did not like us. Every now and then its members would inspect our rooms, and were greeted by dead silence. It was now a crime to be patriotic, to sing *Our Fatherland,* and all patriots were considered "lackeys of imperialism." Mr. Torgomian fled to Georgia. Our new director, a more courageous and able man, was also a member of the outlawed nationalist party, and if the Nor Bayazet communists had known it he would have been arrested and shot.

Before this change in regime we had had classes for about a week, but now there were no more classes. However, they still let us occupy the school building, in the auditorium of which Soviet plays, lectures and programs were given. There were some talented actors in the town. I participated in these programs — the only one from our school who did — by reciting a poem about workers (*Make way, we are coming!*), my chest bared, holding a shovel.

In a few weeks we had sold all of our spare clothing, and more. The local Soviet had neither the means nor the desire to support us. We were the protégés of the former government and, therefore, counter-revolutionaries in their eyes. There was only one solution to our problem — return to Constantinople. But leaving Soviet territory was practically impossible at the time.

We finally managed to get permission to go to the Georgian border, and one day early in February started for Karaklis, a town on the Tiflis-Yerevan railroad, which we hoped to reach in three days. It was like a journey across the frozen wilds of Siberia, but we were cheerful, and sang our patriotic songs.

The Soviet of another town, Dilijan, refused to recognize our permit and put us under arrest. Arrested by our own countrymen, in Hayastan!

They lined us up in the courtyard of a prison, and a man announced in a gruff voice:

"Comrades, before we search you, I request in the name of the Extraordinary Commission Against Counter-revolution and Sabotage that you give up your arms of your own free will. If we find concealed weapons on anyone he will be punished by the laws of revolutionary times."

That had an ominous meaning. It meant the firing squad. Their suspicions about the real purpose of our journey seemed to be verified when they got hold of a few revolvers for which our boys had traded clothing, and convinced that we were plotting a counter-revolution, proceeded to search every one of us.

One of our instructors had two dangerous pamphlets on him in which Bolshevism was described as a Russian pathological phenomenon, alien to the Armenian spirit and inimical to our national interests. They were strongly worded in a learned sociological language.

"For God's sake keep these," he begged me. "They will shoot me if they find them on me."

I pushed them down my belt, next to my skin, and faced them with such innocence that they felt hastily around my pockets and let me go.

To instill some true Armenian spirit in the warden of this prison, who was from Baku, I would show him my boy-scout buckle, with its picture of Ararat at sunrise, recite poems to which he could not object, and I even told him one could be a good Bolshevik and still remain a good Armenian. He seemed to like me, but was very cautious, as if forced to hide his own patriotic feelings. Since then Armenian communists, having discovered Armenian literature and history, have become great patriots.

We sent a telegram to the president of the Revolutionary-Military Committee at Yerevan, protesting against our arrest. It must have had some effect, for we were allowed to go to the latrine without an armed guard. Every day they sent us to a near by forest to chop wood. We marched with axes on our shoulders, singing *La Marseillaise* and an Armenian socialistic song. The Dilijan Soviet was composed of fanatic young communists, several of them mere boys, who hated us, but they could not prove, much as they tried, that we were, one and all, "Dashnags." The communists of Nor Bayazet were patriots compared to these armed brats. Here the Russianization process seemed to have taken a violent anti-Armenian aspect. There were girls among those communists too, shapely, good-looking ones, wearing white sweaters and knitted wool caps. Dilijan with its pine woods and excellent climate was a noted health resort, and many rich families from Tiflis and Baku used to spend their summers here. The town had a tuberculosis sanatorium.

After two weeks we were allowed to leave the prison grounds during the day. Meanwhile we heard in Yerevan the entire Armenian intelligentsia was in jail. Surrounded by a cordon of mounted Russian guards, all the officers of the Armenian Army, including the Chief-of-Staff and the Commander-in-Chief, passed through Dilijan on their way to Baku, where God alone knew what was going to happen to them. Nobody was allowed to go near these exiles, but I managed to buy food and tobacco for them, mail their letters and render them various little services.

Finally an order came for our release, and we went to Karaklis. This was a larger town, with about twelve thousand inhabitants, and being on the railroad had attracted homeless children from the devastated war zone. They were dying in the streets of hunger and cold. Wearing nothing but potato sacks, they lay on the snow of the pavements, whining and shaking like wounded stray dogs, day and night, continuously, until calmed by merciful death. They had wrinkled old faces, looked more like monkeys than human beings, and it was impossible to tell whether they were boys or girls. Nobody ever spoke to them. Could they speak, I wondered? Did they have any names, did they know where they were from? Sometimes two or three of them huddled together, but the only sound they ever emitted was that incessant dog-like whining. Their faces and cries haunted me.

I could not live in Armenia without holding a public office of some kind. And so I became an assistant secretary in the Commissariat of the Interior. Armenian was still the official language of the country. The communists here were mature men, and we found ourselves in a more Armenian and friendlier atmosphere. The character of local Soviets and administrations differed from town to town. Not all communists were of the same pattern. As nobody in Karaklis, with the exception of a well-known young poet from Van, knew as much Armenian as I, and I excelled even him in penmanship, I enjoyed a certain distinction in the Commissariat of the Interior, even though I was its youngest employee.

There were three of us in the bureau where I worked; an engineer was the chief, a poet the secretary, and I was the assistant secretary. I did practically all the writing, and signed and countersigned my name to certificates of birth, marriage, death, to identification papers, to requisition papers, and so on. Soviet Russian laws were now in force in Armenia too. Marriage had become simply a matter of registration. Even leading communists had to come to our bureau and answer my official questions. I felt important. So important, in fact, that I signed only my first name, with flourishes, on the documents I issued, as if everyone knew me by my first name.

The poet, who suffered from tuberculosis, had long, light hair, always beautifully combed, artistic white hands with long, slender fingers like a woman's, and every few minutes he put his hand to his mouth and coughed, gently, gracefully. I had read some of his verses in Constantinople, gentle, gossamer lyrics. Everything about him was gentle, spiritual, "poetic." He was from Turkish Armenia and not a communist. Sometimes he produced from his pocket a new poem he had written and let me read it.

I tried to reform every communist I met, and worked especially hard on the Commissar of Public Enlightenment. I gave him Daniel Varujan's *Pagan Songs* to read in order to infect him with the patriotic spirit of our literature. His wife was a Russian. I thought that once I educated a few men in key positions, I could gradually make the country a truly Armenian state in spite of its red coating. I even thought of joining the communist party, and working my way to a dominant position, in order to humanize the entire communist movement, and secure Armenia's rights.

Karaklis now was the center of the Armenian Bolshevik government, for a widespread anti-communist uprising had taken place, and Yerevan and Nor Bayazet had fallen into the hands of Dashnags. This rebellion had been brewing for some time, but we did not know it when we were arrested in Dilijan. Armenia was plunged into a civil war. Led by the horsemen of Sassoun a handful of men fought tooth and nail against the Red Army. If Armenians had fought so well against the Turks the latter could not have entered Kars.

Meanwhile, Soviet Armenia, Soviet Azerbaijan and Soviet Russia declared war on Georgia and invaded that country from three sides. In a few weeks Georgia was also Sovietized, and the Bolsheviks threw thousands of Russian troops into Armenia and sent armored trains to crush this rebellion. They were the same Russian troops I had first seen in Trebizond except that they now carried red flags with the hammer and sickle. The noisy mobs of the Revolution had been transformed into a disciplined, superb fighting force. They marched through Karaklis, battalion after battalion, and as I watched them I sighed and said to myself, "Woe to the Armenians on the other side!"

As I was now earning my own living — if living it could be called — I roomed with a private family from Trebizond, a middle-aged, grief-stricken woman and her young nephew, a boy of twelve, whose father had been exiled to Baku apparently for no other reason than that he wore a white collar. Her Remington typewriter had been confiscated, worth, she tearfully protested, three million rubles — or perhaps it was thirty. They were destitute. The boy taught me the *International* in Russian, and we would sing it together just for the music and the fun of it.

In a mud hovel near our cottage a member of the Armenian Parliament, a veteran of three wars against Turkey, was in hiding. He was born in Van, for whose heroic inhabitants and pretty girls I had great admiration, and I often visited him in his lair. We would take our shirts off, hold them over the fire, and while our lice exploded like the crackle of machine guns we would discuss the latest political and military developments, talk about the philosophy of life and death.

One day disguised as a peasant this member of parliament came out of his hiding and tried to cross the battle line to save his life, and perhaps join the guerrilla army of the Committee for the Salvation of the Fatherland which was directing the armed revolt against the Bolsheviks.

A few days later, as I was coming out of the Commissariat of the Interior, I saw him trudging along in his cowhide moccasins with a big wool hat on his head and a peasant walking-stick in his hand.

"What is this?" I whispered to him. "What happened? Why did you come back?"

"I could not cross the line. The peasants of a village near the front would not help me. They threatened to hand me over to the Bolsheviks if I did not turn back."

"Russian or Armenian peasants?"

"Armenian."

I could not understand how Armenian peasants would refuse to help a member of parliament, a patriot like him.

"The Bolsheviks have won them over," he said. "It's our incurable Russophilism."

This seemed to have convinced him that the Red regime in Armenia had a substantial popular basis. If our peasants were on "their" side, then we had to respect their will, I thought. But I was certain the Bolsheviks were popular in Armenia primarily because we Armenians, one and all, were under the old spell of "Uncle Russia." Communism in Armenia was essentially a pro-Russian movement.

The Armenian SSR maintained friendly relations with republican Turkey, following a more realistic policy than the former government. The Bolsheviks were determined to "liquidate" national and religious hatreds — and that was the best part of their program. But in this new era of socialist peace and reconstruction we had no one, I thought bitterly, to act as the true, competent spokesman of our people and present our national cause before Moscow, and yes, even before Ankara.

Turkey's former enemies and victors were being so carefully nice to her now. Soviet Russia, France and Italy were helping the Turks, with arms, supplies, diplomatic tricks and honors. In Paris the Turks were old Francophiles, in Moscow they were comrade Bolsheviks. Kemal sat on the fence and collected from everybody on both sides, by throwing a bone now and then in the direction of one or the other, to keep them fighting among themselves. It was an old, old Turkish game.

I read in an Armenian communist paper that according to the chief of the Turkish delegation to Moscow "Communism is making great progress in Turkey," and a young Armenian communist tried to convince me that the Turks had changed, they were our brothers now, and it was only a matter of a few years until the complete Sovietization of Turkey.

In Moscow, Turkey and Soviet Russia signed a treaty of "friendship and brotherhood for the common struggle against imperialism," and gritting my teeth I read the article defining the new boundary between the two states: Kars, Ani, Ararat, formerly Russian, were ceded to Turkey. Kemal also retained the whole magnificent territory of Turkish Armenia.

To the Armenian proletariat was left a bit of land no larger than Belgium, consisting of mountains and arid plateaus. Every Saturday morning we employees of the Commissariat of the Interior, led by a brass band playing the *International*, went to clear the roads of snow, dig ditches and repair buildings. Nobody shouldered a pick or shovel with more enthusiasm than I, nobody marched behind the band with more resolute steps. But my heart bled meanwhile. How could we build a viable, prosperous Armenian socialist state on the small territory left us, with no natural resources, with not enough arable land to support our peasant population, not to mention the hundreds of thousands of refugees scattered in all parts of the world, men without a country, all longing for Ararat?

Turkey had no need of the land she had taken away from the Armenian peasant, and, I was convinced, would never cultivate it. In ten or twenty years there would be gardens and busy villages and towns on one side of the new frontier, and fallow, dead, silent land on the other — our cemeteries. But not all our industry, not all the electrification and irrigation projects in the world, could make such a restricted Armenia a self-supporting country. I pored over statistics, studied the areas, population and resources of Belgium, Holland, Switzerland, Greece, Bulgaria, Hungary, Denmark, Portugal, and could see no way out for us Armenians except the recovery of at least a part of our lost territories. I was willing to give up Trebizond, Erzurum, Cilicia, and would have been satisfied with Kars and Van. And I swore by Ararat that some day I would stand in Van, that most ancient capital of our race, and see the splendid new buildings, the broad, tree-lined avenues, the schools and scientific institutes of the new and forever Armenian Van.

What made me furious was that Armenian communists — and able, influential men were not lacking among them — did nothing about our boundaries. The responsibility for correcting the mistakes of the past and of healing our national wounds was theirs, now. They believed Turkey would follow the example of Mohammedan Azerbaijan and become a Soviet state — after which, our refugees could return to their homes, and between Soviet Armenia and Soviet Turkey there could of course be no boundary dispute. But I knew there was not the slightest possibility of Turkey's going communist, and if Turkey did adopt a Soviet form of government it would be another clever move on her part to gain selfish ends. The "comrade" Turks shot immediately any agent of the Third International that dared enter their country. Having fooled us Armenians repeatedly, they were now fooling Soviet Russia.

At a word from Moscow, Turkey would have discreetly retired from Kars as well as Van, as she did retire from Batum. But Moscow did not give the word.

Even though I had a much better plan for the solution of mankind's political, social and economic ills than anything I read in communist pamphlets, for defeating evil *without* evil, I would have gladly become the reddest of the Reds if only the red flag had flown on Ararat, the fortress of Kars and the old castle of Van.

The Armenian SSR had the picture of Ararat in its coat of arms, for that mountain is the symbol of our race. We had to be satisfied with the picture. What kind of socialist justice for the oppressed small nations of the world was this?

CHAPTER 18

Sixteen: America Bound

My work as assistant secretary in the Commissariat of the Interior of the Armenian SSR became dull and confining, for it was spring, incredibly, miraculously spring. I stopped stuffing communist newspapers under my shirt to keep warm. For months I had thought bitterly that in dividing the earth among the peoples of the world God had given us nothing but rocks and ice for a fatherland. But now the sword-length icicles had melted, and the valley of Pambak was green, shot through with the blaze of the blooming crocus and the other wild flowers of the Caucasus.

I contemplated the picture of Lenin over my desk on the wall, and a communist poster beside it — a worker sailing toward a lighthouse on a raft through a stormy sea at night, *"Capital,* by Karl Marx," written on the raft. The worker represented toiling mankind. But Marx was all cold economic mathematics, and with his bushy hair and beard looked like a cruel Jehovah. I wanted to write a book that would supersede *Capital,* and be the Bible of mankind — *Agriculture as the Direct Road.* I wanted everybody to live in a white cottage with a garden, beehives, chickens, with healthy, merry children running around. But in order to write such a book and lead my fellow men to that idyllic millennium — in order to abolish poverty, ignorance, injustice, cruelty — I had to be the wisest man of my time, I thought, and the strongest, most perfect.

So I wanted to see the world and learn everything. Above all, I wanted to see America. I got up and walked over to the window. The birds were singing in the poplars and acacia trees, unconcerned with the destinies of classes and nations. I whistled a silly White Russian tune, then broke into an Italian operatic aria, with theatrical gestures.

"Ha! Ha! Ha!" laughed a consumptive young clerk in our office, pointing at me. "Comrades, look at him!" He had another paroxysm of coughing. He was not the poet, but another boy.

Next to me he was the youngest employee in the commissariat, being barely eighteen, an intense, pale youth with beautiful eyes, who never took off his filthy, tattered army overcoat. His overcoat and my half-burnt, ragged cap were famous among all the clerks. But when they joked about my cap I declared I was keeping it for the state museum, that some day it would be put in a glass case and preserved for future generations.

I turned and glanced at the tubercular boy coughing his lungs out. I went over to his desk. He looked at me with tears of rebellion in his eyes, which seemed to say: "I don't want to die, I am too young, I haven't lived yet, and it's spring."

"Sirak," I said, "from now on we'll have fine weather."

He expectorated in his handkerchief, wiped his mouth. "Another winter would kill me."

"When are you going to Tiflis for treatment?"

"I am not going," he said, still breathing hard. "Circumstances make it impossible."

"How about your permit? What will you do with it?"

"Nothing; I'll let it expire."

I lowered my voice. "Listen, give it to me. I can use it. I'll go to Tiflis in your place. I'll pay you for it. I'll give you three pounds of bread and my month's ration of tea and soap."

He considered my offer. "But if they catch you, they will arrest both of us."

"Nobody can catch me. But if they do, you can say I stole it from you."

He sold me his permit for four pounds of bread and my month's ration of tea and soap. This transaction was carried out in secrecy, for one of the clerks in the room was a member of the Young Communist League, and we had to be careful. I went to the chief of my bureau, a dark little man, formerly a military engineer, who never took off his engineer's cap. He hated himself for being Armenian, but I was fond of him. We often argued about the comparative merits of Russian and Armenian literature — though he was so Russianized he knew nothing about our great poets. I maintained Daniel Varujan and Siamanto were greater than Pushkin and Lermontov.

"I am resigning," I said. "You had better find another assistant to help you with the Armenian language."

"Why?" he frowned.

"Oh, I have plans. I want to go to Constantinople, to America. I have a lot of things to learn, a lot of things to do. But I'll come back some day. You will see me again."

"You can leave your job if you wish, but I know nothing about your intentions to go abroad, you understand? Nothing whatever. How are you going to travel? Do you have a passport for leaving Soviet territory and going abroad?"

"No, I don't need it. Once I reach the sea I can go anywhere." I did not tell him about the permit I had just bought, with which I could at least go to Georgia for my "health."

He consented to give me a typewritten reference — which I wrote myself, stating I had worked in the Commissariat of Interior of the Armenian SSR, and rendered excellent service. I left Soviet Armenia and reached Tiflis in grand style, on the roof of a boxcar. After spending a few adventurous days in that splendid city, where I slept on the benches of the railroad station as a baggage boy, and meanwhile visualized to myself the white cottages, the beehives, chickens, happy children in the wonderful world I would create, I bummed my way to Batum, the town I loved most next to Trebizond. I was thrilled at the sight of the Black Sea, and the smell of oranges and anchovies was, for me, heavenly fragrance. The first thing I did on reaching Batum was to eat a plate of fried anchovies with Georgian corn bread.

Not finding any of my relatives and friends in Batum, I joined a group of Armenian refugees from Armash, in Turkey, who had camped along the railroad tracks. Some of them wanted to settle down in Armenia, others hoped to return to Constantinople.

I built myself a fire from stolen coal, and pulling my cap over my ears, curled up on the ground beside it. My cap burnt a little more. I began composing in my mind chapter one of *Agriculture as the Direct Road*.

A girl passed by, stopped, and glanced back over her shoulder at a few refugee men huddled around a fire. Then she continued walking, slowly, apparently expecting one of them to follow her.

"There goes another little whore," said one of the men.

"Brother, it's worse than Kemer-Alti in Istanbul," said another.

She looked back twice more, but none of the men moved, and she disappeared in the dark. I got up, and pretending to be going somewhere else, followed her, whistling. She slowed down. I did not care, I was old enough, sixteen. She stopped as I went up to her, and seeing I was a boy, gave me a skeptical, contemptuous look.

"Good evening," I said in Russian, gulping hard. "May I walk with you?"

She hesitated for a moment, then shrugged her shoulder indifferently. "If you like."

She was shivering like me. I took her thin arm. As we passed under a light I saw a pretty, delicate face, pale and haggard. She couldn't be over fifteen. Her features weren't Russian. She had black hair.

"Jewish?" I asked.

"Georgian. Have you money?"

"Sure."

"I never take less than twenty rubles."

"*Khorosho*, all right," I said, and squeezed her arm possessively. Unfortunately she wasn't plump. "Do you live far?"

"No."

We walked for a few minutes along the tracks, then turned into a narrow, dark street lined with large persimmon trees. She may have venereal disease, I thought, I better turn back. But I wanted to be a man, to find out what it was like.

We entered a small one-room shack with a tin roof. She struck a match and lighted a kerosene lamp. I peered around. There was a bed in a corner. An empty sardine can and unwashed dishes on a small table covered with red oilcloth. Cigarette stubs here and there. A potted carnation on the window ledge.

"I didn't know any sardines were left," I said, picking up the can and looking at the label on it. It was Italian. I read it aloud, to show her I knew Italian.

She sat down on the edge of the bed and began unlacing her shoes. I stood by, fidgety, not knowing what to do, how to go about it. She dropped her shoes on the dirty, worn carpet, and pulled herself on to the bed.

"Well, what are you standing there for?" she said, after I had paid her in advance twenty rubles I had earned carrying baggage at the railroad station in Tiflis. I took off my coat and hung it on the back of the only chair in the room. She reclined on the bed, her skirt now way up above her knees, exposing her fancy pink garters and thighs. I knew she wore nothing under her skirt, in the Russian fashion.

I tried to act calm, experienced. But as I was dawdling she looked at me with a thin smile on her lips, and as she smiled, it seemed to me I had seen her somewhere.

"What's your name?" I asked.

"Anna."

I was sure I had seen her before. Strange. "Where are your parents?"

"What are you, a secret investigator?" She looked at me suspiciously.

"Of course not."

"Well…"

"Batum is a beautiful city," I said, to gain time and courage. "I just came from Tiflis. But there isn't another place like Batum in the Caucasus. Batum is almost like my home town, though I was born in Trebizond. I lived here five years ago, with my great-aunt, on Bebutov-Korsakov Street."

She sat up. "Bebutov-Korsakov? I used to live there myself."

We stared at each other. And suddenly I remembered her as a girl in our neighborhood whose mother was Greek and father Georgian. She often came to our courtyard to play with the girls. "Maria Barishvili!" I said, seizing her by her shoulders. "You are Maria Barishvili."

She covered her face with her hands.

"Do you remember the funny watchmaker with the big red nose in our courtyard whom we used to mimic?"

She nodded.

"And the Russian priest with the long white hair?"

She nodded.

I took out my wallet and showed her a picture of myself with two of my former playmates in Batum.

"That's you, with the white cap and pistol," she said. "You always played soldier. But how you have grown since then!"

"That cap!" I chuckled. "I hated to wear it because it wasn't a Russian cap."

She took a deep breath. "Many things have happened since then."

"Yes, many." I pulled up the chair and sat down by the bed. "What happened to your parents, where are they?"

"My mother died. I don't know where my father is. He was a good-for-nothing drunkard and beat my mother all the time. She became sick, she coughed. He went away, didn't care what happened to us. The sailors of foreign ships made me — do this. We were hungry. They gave me white bread, sausage, sardines, clothing, all kinds of nice things."

"Some day there won't be any more poverty and hunger, Maria," I assured her. "People will live in white cottages with flower gardens and beehives; everybody will be kind and contented. You too. You must never do this again, never."

"I didn't want to, the sailors made me."

She was so naive, still a child, really. I did not tell her about my book, that I carried the destiny of nations on my shoulders, but I persuaded her to sell roasted sunflower seeds for a living. I had sold them myself. Satisfied that I had reformed her, I rose to go.

"Where are you going?" she said, seated cross-legged on the bed, with her hands clasped around her knees.

"It's late, time to sleep." I put on my coat.

"Where are you going to sleep?"

"Under the stars."

"It's cold and damp outside. You *can* stay with me." She smiled, timidly.

"But there is only one bed here."

"It's large enough for two."

I hesitated, but she urged me. "Very well," I said.

I blew out the lamp. We undressed in the dark and went to bed. I kept rigidly to my side of the bed, as far away from her as possible. We talked for a while. I told her I was going to Constantinople, and later, to America. That I would study in great universities, and some day come back to Batum in far different condition than she saw me in now.

She wanted me to take her to America with me, but that was quite impossible under the circumstances.

When she turned over and snuggled against me, my heart threatened to burst out of my ribs. I could hardly breathe. I edged away from her. We were silent, and I pretended to fall asleep. About an hour later she was breathing deeply. I touched her lightly. She didn't wake up. I slipped out of bed, grabbed my clothes and shoes, and dashed out of the shack. The fire I had built had almost died down. I put some more stolen coal on it, and slept on the ground, with a clear conscience.

But I saw her again the next morning. "I thought you had already gone to Constantinople, to America," she said, with a mischievous smile. "Are you afraid of me?"

"I was afraid of myself."

We spent the day together. Went swimming — naked — though we

undressed in separate sections on the beach. She was slender like a birch
sapling, with lemon-shaped breasts — a lovely, swift creature in the water.
Then we went to the harbor. An Italian liner, *Roma,* of the Lloyd Triestino,
had docked — a magnificent ship! She wouldn't go near it.

"The sailors know me," she said.

White bread crumbs, beer bottles, sardine cans, floated in the water around
the *Roma.* A few sailors were leaning over the rails of the deck, watching the
Red sentries and the hungry, ragged natives, who like me stared at those
floating pieces of white bread. I wondered how I could board that ship.

When later Maria and I were strolling in the Boulevard we saw three
Italian sailors from the *Roma* seated on a bench.

Leaving Maria behind I went over and greeted the sailors in Italian. I
recited an Italian poem for them:

> *Rondinella pellegrina,*
> *Che ti posi il sul verone*
> *Ricantando ogni matina*
> *Quella flebile canzone?*

I told them in my best book Italian that I myself was like a pilgrim
swallow, with a plaintive song. I sang it:

> *Quando io nacqui*
> *Mi dice una voce*
> *Tu sei nato*
> *A portare la croce.*

Yes, I told them, I too was born to carry the cross. When I next sang *Santa
Lucia* for them, they were visibly affected. We became friends. I learned the
Roma was sailing to Constantinople at six o'clock that same afternoon,
stopping only at Trebizond and Samsun. I frankly told them I wanted to go
to Constantinople as a stowaway on their ship. They assured me they would
not say anything and would help me if possible. But I had to be very careful
and they could do nothing for me if I were caught.

About half an hour before sailing time I was on the quay with Maria,
but she didn't come close to the ship. The passengers were all foreigners,
mostly Persians, well-dressed, prosperous-looking men, with a few veiled

women. I was racking my brains for a method of getting on the ship undetected, every minute counted, when I had a bright idea: as a porter, of course. I was in a way a professional porter. So I seized the baggage of a Persian, two heavy valises, and went up the gang-plank with him, past all the Red and Italian officials and guards. Nobody stopped me. I deposited the valises in the Persian's cabin, thanked him for his tip — and stayed on the deck.

A party of Soviet officials came up for a final check-up of passports. One of them looked suspiciously at me, but I was now posing as an Italian, a member of the ship's crew. My clothes were dirty, but they weren't Russian clothes, they were the kind any Italian boy might wear. At this critical moment, seeing one of the sailors I had met in the Boulevard, I shouted to him a few Italian words. The suspicious officials did not question me, and I was saved for the time being.

The powerful throbbing noise of the engines thrilled every cell in my body. I prayed, "Our Father who art in heaven, hallowed be Thy name. Thy Kingdom come. Thy will be done on earth as it is in heaven." I glanced at Maria — at the snow-capped mountains crimson in the setting sun — the crowd on the quay — the buildings — trying to impress the details of this scene indelibly on my mind so that I would always remember them, even in far-off America. Maria waved at me, and I cautiously waved back.

The gang-plank was drawn up. The thick ropes were released from their moorings. The great vessel began to move. Churning the waters milk-white the *Roma* turned around majestically — a vast leviathan of a ship. Maria, with the shore, receded into the blue of the thickening dusk. Good-bye, Maria! Good-bye, Batum! Good-bye, Ararat!

I found a place to hide on the deck. One of my sailor friends brought me a plate of spaghetti and roast meat, with a few slices of white bread.

"Stay here," he said. "Don't come out. Let nobody see you."

The ship anchored off Trebizond late at midnight. I crawled out of my hiding and looked sadly at my home town. Lights twinkled on the shore. I could make out the silhouette of Guzel-Serai, the old Genoese castle — the cypresses of the Turkish cemetery — the cross of the Armenian church — the white, rock-hewn Byzantine monastery on the Gray Hill. In the background rose the Pontic empire of somber firs.

A fleet of high-prowed rowboats, approaching the ship like black camels of the sea, discharged their passengers. Turks scrambled up the gang-plank.

An old fear gripped my heart.

Suddenly I found myself confronted with the purser. *"Tichetta,"* he said, wanting to punch my ticket.

I shook my head.

"Passaporte," he demanded.

I shook my head again. His jaws tightened. He seized me by my shoulder and angrily pushed me to the gang-plank. Signaling to a Turkish boatman to take me ashore, he tried to disengage my arms from the railing, to which I clung for dear life. The Turkish and Persian passengers gathered around us, watching our scuffle. Twice I nearly fell overboard. Down, deep in the black pit of the water, the Turkish boat waited for me, crashing against the tall iron sides of the ship, and Trebizond was weeping, weeping for me in the night with those twinkling lights. I saw countless dead eyes in the sea, all staring up at me, as if eager that I too should join them, enter the undersea world of the dead whose futile protests and cries for mercy when they were being drowned during the massacre nobody had heard.

The purser succeeded in pushing me two steps down the gang-plank when the captain came to see what was going on, and I immediately appealed to him, as one civilized person to another, in a mixture of Italian and French:

"Monsieur le capitaine, je suis un étudiant Arménien. I want to go to America, to study the science of agriculture. The Turks killed my parents and relatives right here in Trebizond. I escaped. That boatman will never take me ashore, he will drown me. Even if he does, they will shoot me later. We Armenians have been propagators of *la lingua e la cultura Italiana."*

He listened to me, pipe in mouth. The Turks and Persians drew back respectfully. Even the purser's hold on me relaxed.

"Let him stay," the captain said.

I had now the freedom of the ship. It was cold on the deck. A Turk offered me his bed, but I declined it with thanks. The excitement was over, and the passengers returned to their places. Many had brought their bedding and slept on the deck. I stood alone on the prow of the ship, my hands in the pockets of my breeches, the collar of my coat turned up, gazing out upon the sea as the *Roma* cut smoothly across it.

The cry of the sea now sounded like a mass piano concert in the moonlight. My heart is a hard red shield, I said. My heart is a star upon my breast. And my breast is the world. I am sailing on to America, to the great future, on the raft of my thought. A lighthouse — the burning heart of the world — my guide through the starry night.

I saw Maria coming out of the waters and presently we were swimming on together in the path of the moon across the wide, wide sea. All around us moved the protective spirits of the sea, and stars flung down handfuls of orange blossoms on our heads. An angel beat her wings and flew away with a message for Saint Mary. An old hoary god of the sea, his head in the stars, his feet in the waters, married us, and troupes of sirens danced a wedding dance in the waves.

When the *Roma* entered the Bosporus and the control launch came, the captain sent me to the boiler room, where I hid in the coal bin. After the control officers departed and the ship docked in Galata I jumped off the deck, shook the coal dust off my cap, banged it down on my head at a rakish angle, and strode on — ready to conquer the world.

CHAPTER 19

The Great Hoax

My conscience bothered me, and time and again I wanted to make a full confession, but didn't dare. The whole thing had gone too far. And I wasn't sure they would believe me if I did tell the truth.

After taking a Turkish bath and cleansing myself of the dirt, coal dust and lice I had accumulated as a Soviet tramp and stowaway, I was admitted to an orphanage in Pera, where I found my brother clean and safe. With some twenty other orphan boys we attended the Armenian Central School.

My pilgrimage to Ararat had cost me a year. Onnik was in the fifth class, while I was in the fourth.

"Do you remember, it was Father's intention to send us to Central when we grew older?" he said.

I did. It was a famous old school, even though I was shocked to see it located in the gutters of Galata, surrounded by Levantine labyrinths swarming with prostitutes, drunkards and the riffraff of seven seas.

Onnik showed me a camera he had won as first prize for getting the highest marks in the school, which was something, for there were many brilliant students here.

"This would have made Father happy," I said as I examined the camera. "He wanted us to be always first in school."

Onnik's mouth twitched, and we looked away from each other. We took care, even after so many years, not to mention our murdered parents and relatives when we talked. I still could not look at a pharmacy without seeing my father's dark, graying face moving behind a prescription counter, and every time I remembered my mother I suppressed a deep, secret sob.

I considered myself only a temporary student at Central. This was a good chance for me to pick up some mathematics, sciences and English before going to America. English fortunately was a required subject, taught by a graduate of Robert College. Most of our textbooks were French, and our program was substantially that of a French lycée. Like most Armenian schools Central was wretchedly poor.

Dreaming of going to America, I made my plans accordingly — which I kept to myself. Not even my brother knew what was going on in my mind. But how to go to America? I had no money. I could, perhaps, reach New York as a stowaway. That idea fascinated me as a wonderful adventure. But I was afraid some modern Nat Pinkerton or Nick Carter — whose Yankee cunning and exploits I greatly admired — would eventually seize me and I would be sent ingloriously back. For some strange reason the immigration laws of noble, humanitarian America were very strict and impersonal. I could not study agriculture — indeed, the whole American civilization — in hiding.

One day a man came to our orphanage, smoking a cigar. "I am a merchant from Baghdad," he said. "The Armenian Women's Club of Baghdad has raised a fund for the education of two orphan boys talented in the fine arts. It is their desire to send them to the best schools of Europe to perfect their art. I have come here to choose these fortunate boys from among you."

We were amazed. Baghdad, of all places. Well, that was just like Armenian women. Those patriotic ladies, however, had ruled me out, for I had no talent in any of the fine arts. Didn't they know that our national salvation lay in adopting American science and technique? Why waste money on fine arts?

The musicians among us took out their violins, flutes, trumpets and started practicing them vehemently. Others painted furiously. One boy drew lovely heads of Turkish women. The merchant came again, always cigar in mouth, with the lordly air of an Englishman, looking very prosperous and benevolent. He was also a poet and scholar, and a local paper was publishing his translation of the quatrains of Omar Khayyám from the original Persian.

"Art is the only worth-while thing in life," he told us. He listened to the efforts of our musicians, looked over the paintings and drawings, consulted some experts, and announced his decision: to send to Vienna the boy who drew the heads of Turkish women to study painting, and my brother to study violin. So their future seemed assured.

The merchant meanwhile was looking for a wife. He returned to Baghdad with an attractive teacher as his happy bride.

The mathematicians among us hoped to win French scholarships at the competitive examinations conducted by the Alliance Française, and to study engineering at the École des Ponts et Chaussées, or possibly even at St. Cyr. But in mathematics I was the prize dullard in my class. I had made a sudden jump from arithmetic to analytical geometry, which caused me untold misery. The director of our school was a noted mathematician — "The Armenian Poincaré" — and we were given heavy doses of mathematics. The mathematics sharks were the top dogs in our school. As I listened to them chattering about differential equations and Fourier's series I suffered from an acute sense of inferiority.

Two literary boys, Vahram and Ashod, Onnik's friends and classmates, could hold their own against the mathematicians in the hierarchy of the student body. Vahram was our literary genius, and he looked it, too, with his large, curly head, which he never covered with a hat, and flowing Latin Quarter tie. He translated the works of Dostoevski, Maxim Gorki and Leonid Andreyev for *The People's Voice*, whose editor was one of our greatest living poets. Conscious of his superiority and fame Vahram was always laughing at something or somebody. He glowered every time he saw me, and never deigned to speak to me.

Ashod was the Apollo of our school, a sensitive, handsome dreamer who always carried Baudelaire's *Les Fleurs du Mal* in his coat pocket like a prayer book and was given to murmuring melodic lines to himself. But I had not read Baudelaire, nor Verlaine, Mallarmé, Flaubert, Proust, and so he showed no interest in me, though he did not deliberately and savagely cut me as did Vahram.

I wondered what I should do to attract some attention to myself, to make people know I existed. I needed friends who could help me go to America. For a while I practiced running, with the intention of entering the Armenian Olympiad, hoping to win a medal. I thought that as a champion runner I might succeed in making myself the protégé of athletic enthusiasts with money or influence. I also took boxing lessons. But I had to give up this plan because I lost weight, was burning myself out, and I had always been thin. I needed two thousand calories more a day than our meager fare provided.

In my despair I decided to pass myself off as a poet.

Poets were respected even more than athletes and mathematicians. My immediate concern was to win the good opinion of the Armenian Agronomic Society, which from time to time sent deserving poor students to America to study agriculture.

And here is how I became a poet. I sang to myself a Russian song about the Dnieper, which always brought me glowing visions of wheat fields swaying in the moonlight, the slow, broad, fertilizing flow of a great river. That put me in the proper mood. Seizing paper and pencil, I began my poem by declaring that I wanted to be "the red poppy in wheat fields, a cup for the sun." Then I went on and described the other things I wanted to be, becoming in turn a cricket, a rustic bridge, a country road, a village brat, the little silver cross dangling on the breast of a barefoot little girl. The words somehow came by themselves, after that song. I called the poem, *My Wish*. Copying it clean in my best handwriting, I mailed it to the editor of *The People's Voice*, without breathing a word about it to anyone.

The following Sunday, as I returned from a boy-scout excursion to the Princes' Isles, a few small boys in our orphanage ran to me excitedly with a paper. "It's your poem! It's your poem!" I could hardly believe my own eyes. There it was, on the front page, for everybody to read, *My Wish*. I was ashamed, though, now that it was printed. It seemed silly and sentimental. I didn't like to make a public exhibit of my sentiments. The boys, looking at me now as if I were one of the seven wonders of the world, read my printed name over and over again, as if it were also the name of each one of them, shook their heads, sighed, said I was going to be "a great man."

When I went to school the next morning my classmates clapped their hands as I entered the classroom, shouting, "Here comes the poet!" Some of them got up and comically salaamed before me. My ears were burning.

What would Vahram think? I had invaded his province. I thought he was the poet of *The People's Voice* and would consider my poem almost a slap in his face.

"Permit me to congratulate you," Vahram said, holding out his hand. "I began reading your poem with... contempt, mentally ready to tear it to pieces, but I finished it with respect. I liked especially the third and fourth lines of the second stanza."

"It's nothing," I said, nervous and embarrassed.

"I wouldn't say it's a great poem. You still have a lot to learn."

"Of course," I readily agreed.

"But it made a peculiar, an extraordinary impression on me. I had a

strange sensation on finishing it, as if I had read something written by
myself. Odd, isn't it? You have expressed exactly my sentiments. May I walk
with you?"

Was this the great, proud Vahram? And was it *me* he was speaking to? As
we walked together, he continued:

"I analyzed this strange sensation, and realized why I had disliked you.
You don't mind my speaking frankly?"

"Not at all."

"I disliked you the moment I first saw you. You had just come from
Armenia, and were lecturing to a group of boys. Then I noticed you walking
up and down alone by yourself, with your hands behind your back, as if you
were Napoleon on the eve of a battle, and didn't wish to be disturbed. Your
highness got on my nerves," he chuckled.

"I knew, Vahram, you hated the sight of me."

"You did! Ho! Ho! Yes, I disliked you intensely. You irritated me so. And
yet, you will remember that we had not exchanged a word, you and I. I
hated you because you are, the devil take you, so much like myself! I seemed
to see in you my own ghost — and you know the proverb, 'He who sees his
own ghost doesn't live long.'"

"Don't scare me!" I said, and we both laughed.

Ashod also befriended me. We soon became very chummy, thought of
going to America together. But he had a family, wasn't free to travel.

The Armenian Agronomic Society did notice my poem, and others I wrote
in rapid succession, glorifying nature and village life. When I thought the time
ripe, I applied for a "scholarship." I received one entitling me to free tuition
in the agricultural college of a rectangular state called Kansas, which I had
never heard of before. The society also helped me get an affidavit and other
necessary papers, and the American consul promised a visa.

But I still had to buy my steamship ticket, and in America I had to work
my way through college.

A steamship agent proposed to sell me my ticket at less than half the
regular price if I would sign a letter thanking him, to be published in the
papers when I sailed to New York. He thought this would be good publicity
for him and his company would get more Armenian business as a result. I
signed the letter.

A student organization voted me fifteen dollars. The boys who had gone
to Armenia with me were now back, working as apprentices to engravers,

tailors, masons, carpenters, goldsmiths, blacksmiths, scattered in various shops of Stambul during the day, and sleeping in Vickrey Home at night. As they were earning a few piasters a week, they took a collection for me, without my knowledge — enough to buy my ticket at the reduced price, with a few dollars to spare.

I went to Vickrey Home to thank them.

"You shouldn't have done this, fellows," I said, my voice breaking.

"Our education is over, Zavén, you have to study for all of us from now on."

"Bring honor to the nation."

"Petros Tourian!" (The Armenian Keats.)

"Boys, just wait, some day he will be president of Armenia."

"I read your poems to my boss."

They had my photograph — in boy-scout uniform — on their bulletin board. Their manner with me had changed. Even the roughnecks among them were touchingly courteous! I tried to find out who had given how much so that I could pay them back from America, but they would not tell me, insisted I owed them nothing, they were glad to do it. I suspected some of them had chipped in all their savings, earned, literally, by the sweat of their brows. I felt like a cad as I looked at their honest, trusting, strong faces, heroes, daredevils, every one of them.

A few had clipped off my verses and kept them in their pocketbooks. "I am not a poet, this whole thing is a mistake," I wanted to tell them, but could not.

Critics and real poets saw merits in my verses I myself was not aware of. The almanac of the Armenian Patriarchate wanted to reprint a poem by me. A literary magazine in Bucharest wanted to reprint three of them. Somebody in Paris had recited one of my pieces at a patriotic soirée. I didn't know whether to laugh or to cry.

But what could I do when the truth became known? The tricks I used in writing my lyrics. I had no divine inspiration, such as real poets had. I just sang to myself a song or two, then jotted down a lot of words, anything that came to my mind, as one does in taking a psychological test on the association of ideas. These words sprang back at me pregnant with musical images, and juggling them around, combining them into lines and stanzas — always striving for novel, daring effects — I had a new "poem." I plagiarized from paintings, for I saw a poem in almost every picture. This bothered my conscience most of all. It wasn't honest, even if others did not see what I saw. I had it down to a formula, and the whole thing was ridiculously easy. Certainly this wasn't the way real poets wrote.

The editor of *The People's Voice* invited me to lunch. I dreaded meeting him. I thought of writing him a letter and making a full confession, that I had played a huge joke on him and his readers. I had studied his poetry in school, he was in our literature textbook. He was also one of our most prominent political leaders. I had tried to give him the impression I was a grown-up man, a mature poet — not a school kid of sixteen.

The People's Voice was published in one of the massive stone buildings of Galata called han. Just inside the entrance was a little coffee shop, for no important business transaction could be carried on without the ceremony of serving the customer Turkish coffee — a gracious habit, conducive to much good feeling on both sides. I mounted the long, winding stone steps to the office of the paper. It was like climbing a minaret. I hoped to see at every turn a Genoese merchant in spectacular medieval garments thrust his head out through a door and invite me in to view his silks and spices.

The director of our school was in the office, talking with the editor. Our director looked like a mathematical Mephistopheles with his pointed black beard and glittering black eyes. He was over six feet tall, handsome in a satanic way, suave, and had always impressed me as more French than Armenian. The editor, also tall, was an intellectual aristocrat with a noble poetic brow, with blue eyes, one of which was glass. Years before a gang of his political opponents had attacked and beaten him, blinding him in one eye. His brother was an officer in the French Navy, and he had lived in Paris for many years.

They both were cordial. The director acted as if I were not in his class of analytical geometry, and he had never given me low marks. As a professor of philosophy he also took an interest in literature.

"We were just talking about your *Winter Night,*" he said. He quoted a stanza in which I had described an old wolf, headed for the village, and the moon sweetly, quickly, flowing like honey into its footprints in the snow, and the Spirit of Winter, stern and lonely, walking across the snowbound fields with a slow, heavy tread.

"You make the moon very kind to the wolf, almost in love with it," he said.

"It's an Armenian wolf," I said. I told them the poem was essentially a description of a winter night near Lake Sevan, when I had the feeling that even the wolves were like our brothers, being our own.

"What is this I hear about your wanting to go to America?" the editor said.

"To study agriculture," I replied.

"But why agriculture?"

I did not want to tell them about my epochal book on agriculture which would create a state of millennial order and abundance, garden cities of the world. My heart glowed again as I saw my white cottages, with merry, happy children, and myself walking through a wheat field like Christ with His disciples.

"Because agriculture is important," I merely said.

"But poetry also is important," the editor objected. "Leave agriculture to others and concentrate on what is, I believe, your true métier, literature."

"We need poets also," the director said, trying to be diplomatic, I thought. Mathematics was probably the only thing that mattered to him. That's what all mathematicians thought, and they were probably right. Plato and his geometry.

The editor got up, took his hat and cane. *"Allons!"* he said. "Time to eat."

We went to a Greek restaurant, cool and dim like a wine cellar. And over an excellent meal of charcoal-broiled lamb chops, tender hearts of artichokes cooked in olive oil, new potatoes and squash, we talked as if I were their equal, one of them. They tried to dissuade me from going to America, wanted me to graduate from Central; then, if I still wanted to be an agriculturist, I could go to France, they said.

"Will you stay if we arrange for you to have a private room of your own, with a monthly stipend?" the editor said. "It will put you under no obligation except to continue writing poetry."

This was a tempting offer. A private room! A monthly stipend! No more orphanage life. But the stipulation that I should continue writing poems, at least until I was graduated from Central, which meant another three years, appalled me. Three more years of trickery! No, I couldn't do it. A man had a conscience, after all.

I declined their generous offer. I did not look forward to an easy life in America. I knew there was unemployment and poverty in America too. But the Great Secret I was seeking was there.

"American civilization is very powerful," the editor said, worried. "It will swallow you up, as it has swallowed up millions of others. You would cease being an Armenian there. You would be lost to our literature and nation."

"I will never change," I assured him.

But I did want to be born again, in America, away from the evils of the old world, to start my life anew. At the thought of my life in America every nerve and sinew in my famished body became taught like tightly drawn copper wires, and I seemed to be hearing the myriad footsteps of an approaching battle. I was going to America like a soldier, on a supreme adventure.

I held our poets — good men in a world full of evil — responsible for our national disasters, including the massacre in which I had lost my home and parents. I had made a careful study of our political history and reached the melancholy conclusion that we were a nation of Don Quixotes, incurable romanticists. Looking at the editor across the table, I was saying to him in my mind:

"Because you are a famous poet our people chose you to head our national delegation to the Peace Conference in Paris. What did we get from it? Nothing. We were deceived by everyone. Only America, the sole honest Christian Power, helped us with food, clothing and medicines, saving our people from complete extermination, until the pressure of events brought Soviet Russia to our rescue. How can men like you cope with Kemal and Quai d'Orsay?"

Even before the introduction of Christianity we had poet-kings. Our King Ardavast wrote tragedies in Greek, as Plutarch testifies. Though an ally of Rome, Antony seized him treacherously and carried him to Alexandria in silver chains, and had him beheaded by Cleopatra because Ardavast would not bow before that slut and call her "Queen of Kings." Many of my companions thought I would some day be "president of Armenia" because I was a "poet."

"We must be practical like the Americans," I declared, expressing my ideas on agriculture versus literature. "What's the use of poetry? Can poetry feed hungry stomachs? Can it force the Turks to evacuate Kars and Van?"

By the time we had finished our lunch with coffee and *paklava*, I had convinced them I knew what I was doing. The director said he would write a letter about me to a rich Armenian-American rug merchant. "And I will give you a strong school reference in French, for your college," he added.

"You have already given me a French reference," I reminded him. I had it in my pocket, showed it to him.

"Oh, that! That's nothing." He turned to the editor with an apologetic smile. "When I signed it I didn't know Zavén could write such poems."

"All that remains for him is to grow older to add new strings to his lyre," the editor said, convinced I was "an original artist."

I was laughing up my sleeve. But this comedy worried me more and more. I opened my mouth to confess my hoax, but could not.

I spent my afternoon with the editor. He gave me two of his books. We became like father and son.

Walking back to the orphanage, I climbed the hill from Galata to Pera. I could see the sun bleeding over the minarets of Saint Sophia like the torn heart of God. I hummed a symphony to myself, Chopin, Bach, Beethoven, Wagner, Rimski-Korsakoff combined. I had been humming tremendous symphonies for years — they came and went like the wind. I recalled with a pang that my Uncle Harutiun also had gone abroad to study agriculture, that he was a poet, and had died, unknown, of tuberculosis. Petros Tourian also had fallen victim to that cruel disease. It had killed our best lyric poets in their youth. Could it be that even if I was playing a literary hoax I had doomed myself to the same fate? A terrifying thought.

I stopped for a moment and gazed at a couple of poplars trembling in the breeze with a swishing, rustling sound, their leaves reflecting the brilliance of the Byzantine sun. I loved the poplar; it was a noble tree, the poet among trees. A picture of poplars in Trebizond pure and white after the rain flashed through my mind. Then the pageant of a poet's death:

A requiem by nature after a spring shower. White poplars sounding like church cymbals. Dreams arising from the great censer of the good earth. Cottages bowed in grief praying in the gathering dusk. A church bell coughing, coughing, a funeral toll.

Bird-like are the caressing fingers of the evening breeze. The sun is bleeding on the mountain like Christ on His Cross. Night is falling, but there are still music notes in the air, and along the rain-washed road like big tremulous candles the bull-thistles flare.

The sick poet, lover of nature, watching all this from his window, dies softly with the smile of creation on his lips, as the church bell coughs its heart-shattering knell.

Maybe I should write this, I said to myself.

CHAPTER 20

Ah, That Night in Stambul!

"The outward appearance isn't worth describing," Ashod said on our way to Vahram's home on the other side of the Golden Horn. "If I were to write the history of a man it would be nothing but a description of the *mystery* of that man. The mystery is the real thing; it flows like a deep and eternal river under the outward appearance."

"That's too complicated for me; what do you mean?" Vahram chuckled.

"I mean that men have the same noses and eyes and hair. They are uniformly and monotonously alike in their outward appearance, and little physical differences that may exist are of no significance to the artist. But we all vary tremendously in our thoughts, in our inner life, in our mysterious and true existence. Or take a sunset, like the one we are seeing right now. A conventional description of it in terms of colors, lights, and shadows would lack its essential quality — the mystery of the sunset." Ashod was the greatest literary aesthetician I have ever known. I say this in all seriousness.

We passed through the old Levantine quarter of Galata, where the flags of a dozen nations were painted on the windows of cheap beer halls employing blonde Russian émigré girls as waitresses. The smell of raki, perfumes and garlic was overpowering. The hurdy-gurdies, played by men with carnation flowers on the back of their ears, were going full blast.

"Boys, look at that African lover!" Vahram said, laughing. A huge black Senegalese soldier of the French colonial army was devouring the white, tense face of a Turkish woman with his thick purple lips as she leaned against a lamppost, with her veil thrown back. "What is love? How would you define it?" Vahram asked.

"Ah, love!" Ashod sighed. "Love is Alice, or Alice is love. That's my definition." He was in love with a pretty schoolgirl with a doll-like face called Alice.

"That's my definition also," my brother agreed, for he too was in love with her. She was quite a charmer. They would follow her in the streets to my disgust and annoyance. I was a stern Spartan soldier and did not like any display of romantic sentimentality.

All four of us were absolutely chaste and hardly knew what love was, but that did not prevent Vahram from speculating on the metaphysics of love. "Is love a pretty ribbon, a shapely figure or a companion for the soul? Well, it may be any of these things, but it is always and forever self-deception! Ho! Ho! Ho!"

Love... self-deception? I could not understand it. But then Vahram said many things I could not understand. Perhaps because he was two years older than I. He sometimes sounded like a character from a Russian novel.

We paid the toll at Galata Bridge and crossed over to Stambul, bristling with its lance-like minarets. The sun was sinking in the Marmara, behind the Princes' Isles. Turks were washing their feet at the fountains of the imperial mosques, getting ready for their evening prayers. There was the hidden menace of the East in this vast Turkish quarter. After dark its narrow, winding streets were none too safe for Christians, even though the Bosporus glistened with the great fighting ships of the victorious Giaours. The grim shadow of Mustafa Kemal Pasha extended over Stambul. There were disturbing rumors of new massacres in Anatolia.

Vahram's home was an old cottage built a few yards from the ancient Byzantine walls of the city, and like them it was sagging and crumbling under the weight of centuries, but somehow was everlasting in its decay. Its shaky door had two lyre-shaped brass knockers, and there was the inevitable garden in the rear. His mother, a mournful widow, had gone away for the night not to be in our way, and thus we had the house to ourselves, to do what we pleased. Vahram, Ashod, and my brother Onnik were giving a farewell party for me because I was sailing to America in a day or two to study agriculture.

Vahram spread a feast on the table in the garden, and we raised wassail over two bottles of Bordeaux wine. Our revelry began amid the varicolored mosaics of a Byzantine sunset and continued under the brilliant jewelry of an eastern sky. We raised our glasses and sang a drinking song:

Oh how sweet it is
To be a drunkard,
To drink all day wine
And to be cockeyed!
La-ree, tumbara la-la, ha, ha, ha!

The wine quickly went to our heads, for we were not used to it. My brother took out his violin and played *Black Eyes*, after which, waving my glass, I poetized:

"The sun of Stambul fell like a bloody head... and the day is dying like a Circassian dancer drunk in the agony of her death, with passionate grace... O God, will the sun ever come back again? Boys, look at the moon! The moon is coming up to promenade in the golden streets of the heavens... Look at her, look at her, she is dancing to the music of the night ... she is the spirit of the Circassian dancer, the moon is..."

"All right, that's enough!"

"More cheese and less poetry!"

"Pass me that bottle and the olives!"

We ate and drank and shouted, banging our fists on the table.

"Who will lead me to the altar of mysteries?" Ashod presently asked earnestly. "Let us sip the languorous coolness of the night like blue absinthe, for tomorrow I shall have to cover the nakedness of man." (Ashod was a tailor's apprentice.)

"Speech! Speech!" we demanded.

He rose to his feet with a solemn expression on his handsome face, a far-off, dreamy look in his fiery dark eyes. "I have devoted myself," he declared, "to the pursuit of the mystery."

"It's mystery again. I give up. Ho! Ho! Ho!" Vahram roared.

"Silence!" my brother commanded, bringing down his white fist on the table. He had delicate, soft hands, like a girl's. "Silence, I say! Let's hear him. Let's hear this great mysterious speech of the great Ashod." He was feeling good.

"All right, I apologize," Vahram chuckled. "Go ahead, Ashod, and tell us everything about the mystery."

"I have devoted myself to the pursuit of the mystery," Ashod repeated firmly. "Because the mystery is the only thing that differs from man to man and at the same time it's the only bond between one man and another. It's only my enthusiasm for the mystery that makes life bearable for me — otherwise I would kill myself. Without the mystery there would be such an emptiness in me that I couldn't bear it. Is it madness to seek the real truths, the truths of the mystery?"

"It is!" Vahram said.

"This historic generation of ours," Ashod continued without paying attention to Vahram, "has the instinct for victory and song. There aren't many of us left, they killed most of us, but we survivors are strong, by God we are strong! Our orphan generation has the genius of sorrow, and the indomitable power of it. You know, I have always been alone in the world. I don't want to sound maudlin and sentimental, but now that one of us is going to America and we may never see him again I don't mind telling you that I love you boys as a brother. No other love in my heart will ever surpass the affection I bear for you. Yes, I do love Alice, but she is merely an inspiration to me, an ideal. I don't know her at all as an individual girl; she is nothing but a lovely symbol personifying in herself the mystery of her sex." He turned to me: "After you go to America, on a certain hour every day I shall communicate with you in spirit."

Ashod had ended his speech, and shaking with emotion sat down.

"Will somebody pass me a handkerchief? This calls for a good cry," Vahram wailed. Then he got up, scowling fiercely. Strong like an ox, with a shock of curly hair, he now looked like a young Assyrian monarch capable of conquering the world. *"Chort vozmi,* the devil take it," he said in Russian. "Here we were enjoying ourselves, and Ashod gets up and spoils everything. All that sentimental rot! Why weren't you born a woman? In fact, you are beautiful enough to pass for a woman. All you would need would be a little make-up on your face. Now, if I had your rosy cheeks I would positively want to be a woman." And he howled with laughter.

"Forgive me, boys, I can't help it. I can't help laughing at everything and everybody because everything and everybody is so comic, really. Some people think I am crazy because I laugh so much, and laugh to myself too, which exasperates them the more, and that adds to my amusement. But I am going to make a confession — and don't blame me for it, because Ashod started it. I fought in the trenches at Van, but three times in my life I have seriously contemplated suicide, and my dominant inner mood is one of profound pity for mankind.

"Permit me to make another declaration about myself. One of us is a violinist, the best young violinist in Constantinople, and he has won a scholarship to study music in Vienna. I envy you, Onnik. One of us is not a peasant, but he is going to America to study agriculture. Worthy ambition. Ashod will always and forever study the mystery, and who can tell, some day he may write a new *Koran*. But what I want is to be a sailor on a battleship! There is a tremendous career for you!"

He was silent for a few moments, grinning and scowling. "Seng-See," he suddenly said. "Boys, have you ever heard the story of Seng-See, the Chinaman? It's a poetic parable on the fundamental values of life. Seng-See is an adolescent youth, just like us, hungry for power. And when the gifts of life are brought to him on a camel he chooses power and shuns women. He roams all over the world, gets everything his heart desires — but he walks alone. He is a stranger to beauty and women. Seng-See spent all his talents and efforts on his stick, the symbol of his power. But when he became an old man he saw everything in a moment of supremely clear vision. He saw playful, merry children who were not his, he saw women laughing at his doddering old body. I'll write this story some day.

"Which reminds me, we should publish our own magazine and clean up all this mess. I have in mind a thick, substantial magazine, angry, vicious, shouting at first, quiet and melancholy later. We will call it *The Broom*, and sweep with it all the cobwebs off men's minds, throw out all the dust and dirt. Zavén is right. We must return to the village, we must go back to our people. All this high culture and sophistication and Byronic ennui disgusts me. My most cherished dream next to working on a battleship is to sit on the grass after a hard day's work in the fields and eat bread, salt, and onions."

Vahram reached for his wine glass on the table, examined its contents with screwed-up eyes, and emptied it in one gulp. Smacking his lips, he continued:

"I want to live like a song, like the song of a violin. Yes, boys, let us resolve to be the strongest, kindest, and most perfect of men. And in conclusion let me say this: I must grow a mustache. I am old enough to have one and I consider it necessary for diverse reasons. For instance, there are women who love the devil because he is covered all over with hair!" and roaring to himself, he sat down.

Then it was my brother who rose to his feet. "I can't make any fancy speeches," he said, "but I will play something Zavén likes." My brother had carried his violin with him during seven years of wars, massacres, revolutions, and migrations. His violin was a part of himself. He played my favorite number, the overture to *Tannhäuser*, while we drummed the table with our fingers and sang the music, without knowing the words. Then for half an hour or so he played Russian gypsy and Armenian songs, we drank more wine, ate more cheese and olives, and finally it was my turn to make a speech. I was the clown of our group and its youngest member. I hardly ever opened my mouth without making them laugh, and in my patched-up uniform of an American soldier, a gift of the Near East Relief, looked like a scarecrow. I was just skin and bones and my uniform was too large for me and my wild black hair was impossible to comb. But that night I was dignified and serious.

By now the Dostoevskian Vahram was measuring the size of the moon with his fingers, Ashod seemed to be groping desperately with the inner meaning of things, and my brother's violin was a bit cockeyed. I had difficulty standing on my feet. The wine had done its work.

"I have located on the map the college I am going to," I said. "It's in the very center of America, the agricultural college of a strictly geometrical state, four straight lines, absolutely straight, like a piece of cheese. You think I am funny-looking, but what do you bet if I return with a beautiful rich American wife, a millionaire widow? A widow with red hair. I think she lives in Chicago. Yes, I can see her at this moment. There she is! Talking to her parrot. She is lonely, waiting for me. She lives on the top floor of a building which is so high that if you looked up at the windows of her apartment from the street below your hat would fall off. They say, boys, in Chicago there is a society of women millionaires with red hair who have their own constitution and club-house."

Pause. Another swig of wine.

"We must live like the ancient gods!" I thundered. "And like the troubadours of old. Forward march! We are in the trenches. To hell with art! I am for shooting down all the poets we have. I would rather plant trees in Armenia than write the greatest poems in the world. Long live the trees! If we must have poems, then let's have agricultural poems, poems about cows and bees, tractors and steel plows.

"American machinery will save us! I am going to America to study scientific agriculture because that is the proper foundation on which to build our nation. The soil, the holy and eternal soil. Let the cowards and the fools retire to their ivory towers. I am a tree. With my arms spread to the winds and my feet clinging to the sacred cross-embossed tombstones of our land I stand like Jesus upon the mountain. Yonder, below, I can see harvesting machines marching through the wheat fields like giant birds with their wings outspread, and the knives of steel plows are flashing in the sun of our land, and under their passionate kisses is split open the black belly of our soils. The belly, boys, the belly of the virgin soil, the virgin belly of the soil. The holy and eternal soil.

"Ah, every night in the moon-sweet vineyards lithe and handsome village lovers will go a-harvesting. Every drop of tears from the eyes of our dead mothers will be a grape, a fine, translucent, moon-sweet grape. And the crickets will be cymbals to this blessing, to this blessing of our hearts, to this blessing and this singing of our hearts. *Laree, tumbara la-la, ha, ha, ha!* Four straight lines, absolutely straight, near the Missouri River. But we are soldiers in the trenches, forward march!"

I was now fairly leaping through the air and brandishing an imaginary sword. I saw my companions through a haze of unreality. They had become spectral figures in a dark, revolving, receding and approaching void. Their voices came to me from afar, traveling across vast, mysterious cosmic distances. I heard my brother playing his violin again and Ashod reciting some lines from Baudelaire, while Vahram was laughing his head off, but the music and their voices sounded as if coming from another world.

CHAPTER 21

Off on the Supreme Adventure

My sister Nevart came to Constaninople from Novorossisk, and for a few days we two brothers and two sisters were reunited again. A friend, an expert on Byzantine gems and antiquities, invited us to his home in Arnavut Koy, one of those pleasant suburbs on the Bosporus, which now in early summer were like bits of paradise left over from ancient times.

Houses of fragile wood darkened to the color of icons tumbled down the hills with their terraced gardens. On our side of the Bosporus was the round, crenellated tower of the Castle of Rome — Rumeli Hissar — and on the other side, opposite it, rose the Castle of Anatolia — Anadolu Hissar. One of the first books I had read was a history of the siege and capture of Constaninople by the sharp-nosed, rat-eyed Sultan Mohammed II — Fathi, the Conqueror, as the Turks called him. Every time I looked at these twin castles he had built I remembered the tragic yet not inglorious end of the Roman Empire of the East, and could see the last of the Caesars lying dead on the breached walls in his purple boots.

To Nevart, wholly educated in a Greek school, Constantinople had a strong emotional appeal. And it made her feel good to know that many Byzantine emperors and generals were Armenians. She brought some of our family jewels with her which Greek friends had been able to save during the massacre. We sold a few of them, needing the money, and divided the rest among us. My share was our mother's wedding ring. I could not bear to look at it. Its diamond, set in a crown of gold filigree, was like a tear drop from Mother's eyes. Our reunion was brief. My sisters were going to some relatives of ours in Egypt.

Our antiquarian friend was an elegant man with a long priestly beard, who wore spats and a flower in his lapel, and called everybody *"Mon cher."* The list of his protégés was a long one, but he practically adopted us. When a charity ball was to be given, he took charge of all the arrangements. He pinned medals on winners of athletic contests, hired teachers, found jobs for new graduates, was a trustee of orphanages and schools. For a few weeks, while living in his home, I had a taste of the city's social life, going to parties, arguing politics with merchants and lawyers. He would often take me to their homes just for that purpose. At night, after he came back from his store in Stambul — a museum from the treasure-trove of Byzantium — and we had eaten our supper, we would go for a stroll with him along the Bosporus. We enjoyed the night-time pageantry of Constantinople, where life, true to its Turkish name, *Der-Saadet,* was somehow one of constant felicity. There was the romantic music of a Greek mandolin orchestra splashing on the Bosporus from a waterfront casino; ferries moved like giant fireflies in the dark; the air rang with the voices of Greek fishermen as they spread their nets on the sand, and of Turkish boatmen as they towed their boats up the current, which was so powerful here it was impossible to row against it. The latticed windows of the Turkish houses threw arabesques of lights on the waters, and the Castles of Rome and of Anatolia shone in the moonlight with their gilded teeth. I knew I would miss all of this in America, and I observed them with the awareness of an approaching farewell.

Every day Onnik and I swam in the bay of Bebek. Among the marble palaces of Bebek were those of the Persian Shah and the Khedive of Egypt, whose white-and-gold yacht, anchored here, served us as a swimming target. I struck up a friendship with a pretty Russian blonde swimmer, which, however, came to an abrupt end when I tried to embrace her in the water.

Bebek, with ancient plane trees and a marble fountain in the center of the village, was a Turkish suburb. Cool, shady, it had a special antique charm carrying one back to the seventeenth or eighteenth century. Black eunuchs in blue uniforms, with polished brass buttons, still sat at iron grilled gates, withered old men, relics of a past age. Here, too, was a Turkish orphanage, and every time I saw the Turkish orphans playing on the beach or marching along, I had a feeling of fellowship for them. I was sincerely sorry for these boys. The Turks, too, had a generation of war orphans.

There was no visible animosity between Turks and Armenians in Constantinople. The Turkish upper class was sufficiently Westernized here to bridge the cultural gap that separated the Moslems and Christians in the provinces. Influential Turkish families sent their sons to Robert College or the Galata Serai, where classes were conducted in French. I had always held the Turks in contempt, and like every Greek or Armenian boy felt immeasurably superior to them. But in Constantinople I gained a new respect for them. Islam lost much of its terror when I saw the great mosques of Stambul, with their four minarets. They had a soaring, overwhelming beauty. Even though the Turks had borrowed this style, minus the minarets, from the Christians they conquered, Saint Sophia being their model, their very glorification of it elevated them in my esteem. And by now I knew something about the medieval Arabs, the contributions they have made to mathematics, medicine, geography, philosophy, poetry, the flowering of Arab arts from Granada to Samarkand, to appreciate that worthy side of Islamic civilization.

And then there were the Turkish ladies of Constantinople — chic, clever, articulate, highly versed in all the diplomatic arts, including those of their own sex. No man could resist their charms. On Turkish tag days they pinned carnations on everybody in the streets, making no distinctions between Turks and Christians, and even I dropped a few coins in their boxes. I thought the Turks owed their national regeneration to these women — such fascinating creatures!

Though no one knew it I was under the spell of a couple of grey Turkish eyes I had seen in a rose garden. There were generations of Circassian slaves on her white face. As our eyes met I perceived a faint smile on her lips. She was gathering roses and held a bunch of them against her breast. What quickened my blood, and made me wonder, was the wanton innocence, the dangerous invitation, in her eyes. She could have lured me to my destruction.

It was taboo for Christian men to associate with Turkish women, and hence they had the added attraction of forbidden fruit. In flights of wild fancy I would see myself carrying on a secret romance with a Turkish girl. She would send me red roses from her garden, exchange love notes with me, a faithful old servant of her household acting as messenger between us. I thought of writing a sensational Romeo and Juliet type of story with an Armenian boy and a Turkish girl as its chief characters.

I often went to the campus of Robert College, close by Arnavut Koy, to visit with Bagrat Yergat and my former Mekhitarist classmate Aram. This was the only school in Turkey where Christians and Turkish boys studied together. Aram wanted to be a chemist. He was bound to invent something even more wonderful than his electric tram, judging from his talk about his chemical experiments. He had grown from a "shivering rabbit," as we used to call him in Yeisk, into a big, rugged fellow. That's what good food had done for him. His father, on the staff of the American embassy, could afford to send him to Robert College, where tuition alone was about four hundred dollars a year.

But how Bagrat Yergat managed to be there was a mystery. Aram had not known him in Russia, having left our school before he became our proctor. I understood an English officer, a graduate of Oxford University, was financing his education. He seemed well supplied with funds. He was the champion weight lifter in the college, and had acquired a certain polish, the Kurd becoming an aristocrat. He carried himself with the air of an English gentleman. Though more human now, he was as close-mouthed and secretive about himself as ever. I suspected the English officer was one of his new converts. In my conversations with him I avoided the painful subject of the Society of Self-Gods, and he himself made no mention of it. He published a poem almost every week, several of his Zarathustra effusions appearing in *The People's Voice*, on an inside page on week days, while mine were on the front page on Sundays, which I thought very funny. Two years before Bagrat Yergat was one of the world's greatest poets in my eyes, but now I smiled at the hollow rhetoric of his verses. But I did not doubt his extraordinary mental powers, and wondered how he would end up, with that evil genius of his.

The campus of Robert College on a hill near the Castle of Rome, with its modern buildings, laboratories, gymnasium, tennis courts, track field, was an impressive example of American education. Nowhere in the city were there such fine school buildings, such an exhibit of wealth and organization for the training of youth. But to me the most remarkable thing about it was this: here Armenian and Greek boys sat in the same classrooms with Turkish boys, were in intimate daily contact as members of one civilized society, with no fights, no racial catcalls between them. There were also Bulgarian, Russian, Jewish, English, Persian students, all living in harmony. As America had no territorial ambitions in our part of the world, she enjoyed a unique moral authority. And more than the mechanical wonders, the industrial progress and power of America was this moral authority, possessed by no other nation on earth. In my own mind the concept of America was fundamentally based on that, much as I esteemed America's machines.

After many good-byes, the great day of my departure arrived. I wore a new suit, the cheapest I could find in the Grand Bazaar of Stambul, where prices were lower than in Pera and Galata. Unfortunately it was not cut in the smart American style, and I suspected was made of an army blanket, but my new shoes were brown Oxfords with pointed toe-ends, like the Americans wore. The trouble with them was that they squeaked like the wheels of an ox cart, and I had to walk carefully. I shaved myself for the first time, with an American safety razor, brushed my teeth with an American toothpaste, having already begun to Americanize myself. I carried all my worldly belongings in a valise of imitation leather: a few French and Armenian books, my mother's ring, our family photograph, an extra shirt and some clean underwear. I had in my pocket $29.00 in American money, $4.00 more than the minimum required by immigration laws.

My sisters had already gone to Egypt. My brother, Vahram, Ashod and a few other companions went to the harbor to see me off. The ship on which I was sailing was owned by a Greek company but flew the American flag. My heart was heavy now, and tears blurred my eyes as we embraced at the foot of the gang-plank. Alone on the deck, I felt I was off on the supreme adventure of my life.

Our first stop was Piraeus. I had about six hours in which to see Athens and visit Dr. Metaxas. I was so anxious to see the Acropolis that before calling on the doctor I climbed with a group of other passengers the dusty road that led to those immortal ruins. I touched them with reverent hands, and sitting under the columns of the Parthenon felt myself back in old Athens.

The doctor completed the picture for me: he might have been an old Greek statue come to life. He had grayed completely, but was still vigorous and alert. His family were at a summer resort, and only his eldest daughter was in town with him. A healthy, good-looking girl of twelve, she rose on her toes and kissed me, much to my embarrassment. He gave me his picture, signing it *"Votre vieux père, Andreas Metaxas."* We conversed mostly in French because I had by now forgotten most of the childish Greek I knew.

He took me on a walking tour of the city, showing me its public buildings and historic monuments. Modern Athens was a charming city, but the environs were parched and treeless.

We sat at a sidewalk café in Constitution Square and he told me in

detail of his futile efforts to save my parents. My father's death seemed to
have affected him deeply; he was a sad, almost broken man. They had
been close friends for thirty years. This was the first time that I really
became acquainted with Dr. Metaxas. As a child I had been afraid of him.
He knew my sisters and brother much better; unlike them, I had never
lived in his home. He suggested that I change my first name, and christened
me Zeno, after the Stoic philosopher, thinking it would be a familiar name
to Americans, one they would easily remember... that was the Greek in
him. But he wanted me to remain an Armenian. *"J'espère vous voir devenir un
grand homme de science et un grand patriote,"* he said. *"N'oubliez ni votre pays, ni
votre nation."*

He was a poor man now, having lost his fortune on our account, and was
trying to re-establish himself in his native city as a practising physician. The
Athenians did not know what an heroic man they had in their midst — one
of the noblest sons of Hellas. I imagined myself delivering a eulogy on him
in the Greek parliament — receiving him in Armenia with a guard of honor
of five thousand cavalry, and after his death, erecting his monument in
Athens with a quotation on friendship from some Greek poet or philosopher
inscribed on it. (He died two years later of a heart attack while on his way
to the American hospital in Athens, on the staff of which he was serving.)

I felt perfectly at home in Greece. The Greeks too were my own people,
and I was, like my brother and sisters, a person with a double national
consciousness — at once both Armenian and Greek. In some respects the
Greeks were even closer to me than Armenians because of childhood
associations. I had learned to speak Greek along with my mother tongue,
my first and dearest playmates were Greek children. And I owed my life to
the Greeks.

It wasn't until we sailed away from Greece — after stopping also at a
Greek island — that I began to experience that panicky sensation of being
uprooted from one's own world. I felt as if I were leaving myself behind,
and it was another person, not me, going to America.

An Armenian girl on our ship, attractive and serious, asked me to write a
poem in her album. Retiring to my berth in the pit of the ship — I was
traveling "fourth" class — I wrote *Last Prayer.* There is a feeling akin to the
agony of death in long voyages to foreign lands. And it was this feeling I was
expressing when I wrote:

My soul is a huge cathedral this evening, vacant after the mass, in which there is only a pure-white girl with long, loose hair, shining like a holy light. God, forgive me, I am ill and innocent tonight, a dying monk in love. I want the souls of sick flowers in my soul; I want the moon to hang low, large and pale like ivory; I want the little stream to stop under the moon, like a wounded silkworm. And when men hear the news of my death, let none pity me, nor come near me, except that young girl. Let her come holding a lily instead of a candle in her hand.

I thought, perhaps it's necessary to die, in order to be born again.

CHAPTER 22

The Grandeur and Misery

Faster ships covered the distance between Istanbul and New York in two weeks, but it was only on the twenty-fourth day that sea gulls came to fly around our ship, and I saw a long, low strip of mysterious land stretching out over the horizon — America! The breeze was the breath of the New World, mild and sweet on that first day of September. Everybody rushed to the deck. A few women crossed themselves, but few spoke, the occasion being too solemn. The attention of all was riveted on that strip of land in the distance.

Sailing boats flying the American flag scudded past us, different from our lateen-rigged boats, but with a gay, reckless beauty of their own. Watching them I experienced a sensation of aerial lightness — as if I could fly forever like some deathless bird of the sea, relieved of all human cares and worries.

New York emerged from the now tawny waters of the Atlantic with the soaring towers of its cosmic crystal cubes — immense geometric shapes of silver-gray, high as mountains of mathematical precision. Could it be possible that these were buildings? I gazed with frenzied interest at the spectacle of the New World, the Statue of Liberty symbolizing its spirit.

The smoke that rose from these skyscrapers made New York look like a twentieth-century Nineveh or Babylon on fire. What imperious battle march of industry! America was marching before us with banners and guidons of smoke flying. Puny, mortal man, so insignificant in the elemental vastness of the ocean, had created this titanic miracle on land. Come, I wanted to cry, gather all ye gods of Greece and Rome, Egypt and Babylon, and behold what man hath created here, the man of the old world on the soil of the new. As I came face to face with the overwhelming reality of America, Europe paled into insignificance, faded away, became like an historic myth, almost.

It seemed that all the ships of the globe had gathered in the harbor of New York. All the nations had come to lay at the feet of the Statue of Liberty their products and their people in a universal pageant of homage. And above all this Lilliputian confusion and activity, all this busy festival of human pigmies, marched the proud new world, marched through epic skies with banners and guidons of smoke flying.

Our ship stopped with a loud rattle of its anchor chain. A tender drew alongside her, and immigration and quarantine officers came aboard. The passengers lined up on the deck to show their papers. After this inspection was over, our ship was allowed to proceed, and docked in the harbor proper — a thick jungle of ships.

We went ashore with our belongings. The first- and second-class passengers were allowed to go after clearing the customs, unless there was something wrong with their papers, but those of us who had come third and "fourth" class were segregated and kept under guard. We were, apparently, the undesirable ones, even though I was a student.

"They will send us to Ellis Island," an Armenian said.

"Because they found a louse on a fourth-class bum," said another man, which caused general laughter in our group.

"Proletarians of all countries with lice, unite!"

The guards ordered us into a launch. We were a motley crowd of Greeks, Albanians, Jews, Hungarians, Rumanians, Yugoslavs, Czechoslovaks, Russians, Armenians, and there was even a Turk among us. All of us were bewildered and worried as we were taken to Ellis Island, where I had to declare again that I did not believe in polygamy, anarchy, in overthrowing organized government by force; that I had never been an inmate in an insane asylum, imprisoned for a crime, and nobody in America had promised me employment. I showed my letter of admission from the vice-president of the great American college in Kansas where I was going to study agriculture.

Colored papers were pinned on our coats, and we were carefully examined by red-faced American doctors.

"They are still after that louse," one of us cracked again. "They won't let us free until they find it."

In the dining hall the eyes of many popped out as they saw the food: meat, butter, potatoes, bread, milk, coffee, prunes. There was a separate section for Orthodox Jews. We ate with paper forks and spoons, from paper plates, and drank the milk and coffee from paper cups. It was all very sanitary, but the food also tasted like paper. Some insisted the butter and meat were synthetic, chemically produced by machines, which I myself was inclined to believe.

We stared curiously at the Negro employees of Ellis Island, marveling at the progress the African blacks had made in America — speaking English, wearing clothes and horn-rimmed glasses like other Americans. At night, a giant café-au-lait mulatto with long, swinging arms and an organ-like voice handed to us our fumigated blankets.

Another Negro with horn-rimmed glasses announced the names of those who were to be admitted. He was very popular. Every time we saw him we flocked around him, each one wondering if his name was in the new list. We called him "Baggage." He always said, "Baggage!" after reading off a name.

I did not know why I was being detained at Ellis Island. The steamship company had spelled my name wrong, which perhaps was the reason. After I fretted and worried for a month, my case was straightened out, thanks apparently to the efforts of the Armenian secretary of the New York YMCA, and "Baggage" at last called out my name also. With a feeling of glorious freedom I got off the ferry boat and set foot in New York City. "Now remember," I said to myself, "you are actually in America, this is New York. Forward march!" I marched a few blocks, feeling a realized dream under my feet.

Getting on a streetcar I managed to reach the office of the Armenian secretary, in the YMCA, a Protestant minister, and a hustler. He told me the patriotic rug merchant, to whom the director of my school in Istanbul had recommended me as one deserving of his support, would pay for my railroad fare to Kansas, but had declined to undertake the cost of my education in America. He was already supporting seven Armenian students in American colleges and was dissatisfied with them. They had turned out to be "Bolsheviks," and were so extravagant that they wore ten-dollar hats, while he himself wore only a five-dollar hat. I laughed, that was funny! I wanted to meet him, but he seemed inaccessible to favor seekers like myself, and the secretary advised me to stay away from his store, which I understood was an elegant establishment with many American employees.

I was disappointed, for I had expected to get five hundred dollars a year from him, the sum he was paying the other students, but it did not matter. I felt that from now on the world belonged to me.

I spent a sleepless night in a cheap hotel, paying one dollar for my bed. Trains and trucks trundled along all night, and the noise was so awful that I wondered how people could ever sleep in New York.

By next morning I had sufficiently calmed down to really see New York and get the feel of America. The policemen directing traffic on horseback, the drugstores, the cornucopian groceries, the clothing stores, the Negro postman with the morning mail in his leather bag, the vending machines for cigarettes, apples, oranges, chewing gum, the newsstands — all these were objects of much interest to me. And New York was a friendly town, its citizens were human, and not like creatures on Mars, as they might have been. I had not seen elevated trains and skyscrapers before, nor newspapers with sixty or a hundred pages — but otherwise there was nothing particularly strange or startling to me. Istanbul had a subway, the Galata Bridge was long too and sections of it could be opened for the passage of steamers, the ferry boats on the Bosporus were just about as fast and comfortable as those in New York. From the inside, the city lost much of its fantastic otherworldly quality, became quite familiar. And it was that very familiarity that bound me to it immediately, made me want to live there. I now wished I did not have to go to Kansas, the very thought of it filled me with a vague dread. I imagined Kansas a sparsely populated agricultural region, with a few small settlements here and there, of its towns only Kansas City being large enough to be marked on a French map of the United States I had consulted in Istanbul.

My ticket was ready and my train was leaving for Kansas at two in the afternoon. Now, I felt, the real adventure begins! I reminded myself that I was a "soldier" and had to be brave. I bought cheese and ham sandwiches, individually wrapped in tissue paper, to eat on the train. I also attained a childhood wish and bought a large one-pound bar of chocolate — for which I was prepared to pay at least a dollar, but the price was only twenty-five cents.

I managed to get by with a few words like how much, thank you, yes sir, no sir, please give me, I wish to go to — and the most useful phrase of all, from the Berlitz manual — What is this? By asking that question I learned the names of many articles when I made a purchase.

I rode to the railroad station in a taxi — feeling like a millionaire. The station was a cathedral-like building of such colossal proportions that just glancing up at its ceiling made me dizzy. There was something of the music of the spheres about the air here, the station vibrated with a cosmic drone. I felt like a human ant in it, crawling along with thousands of other human ants, and all of us insignificant and absurd. This was a place for God to set up His throne, close to the skyey ceiling, in that cosmic music, with angels flying at His feet. And to think that this was nothing but a railroad station! Well, in America industry after all is God, I reflected, catching my breath. This great temple is dedicated to that divinity. How strange that Americans should be Christians — and how fortunate! Christ seemed out of place in the New World.

I was wandering in the vast spaces of this station when a Negro porter came up and reached for my suitcase.

"Carry yo' bag, suh?"

"Please, thank you," I said, giving it to him, though I had to count my pennies and would have preferred to carry it myself. "I wish to go to Manhattan, Kansas."

"Kansas? Yassuh. This way." I gratefully followed him to my train, and sat in a day coach, next to a window. I admired the quiet behavior of the people as they came in with their bags. They took their time, there was plenty of room for everybody. The train started on schedule, and for an hour or so I could see nothing but tracks and cars gliding by.

A man in a white coat and cap walked through the car, carrying a basket loaded with food and drinks. "Get your peanuts now, folks, nice, freshly salted peanuts," he said in an intimate, persuasive voice. I bought a bag of peanuts, and drank my first bottle of Coca-Cola, which I had seen advertised everywhere. A novel American drink, of a peculiar taste, which made me feel more American.

At Albany I bought a paper, and discovered the comic strips. But those odd drawings, with words coming out of the mouths of the characters like elongated bubbles, puzzled me. They were, I perceived, intended to be humorous, but I had seen nothing like them before, and after faithfully translating some of the bubble words with the aid of my pocket dictionary — many others were not in it — I was still mystified by them.

I changed trains in Chicago and Kansas City, and after two anxious days, always fearing I had missed my station, arrived in Manhattan, Kansas, a nice, peaceful place — strangely silent after the noise of New York.

The campus of the college was on an elevation at the edge of the town. So palatial were its white limestone buildings — I counted some fifteen of them — that I was awed. The nerve of me to come to an institution like this with, now, only seventeen dollars in my pocket! In a field student cadets, rifles on their shoulders, were drilling like a battalion of real soldiers, while a band played. I had never thought of the American youth martially inclined. On another lawn young ladies in white turtle-neck sweaters were practicing archery, and other girls were playing baseball, croquet, tennis. What comedy was this I was playing! How could I expect to associate with these mature, aristocratic students?

The taxi deposited me at the gate of the ivy-clad administration building. With my battered valise and squeaking shoes I went in to find the office of the vice-president, when electric bells began buzzing from all sides and the long corridor was filled with a torrent of gay, carefree youth. It flowed in from one end, and flowed out of the other, the main stream augmented by tributaries cascading down two stairways. It carried me along with it for a while, until I found a passage into which to retreat. I had expected to see only a few girl students, but there were thousands of them here — sophisticated young ladies, looking like millionaires' daughters. The prospect of sitting with them in the same classrooms was disconcerting, but perhaps the rich, kind-hearted widow with the red-gold hair I had dreamt about was here... I noticed the athletes, the campus lions, wearing white sweaters with a big purple "K." There were also women athletes, Amazonian females, similarly attired. They all glowed with health and animal vitality, they all seemed so happy, like grown children who had never known sorrow, had never suffered, gone hungry. What a Utopia of youth!

When the corridor was clear again, I composed myself, gathered enough courage to ask a passing student where the vice-president's office was, by showing his letter. He led me to his door.

The vice-president, a dark man with graying mustaches, European in appearance, rose from his desk and shook my hand. At first I pretended to understand what he said, for how could I be admitted to college without speaking English? But I soon gave myself away, being unable to answer his questions.

"*Sprechen sie Deutsch?*" he asked me.

I shook my head. "*Mais je parle un peu français.*"

He called the professor of French, and our linguistic troubles were over. This man had taught in Robert College and also knew Turkish. I had to tell the whole depressing truth — that I had no money, no friends in America.

Could they give me work? I would do anything. I told them how much chemistry, geometry, botany, zoology, anatomy and physiology I knew.

The vice-president looked as if he had a big problem on his hands. He explained that the college did employ a number of students, and he would have been glad to recommend me for a job, but I was three weeks late and all the positions on the campus had been filled.

He took me around and introduced me to my dean, the registrar, various other officials, and after helping me fill out the registration blanks, turned me over to the secretary of the college YMCA who was also men's adviser and assistant football coach. This gentleman took me to a pep meeting, and made a little speech about me, which I could not understand. There were other brief speeches, and much rhythmic yelling, led by two dynamic cheer leaders who jumped up together, bent now to the left and now to the right, went through some amazing contortions, as the room shook with explosive roars. These official cabalistic yells were in the student handbook, a copy of which was given me.

> Jay Rah, Gee Haw,
> Jayhawk Saw.
> At 'em, eat 'em,
> Raw, Raw, Raw!

It was great stuff. This is what student life should be, I thought. And that night, from my room in the YMCA, I watched a football rally and bonfire. But much as I yearned to join them in this celebration, and cut up with them, I remained dignified and aloof, being an outsider.

I liked my room, it was ideal for a student. I had paid a week's rent in advance — but after that? I didn't want to think of it. I wrote enthusiastically to my brother and companions in Istanbul of my first impressions and experiences in America, without mentioning my worries, and started a diary. My room was a vantage point for my future conquests. I would start from here — had already started. Forward march!

The following week I had to move down to an unused damp room in the basement, sweep the hallways in the YMCA and do other menial tasks about the building — my forced cheerfulness hiding my shame and humiliation. But I said to myself all this is good for my soul. For several days, until I got a job in a downtown restaurant where fortunately six other students also worked, including two football stars — I lived on bread, cheese and water.

After the novelty and initial glamour of this college town wore off, I became desperately lonely. Not so much because I was cut off from my people and friends, but because I did not meet a genuinely intellectual American student, one who wanted to devote himself to the welfare of his country or humanity, and was interested in more than getting "credits" for a degree. These young Americans had bright minds, were keen in laboratory work, and wonderfully healthy. They were free from those mean traits so common in the youth of other countries. There was a certain large, spacious quality about the American character. But culturally and spiritually they were far behind my companions in the old world. A single American comrade would have made me happy, in spite of all the difficulties I had to contend with. As it was, I sought intellectual companionship only among faculty members.

I was very busy, always on the go, caught in the perpetual motion of American life. Translating Emerson was my main comfort. He expressed many of my own sentiments and ideas. Emerson's America was much closer to my heart; I loved it. I was sure I would have felt perfectly at home in old New England.

Sundays were the hardest. On Sundays I could have battered my head against the walls of my room, gone mad with loneliness. Anything from Europe, such as French magazines in the college library, which apparently no one besides myself read, caused an attack of acute nostalgia. I counted the days and the hours when I should receive a letter from Europe.

My brother was now studying music in Vienna, and Vahram and Ashod were in Paris. They, too, had their troubles and suffered disillusions. France was not the country we had thought, and loved. We had thought of ourselves as belonging to a backward little nation of the East, not knowing that we were, in fact, the true Frenchmen, or Austrians, or Americans, ahead of our models in Christendom. They had lost what we preserved and cherished.

Now, for the first time, I felt really homeless. I sighed to myself when I saw American children playing before their homes and witnessed scenes of happy family life behind lighted windows at night, as I walked alone through the streets, sick with loneliness and memories. One evening, returning from my work in the restaurant, whose proprietress, a severe taskmaster, haunted me in my dreams like a witch, I paused before a house, and listened, enchanted, to the music of a piano. It was played hesitantly, by a young girl practising her lesson, I thought — as girls in our street in Trebizond used to do. Those familiar repetitious notes were infinitely sweet and perfect to me. When the piano stopped, the magic was gone. I blessed its player in my heart, and lingered before that house, hoping the young girl I imagined would come out, and I would see her and thank her. I had the feeling she would recognize me, would remember we had played hopscotch and skipped rope together — in a dream world long ago. Yes, we knew each other very well, though we had never met, and she was American and I Armenian.

I walked on to my room, for another solitary night.

All that winter I could neither laugh nor smile, and would have fled back to Europe, or at least to New York or Boston, so much closer to Europe, if I could, or were not ashamed.

But I did not wish to acknowledge my defeat — no, I was not defeated. Forward march, forever! What I sought in America was here, somewhere — I would find it. The children I passed by but never spoke to in the streets, and the recurrent music of that piano, gave me courage, allayed in some measure my great hunger and longing. We were alike. Remembering the poem I wrote on the ship, I said to myself, I *am* dying — but to be born again.

CHAPTER 23

America in My Blood

Hope had returned with the spring. After the bewilderment, the loneliness of my first winter in America, I began to live again when I saw the lawns turning green and dandelions growing exactly as in Trebizond and Constantinople. The old familiar dandelions — they were with me again, hundreds and thousands of them, smiling at me in the streets. I felt a personal triumph in them like a convalescent who has defeated death after a long illness. I picked them with trembling fingers, to make sure they *were* dandelions.

Yet now, on the train hurtling across the Kansas countryside in the summer night, the renewed pain of my being in a strange land became a sharp physical anguish. The farm where I was to get the practical experience required for my degree in agriculture was more than a hundred miles away. Always I was going farther from Europe. The college town of Manhattan, however unhappy I had been there during the winter, now seemed a place of civilized security, a sort of European oasis in the wilderness of America. Outside in the darkness was the terror of the unknown, as the great train thundered on with cataclysmic force. Now and then, looking anxiously out of the window, I caught glimpses of weird, gaunt silos rising like wooden minarets in the gloom. They might have been primitive tombs inhabited by lonely Indian ghosts. Somehow these wooden towers of Kansas made me think of Turkestan and filled me with the dread of Moslem Asia.

When I got off at the little country station where Harry, my college friend, was waiting for me in the family Ford, I felt like a man deposited by a rocket on the moon. His presence in this strangely unreal world had comforting substance.

We drove through the streets of a small town and then across open country. Fields and woods shone phosphorescent in the moonlight. I smelled June-in-the-country, the familiar fragrance of moon-drenched earth when the wheat is almost ready to be harvested and red poppies are knee high. Was this really Kansas, really America?

In vain I looked for a village. Everywhere was open country, though we drove past isolated houses now and then. "No villages in Kansas?" I asked Harry, who piloted the Ford on the rutty road with marvelous skill.

"Sure we have villages. Just passed through one. Where you came in on the train. Knox Springs is classified as a village by the census."

But it hadn't looked like one to me. It was a town, with banks, barber-shops, stores, filling stations.

"I guess your villages are different," Harry said after a silence.

"Well, you see, in ours farmers live together," I explained. "Not one house here, another house there, a mile away, behind that hill. You can see our farmers walking to their fields in the morning and coming back in the evening, though there are fields also in the villages. On Sundays the people gather on the green and the young folks dance, all together, hand in hand, not two by two. The musicians play wooden flutes attached to sacks of calf skin — what do you call them — bagpipes? Also little violins, which they hold like violoncellos. They play very well. Our farmers are poor, but happy. They sing when they plow or sow" — (which I pronounced *sau*) — "or harvest their crops. Folk songs, you know. Everybody in my country knows them."

"Sing me one," said Harry.

"But you will not understand."

"Sing it just the same."

I cleared my throat and broke into a gay peasant song, addressed to birds. But the words sounded strange. I had not heard Armenian for so long I felt as if somebody else were singing. I was so deeply moved by what I sang — or rather heard — I could have cried.

At the Schultz farm, Harry's mother, a short, chubby woman, and his two very attractive sisters, met us in the yard. I wondered what they thought of me. My heart was thumping with deep hammer blows and I felt like running away.

"Where's Dad?" asked Harry.

"Gone to bed," his mother answered.

As we entered the house, I noticed the radio, phonograph, sewing machine, and book shelves in the living room. To my intense surprise there was nothing rural about this house except that it was lighted by kerosene lamps. This delighted me. I hadn't seen a kerosene lamp in America.

The two girls were friendly enough, but I scarcely dared to look at them! One was a milk-white blonde, with hair the color of yellow corn. I took her to be about eighteen, my age. The other, a brunette, was younger, and looked like a Greek or Armenian girl to me, so that I was more attracted to her than to her fair sister, though the latter was obviously the beauty of the family. Both were dressed simply, like two neat city girls. This was like any middle-class city family, and I realized that the American urban and rural populations were substantially on the same economic and cultural level. It was so different in the old country, where villages were a thousand years behind the cities.

We talked for a while, and I had to answer the usual questions: How did I like America? Were the houses in my country like American houses? Did people over there wear the same type of clothes?

"Harry, you'd better show him to his room," Mrs. Schultz said, after I had told them nearly my whole life story.

"Yes, you'd better get all the rest you can tonight. We have to get up mighty early in the morning," Harry chuckled. "Four-thirty. That too early for you?"

"No, not at all," I said, eager to please.

"It's early to bed, early to rise with us," Mrs. Schultz said. "Early to bed, early to rise, makes a man healthy, wealthy, and wise," she added, smiling. "I'll have a pair of overalls ready for you in the morning. You're just about Harry's height."

Harry took me upstairs to a large, airy bedroom, with a wide double bed, a writing desk, a dresser, and a framed religious motto hanging on the wall. The windows had shutters like the village houses in Trebizond. The room was flooded with moonlight and the good smell of the cooling earth on a summer night.

"How do you like it?" Harry asked, putting down the kerosene lamp.

"I like it very much," I said gratefully. I had wondered if I was to live in the same house with them, or be treated like a servant.

Alone in my room, I touched the window shutters caressingly and looked out to see the environs of the farm. In the yard, a water pail by the pump cast a shadow just like a water pail in the old country — an exciting detail in this nocturnal phantasy of Kansas-Trebizond. I filled my lungs with the intoxicating odor rising from a freshly-mown alfalfa field, and listened to the thrilling night sounds of my childhood; for, amazingly enough, the crickets and frogs of Kansas sounded just like the crickets and frogs of Trebizond. It was the same resonant silence of the night that I was hearing again, the same sweet summertime music of the earth's dreams.

I looked up at the sky. It had sprouted and bloomed with stars, like dark-green fields covered with dandelions and the little golden flowers, the holy yellow flowers of Trebizond we called the Tears of the Virgin. Like a girl reaper with a white kerchief around her head, the moon moved across these flower-fields of the sky. All about me was the quivering, lyric translucence of an enchanted world that was dearly familiar to me. What miracle was this, what magic transfiguration? For the first time in America I did not feel a stranger. I had discovered the earth I had lost, the stars and the moon of my childhood: my exile was over.

Early the next morning I began my apprenticeship on an American farm, wearing overalls. In them I felt like an American. Harry and I went to the pasture to bring in the cows. It was a golden June morning. The young corn crackled in the breeze, and the orchard was ablaze with ripe sour cherries. I was in secret raptures over those cherry trees.

"Do you know," I said to Harry, who majored in horticulture, "cherries come from a place near my home town, from Cerasus, or Kerasund, on the Black Sea. That's why they're called cherries."

He was surprised.

"And do you know the scientific name of the apricot?"

"I'll be damned if I do," he said.

"*Prunus armeniaca*. Armenian prune. Oh, a lot of other fruits come from my country! Chestnuts, for example. The English word chestnut is derived from the Armenian word *kaskeni*, which mean chestnut tree."

A little brook ran through the pasture, where I saw blackberry and gooseberry bushes, and even loquat trees. To complete this miraculous picture, a spring flowed from under a rock through a narrow wooden trough, with a leaf dangling at its end! I wondered if I was dreaming, if this would vanish like an hallucination.

The sleepy cows struggled to their feet, heavy with milk, their big udders tight and full. We drove them to the barn, where Harry's father was waiting. He was a man of dignity, given to few words, tall, impressive, with keen blue eyes. But he looked ridiculous when he sat on a small stool, put a pail between his knees, and proceeded to milk, just like a woman. Yes, preposterous as it seemed, we three men had to do the milking. Mrs. Schultz and the girls were nowhere near the barn.

They were busy preparing breakfast and setting the table. It was an excellent breakfast they served when we finished milking — grapefruit, bran flakes and cream, home-cured ham and eggs, fresh country butter, home-made bread, good hot coffee. Mr. Schultz said Grace, thanking God for His many blessings — the God of America. Yes, America seemed to have a different God, a more generous one.

My first efforts as a milker supplied the conversation at the table. Of course I was clumsy and nervous, but in a week I could milk as well as Harry.

After breakfast we put two full ten-gallon milk cans in the Ford and drove to a collection point on the highway where they were picked up by a truck. That drive was another thrilling experience. The road, with its startlingly familiar bends, the bushes and trees that bordered it, the chip-chip of the sparrows, the tufts of wool caught on the wire fences — all these might have been in a village of Trebizond, and were infinitely dear to me. I felt that at any moment my childhood playmates, Vahe, Nikolaki, Anthula, Penelope, would come running down a field with bows and arrows, sling shots and sticks, wearing wreaths and baldrics of wild flowers. "Hey, where have you been?" they would ask. "Come on, we're going to pick wild strawberries and have a picnic lunch."

The real toil began after these preliminary morning chores. A field had to be plowed, and I begged Harry to let me do it. Plowing was the fundamental art in agriculture I had to learn, and I had very romantic conceptions about it. What a thing of beauty and precision the modern steel plow was! Harry showed me how to cut furrows of uniform depth and width, turning the surface completely under.

A no less heroic task was pitching hay in the afternoon. This was sheer poetry. True, my hands became blistered, my face, neck, and shoulders sunburned, and the blue shirt on my back wringing wet with perspiration. The mighty Indian sun blazed down upon the immense fertility of the Missouri Valley. But I exulted in the powerful heat of the earth, in the dust and odor of alfalfa hay.

By nightfall I was dead tired, with a fine fatigue.

Something important had happened to me, but I did not know how to word it, not even to myself. Somehow I felt as if the earth and sun of Kansas flowed through my veins, that I had suddenly become an American, that I had been born again and wedded to the American soil.

This kind of Americanization has nothing to do with speaking English, taking out first and second papers, and swearing allegiance to the Constitution. Those are comparatively insignificant and superficial processes.

When, three months later, I returned to college, I was not only thoroughly Americanized, but, paradoxical as it may seem, was my former Old World self again. The nightmare of the previous winter was over. I could laugh and clown. I was happy, a boastful, rabid Kansan. If anybody said our college wasn't the greatest and best in the world, I felt insulted. I yelled myself hoarse at football games, avidly read the sport pages of newspapers, which had meant nothing to me before. I wrote two poems about Kansas which I sent to the *Topeka Capital,* and to my utter astonishment and joy they were published.

What is it soldiers fight and die for? What is it that makes nations? Language, history, traditions, political organizations? These are contributing factors, yes; but, fundamentally, it is the land, a common identity with the earth — with dandelions and moonlight and crickets and the crackling of young corn in the morning breeze.

That summer I saw how the sun made love to the earth in the Missouri Valley, and how from that love poured forth rivers of golden grains. I heard the droning of bees among wild flowers in the stillness of the noon, the sound of the woodpecker. I listened to the song of bread sung by millions of invisible lips in miles of scented wheat fields at night.

America flowed into my blood; the earth and the sun, the wind and the rain, the moon and the stars of America were within me.

CHAPTER 24

I Ask You, Ladies and Gentlemen

Tonight is New Year's Eve, and I'm drunk again. I realize that I'm a disgrace to this society, of which I have the honor of being a member; I'm a disgrace to America, of which I have the honor of being a citizen. Ladies and gentlemen, I'll fight for America any time; I'll not hesitate to lay down my life for the land of Jefferson and Lincoln.

But I ask you, ladies and gentlemen, what can I do, when once upon a time the world was no larger than the little side street where I was born? Where I led my armies to incredible victories on my spirited broomstick horse. When stalwart men in hobnailed shoes sold vegetables, carrying primitive weighing instruments with pebbles of various sizes for weights, and sang the praises of their string beans and eggplants and tomatoes and artichokes in booming, hearty voices. And beautiful village women, wearing costumes like Byzantine frescoes, cried *"Xino ghala!"* as they came to the city to sell milk and yoghurt, carrying on their backs baskets loaded with clay pitchers and jars of classic forms.

I ask you, ladies and gentlemen, speaking as a sincere and patriotic American citizen, what can one do on New Year's Eve, when once upon a time the world was a fairyland on New Year's Eve and life lovelier than mortal life can be? When scenes of that vanished yet immortal life come back to me in softened and spiritualized hues, out of the dream-like haze of a measureless past… We stuck a large olive branch in a loaf of bread, cracked hazelnuts and hung them from the leaves, and fastened to the twigs pretty little candles, pink, blue, and white. People gave and received gifts; poor boys with lanterns went from door to door and sang ancient hymns of rejoicing, while inside, in our living room, was that olive branch with the hazelnuts and candles; and oranges, dried figs, St. John's bread, almonds, walnuts, apples, cakes, and sweetmeats were piled up on the table, and the room was bathed in golden lamplight and kept warm by a roaring iron stove.

What can one do on New Year's Eve in America, when once upon a time there was a city built on the lower slopes of a towering cliff, on the dark, serene face of which an old Byzantine monastery seemed to ascend like a white stairway to the throne of God? The top of the cliff was flat like a table, covered by a bedding of grass over which we schoolboys romped and somer- saulted, intoxicated by the odor of the old springy turf and the little yellow flowers we called "the Tears of the Virgin." Some nine hundred feet below us was the anchorage; and across the sky-blue expanse of the sea, the swift, lateen-rigged Turkish coasters scudded like great white-winged birds, kicking back showers of spray.

Ladies and gentlemen, it's great to be in America, and as I said, I'll fight for America any day, but what can one do on New Year's Eve when once upon a time there was a monastery called Vank, dedicated to a Redeemer who did not redeem His people? Vank was built upon a hill, girt with strong walls like a fort, overlooking Xenophon's Camp, where rested the caravans of Bactrian camels that came and went on the golden road from the Black Sea to Tabriz. We went to Vank for a few days' outing to celebrate the Ascension of our Lord Jesus Christ. The old cloister was crowded by pilgrims. Magnificent rams with Roman noses and spiral horns were butchered under chestnut and walnut trees, cooked in huge copper caldrons, and eaten in communal meals for the salvation of the souls of our dead. Cock fights, games of skill, and wrestling matches kept us boys in a state of constant bubbling excitement. The men pilgrims from the villages wore tight jackets ornamented with two cartridge pockets across the breast; they wore operatic breeches with balloon seats and glove-tight legs. They wrapped a jaunty cloth-hood around their heads, leaving the two ends flapping behind over their shoulders. Their women sported gorgeous costumes of wine-colored velvets and green silks, their small disk-like head- dresses bedecked with gold coins. They danced in a circle, to the music of drums and bagpipes, the girls coyly exhibiting their charms and the young men picking and wooing their future wives. And there was a blind minstrel with a wailing violin who sang old Armenian rhymes of wisdom and metaphoric rhapsodies of love.

I'm drunk, I'm a disgrace to this society, and believe me, I'm ashamed of myself. But what can one do on New Year's Eve, here in Hollywood, California, when, with the thawing of the snows in the mountains of the interior, great bands of sheep came to Trebizond from the highlands of Erzurum? They blocked the streets and kicked up clouds of dust as their shepherds drove them down to the harbor, broadtail sheep of the hardy karakul breed, each band led by a vanguard of proud bucks, bearded warriors wise in the ways of the range, and carrying bells of deeper tone. The shepherds wore sheepskin capes and carried long crooks. Their dogs, big, hairy beasts with bushy tails, wore spiked steel rings around their necks to tear the jaws of attacking wolves.

I voted for President Roosevelt and I repeat, I'll fight for America any time. But what can you do on New Year's Eve, when, though you are wearing a tuxedo and own an automobile, you remember the baker who kept his accounts by cutting notches on a tally stick, and collected once a month? When you remember the vendors of cold beverages who hurried along the narrow streets, looking as if they had just arrived from Mohammed's paradise to serve the faithful with refreshing drinks? They were dressed in white, and wore white caps, delicately embroidered with fancy flower-work; and strapped across their backs they carried enormous brass pitchers with long, graceful spouts, adorned with little bells which jingled as they strutted in characteristic pompous gait, shouting *"Airan! Buz kibi! Vishne sherbeti! Buz kibi!* Buttermilk, ice-cold! Sour-cherry sherbet, ice-cold!" When you remember the wreaths of daphne leaves and wild flowers on May Day, framing winged cherubim, that hung from every door in a blessed street; and going to the hills with hundreds of happy school kids to gather violets, and then pressing them dry in books. Have you ever picked a wild strawberry from under a hazel tree? Have you ever smelled anything more heavenly delicious than a wild strawberry? Or aren't there any wild strawberries in America? Where can I find a little wild strawberry, a little wild strawberry that will look and smell like the wild strawberries of Trebizond?

America is a great country. The Promised Land, the hope of mankind. It's a great privilege to be an American in these perilous times, to be protected by the Constitution, the Atlantic and Pacific Oceans, to live in a country that has 80 per cent of the world's automobiles, 60 per cent of the telephones, 30 per cent of the railroads, 90 per cent of the bathtubs, and produces 85 per cent of the world's moving pictures. But tonight is New

Year's Eve, and I remember my father compounding drugs behind his prescription counter. My father was the best druggist in the world. There were two glass globes on his prescription counter, one on each side, and filled, I guess, with a liquid solution, one of a wonderful red color, the other of a wonderful blue. He never told me what was in those glass globes, and why they were there. Whenever I asked him, he just smiled mysteriously. Who will tell me where in this country I can find such magic globes? They haunt me. When my father came home in the evening, he took off his black shoes with elastic sides and, sitting cross-legged on a thin mattress, drank raki and declared to his family that he was an English lord. After dinner he read his paper, which was called *Byzantion* and was printed in Constantinople, a conservative journal with a long editorial on the front page interpreting the latest move in the diplomatic chess game between the Sublime Porte and the Great Powers. I can hear his voice saying, *"Quarrrraanntttte!"* and see him waving a card as he played baccarat with the important guests gathered in our home. He roared when he announced his stake, and we kids couldn't help laughing with Mother.

It would be quite impossible for me to speak of my mother. When I caught a hazy glimpse of her tonight, I drank four martinis one after the other...

I see some socks, thick, rough army socks on a long, bare table. It is New Year's Eve in Yeisk, Russia, a town with windmills on the Azov Sea. The guns of the Red artillery are booming across the bay of Mariupol, the Azov is frozen, and so is the eternal Russian steppe. An Armenian priest from the Island of San Lazzaro in the lagoon of Venice is there, the founder and director of our fugitive orphanage from Trebizond, stranded in that godforsaken town of Yeisk. We called him Vardapet — Doctor — loved and feared him. Vardapet spoke twelve languages, and though he wore the black Benedictine habit, even the Bolshevik commissars who couldn't sign their names respected him. He had the manner of a cardinal, the go-getting qualities of the old Jesuit missionaries who penetrated the domains of the mighty Tartar khans. Every door was opened before him, and he managed to feed, clothe, and educate us while we roamed across the Russian steppes, from town to town and from village to village, at the height of the civil war. But on that New Year's Eve in Yeisk, our Christmas Eve, he presented each of us with a pair of Russian army socks. I was glad to get them, though they were too large, but I felt sorry for Vardapet, who was trying hard to smile and be cheerful. I wondered during our mournful party that New Year's

Eve, as we rubbed the new socks against our cheeks, if the day would ever come when we would have a real meal: beans, lentils, chick-peas, cabbage — it didn't matter — as long as we could sit down and eat and eat and eat. It seemed as if that day would never come. We had forgotten how it felt not to be hungry — what white bread tasted like.

I ask you, what can you do on New Year's Eve in free and happy America, when your playmates and schoolmates, the kids you grew up with, your companions in grief and joy, in hunger and misery, fellow dreamers during your dream age, are gone, lost? When you see mountains carrying silver shields and lances, or holding eternal war council on the watershed of the Caucasus — hoary warriors with white, pointed beards guarding the boundary line between Europe and Asia? When you see the old swimming hole in far-away Pontus, seeds of ripe pomegranate, the purple cascade of noble wistaria over porches and doorsteps, yellow roses climbing garden walls, and hear the melancholy cry of popcorn vendors on winter nights? When the pretty girls you loved in kindergarten and grade school are dead and their bones lie unburied, or they are in captivity, forgotten by their own nation?

I don't like to drink. I assure you I have no constitutional craving for alcohol. But once in twelve months, on New Year's Eve, I must forget my past, the New Years of long ago. I'm an American citizen, sincerely attached to the Constitution, and I'll fight for America any time; but I ask you, how can a guy forget his childhood? There are millions like me, tonight, in free, happy America, haunted by their early years, which are always, everywhere, the happiest. The world is full of sorrow and memories, of stories that cannot be told, of poignant images that have no stories. Forgive me, ladies and gentlemen… I must have another drink.

CHAPTER 25

Seven White Hairs

This morning while shaving I saw in the mirror of my bathroom a glistening white hair over my right temple. Upon further scrutiny, I found six more — over my left temple, and here and there on my head. I suppose I have a few others but these seven I could see distinctly — palpable bonds that link my destiny with yesterday's seven thousand years.

Well, I'll be damned! I said to myself. So I'm graying, getting old! These are the first warnings of the coming frost...

As I stood before the mirror, crushed by this discovery, I took a good look at myself and saw behind the rough stubble of my beard the fresh, smooth, eager-eyed, dream-lit face of a young boy, and it is very strange, I thought, that I should have a beard and white hairs on my head. What is time? It was like yesterday that I came to America, and also like centuries ago. And today, after the timeless ages that preceded and followed my pilgrimage to the New World, which was literally so to me, like a world on another planet, what I want is to recapture the wonderment and delight with which I first experienced the everlasting miracle of life — of the days, and the seasons, the wind and the rain, the sun and the stars.

I have meditated much on the beautiful mystery of life and death. And this morning, on looking at the white hairs on my head, I want to be again every moment the child I was, before I end this mortal journey, with, who knows? perhaps a Japanese bullet in my breast. Or blown to bits by a Nazi shell. The child I was in Trebizond, in the white, red-roofed city on the Black Sea, that exists no more, but nevertheless will live forever.

As children all of us were great, and all of us alike. We lived the same true life, and spoke the same true language, though the sounds of the words were different. In children all the world is one. And the real poets, philosophers, saints and heroes in all ages, everywhere, in Kansas or Trebizond, Nome or La Plata, Tipperary or Hengchow, have always been children. We were fit for the company of gods as children. But now — well, I can ask even the best, most successful among us, just look at yourself, brother, look at yourself and weep.

I want to live as a child the day, the hour, the moment — and to be beyond limitations of space and time, logic and geography, races and history. I want to be, and not to have. For being is all the having. I want to be like the apple tree that bears apples without trying — like the red flower growing in the fields, a cup for the sun. Like the crocus that blooms in early spring after the icy winds and the bleak, gray desolation of winter, bright and optimistic. *They* are not failures. They are not frustrated, and bitter. Theirs is the real success, they know how to live the good life, and they are serene.

For even if the end of all our living, of all our struggles and work and happiness and love and knowledge is death, even if death is the supreme and final monarch of our lives, and every triumph and defeat, every gain and loss, every delight of the mind and body, every book read or written, and sunset seen, and tree planted, brings us closer to our irrevocable fate, a day is a day, the hour an hour, the moment a moment, no matter how long, or short, we lived.

And death is better than wine, better than philosophy. It's a wonderful stimulant, and its consciousness like vaporous absinthe warming inside us. I can say for myself that I never lived better and more wisely, I never saw things clearer, and enjoyed them better, than when I came directly face to face with death. For then the veil was lifted from the world and everything came out in sharp relief, in true perspective. The earth became more earthy. The sea more sea-like. The trees more tree-like. I saw, heard, smelled, touched, and remembered everything with exquisite precision.

And remembering death I should be most humble. And strong. Absolutely invincible. This kind of humility is the straight path to peace, the sweetness of life.

I want, I said to myself, to be conscious again of the earth's never-ending wonders, of the all-inclusive, ever-healing and creating mother earth, gracious giver and final receiver of the stuff each of us, the good and the bad, the great and the small, is made of. And the earth is the same kindly mother everywhere, the moon and the stars, here, in America, are exactly the moon and the stars I knew in the old country, that every child knows everywhere, though grown-ups forget. The sun and the rain, the mornings and the nights, are the same here as in the dream-like regions of my everlasting past.

Not to take my life for granted, but always remembering death, to experience mortality for all it's worth, as I did once as a child — that's my ambition from now on, I said to myself, as I stood before the mirror and contemplated my white hairs, the first signs of the coming frost.

> The Bird of Time has but a little way
> To flutter — and the Bird is on the Wing.

Recalling these lines, I must hurry, I said to myself, I must hurry and live again before it's too late. I must become as strong and perfect again as the young boy who stared at me from behind my beard. From now on, I resolved desperately, no matter what happens I'll live again as a child — I'll go lie on a bit of country ground and smell the earth, bury my nose in the good odor of growing grass. By God, I said, I'll let those dear old friends of mine, the little red bugs with brilliant black spots on their backs, crawl all over me as I lie in an airy chamber of checkered sunlight under a thorny bush, and listen to the blackbirds playing brief notes on their flutes. Then I'll get up and run on the cool grass in my bare feet, hug the trees as long-lost sweethearts of mine, and rolling up my trousers wade through a stream. I'll find some willows and cut whistles out of their twigs, chase butterflies and glowworms, and gather nameless wild flowers.

Then I'll go down to the sea and listen to the sound of the waves, and watch them racing shoreward like white horses, shaking their manes — as they used to do in Trebizond. I'll hunt colored stones, and roll on the sand, and hug the sea. I'll watch the sun go down like a great galleon in flames, and the moon cut a golden swath across the black waters.

If I could do these things again with a simple girl who shares my hunger for the earth and the sea, who can get the same electric thrill by running barefoot on the grass and the wet sand, then I'll surely be a Success, richer than the richest man, wiser than all those who have forgotten these things. And at nights we'd sleep under a sky throbbing with stars.

Perhaps after this war the peoples of the world, remembering death, would live a life of peace, dignity and wisdom by becoming children at heart. That is my earnest wish, and hope.

The good world is renewed in children. In them takes place the miraculous resurrection of the race. The soul of the child is like the crocus that blooms in the sun. Therein lies the secret of that world-state we've been hearing and reading and thinking about. For the brotherhood of man will be an accomplished fact when we become children again, and our final emancipation shall consist in regaining the world we possessed as children.

Illustrations

Photograph of the author dedicated to his brother Onnik (Onnig), 1958.
Courtesy of Hasmig Surmelian, Toronto, Canada.

Scene from Trebizond (Source: George H. Hepworth, *Through Armenia on Horseback*, London, 1898). Courtesy of Houshamadyan.org.

Panorama of Trebizond, Postcard (Source: Michel Paboudjian Collection, Paris). Courtesy of Houshamadyan.org.

Surmelian family photograph, Trebizond, 1913. The author is in a white shirt holding a wheel.
Courtesy of Hasmig Surmelian, Toronto, Canada.

The author's mother, Zvart Surmelian, 1913. Courtesy of Hasmig Surmelian, Toronto, Canada.

A group of Armenian orphans, Trebizond, circa 1918. The author and Onnik (Onnig) are among the group. Courtesy of Hasmig Surmelian, Toronto, Canada.

The northern yard of the St. Stepanos Armenian Orthodox Church, Trebizond, circa 1918. The photograph shows survivors photographed among furniture looted from Armenian homes. The author may well be one of the children in the image. Courtesy of AGBU Nubar Library, Paris, France.

The interior of St. Stepanos Armenian Church in Trebizond with looted and destroyed furniture, circa 1918. Courtesy of AGBU Nubar Library, Paris, France.

Three Surmelian siblings: the author, Eugenia (Yevkiné), and Onnik (Onnig), perhaps Constantinople, circa 1920. Courtesy of Hasmig Surmelian, Toronto, Canada.

The author's sisters, Eugenia (Yevkiné) and Nevart Surmelian, perhaps Constantinople, circa 1920.
Courtesy of Hasmig Surmelian, Toronto, Canada.

The author with the novelist and critic Hagop Oshagan (Kufedjian, 1883-1948, left), and the poet and educator Vahan Tekeyan (1878-1945), perhaps Armenian Central School (Getronagan Lycée), Constantinople, 1922. Courtesy of Hasmig Surmelian, Toronto, Canada.

The site of Karapet (Garabed) Surmelian's pharmacy, Trabzon, perhaps circa 1970. Courtesy of Hasmig Surmelian, Toronto, Canada.

Photograph of the author and Clark Gable with a copy of the book's first edition dedicated to the author's brother Onnik (Onnig), 1945. Courtesy of Hasmig Surmelian, Toronto, Canada.

Glossary of Terms

A **à la Franca:** in the modern, western, European style.

à la Turca: in the Turkish style.

agha: an honorific title of address for a male person.

Alashaghah: a war-like cry.

arzuhalji: petition-writer.

B **bakshish:** gratuity given for services rendered.

balalaika: a Russian string instrument.

bash chavush: head of chavushes (an Ottoman military rank approximately equivalent to that of sergeant).

bashibozuks: irregular soldiers of the Ottoman army. The word was colloquially used to mean undisciplined bandits preying on defenseless civilians.

bashlik: a headdress in the form of a hood with long ends used as a scarf.

bey: an Ottoman title for district governors, also used as a courtesy title.

bulbul: nightingale.

B **cahveji:** mostly itinerant coffee-sellers in the Ottoman Empire.

charshaf: dress with veil worn by women in the Ottoman Empire.

cheta: member of a band of irregulars consisting mostly of criminals released from prison.

Circassian: ethnic group inhabiting the north-western Caucasus. Following the Russian occupation of their homeland in the early 19th century, many Circassians emigrated to the Ottoman Empire and some settled along the shores of the Black Sea.

comitadjis: members of a secret revolutionary society.

B **dacha:** a holiday cottage in the Russian countryside.

Dashnag: member of the Armenian Revolutionary Federation party (Dashnaktsutioun in Armenian).

décolleté: a woman's dress with a low neckline.

dervish: a religious mendicant or member of a religious fraternity in the Islamic world.

devas: a divine being.

domóy: a Russian word meaning 'homeward'.

E **effendi:** a courtesy title in the Ottoman Empire given to men of property, authority or education.

F **Franks:** a term used in the Ottoman Empire and elsewhere in the Middle East to refer to Europeans in general.

G **Gehenna:** a place or state of misery; another world for 'hell'.

giaour: a derogatory term for non-Muslims, especially Christians.

Grand Vizier: the title of the Chief Minister or head of government in the Ottoman Empire.

H **halva:** a sweet confection popular in the Middle East and the Mediterranean world. It is generally made of sesame and sugar often with nuts added.

hamal: a porter or bearer of heavy goods.

Hunchak: a shortened name for Social Democrat Hunchakian Party, an Armenian political party founded in 1887.

I **imam:** a cleric leading the Islamic worship service.

Ingush: indigenous ethnic people of the north-east Caucasus.

Ittihad: short for the political party Ittihad ve Terraki Cemiyeti (Committee of Union and Progress), also known as the Young Turks.

K **Kalimera:** a Greek greeting, meaning 'good morning' or 'good day'.

karakol: police station.

karakul: tight, curly-patterned mainly black coat of a very young karakul lamb from Central Asia.

kaimakam: governor of a provincial sub-division in the Ottoman Empire.

khan: a roadside inn or caravansary.

kvass: a drink made from fermented rye bread, popular in Russia.

L **Laz:** indigenous ethnic group inhabiting primarily in south-western Georgia and north-eastern Turkey along the shores of the Black Sea.

Lazistan: homeland of the Laz people stretching along the south-eastern shore of the Black Sea.

lezghinka: a Caucasian folk dance.

M **Maydan:** town square.

mejidieh: a sub-unit of the Ottoman currency, the lira.

mudir: governor of an administrative district in the Ottoman Empire.

muezzin: a person associated with a mosque whose duty is to call the faithful to prayer at appointed times.

mullah: a Muslim cleric.

N **narghile:** another word for a hookah (waterpipe).

neneh: grandmother.

O **oka:** A unit of weight in the Ottoman Empire, equivalent to approximately 1.2 kilograms.

P **paklava:** a dessert made from layers of filo pastry interspersed with crushed nuts and sweetened with honey or syrup.

palikaria: an affectionate term used to compliment a young boy or man.

paschal cake: a tall cylindrical-shaped Russian sweet bread or cake made at Easter.

pasha: a high administrative or military rank in the Ottoman Empire.

pât d'Espagne: a type of flaky pastry. (please note correct spelling is pâte).

peshdimal: Turkish towels made of cotton and used in baths.

piaster: The European term for a monetary sub-unit of the Ottoman lira (1 lira = 100 piasters). The Turkish term for piaster was *kurush*.

Q **quadrille:** a dance popular in Europe in the 19th century.

R **raki:** an alcoholic anise-flavored drink popular in the Middle East.

Ramazan: Muslim month of fasting.

S **salaamed:** a salutation in Islamic countries, in the form of a low bow with the palm of the right hand placed on the forehead.

serai: a mansion or a palace, generally referring to a government building in the Ottoman Empire.

shaitan: Arabic for 'Satan'.

simit: a circular bread with hollow middle topped with seeds (often sesame).

simitji: itinerant bread-seller.

T **tonir:** hearth.

V **vakh:** an exclamation or interjection of showing an emotion such as compassionate surprise.

vallah-billah: an interjection meaning 'I swear to God'.

vardapet: a clerical rank in the Armenian Church bestowed on a learned celibate priest.

Y **yavrum:** an affectionate term (e.g. my dear) when addressing a child or a younger person, literally meaning 'my little one' or 'my child'.

Acknowledgments

The republication of Leon Surmelian's classic was truly a team effort and benefitted from the combined passions and skill sets of a variety of people. First and foremost, Susan Pattie, Gagik Stepan-Sarkissian and Vazken Davidian's input, contributions and insights have been crucial throughout. We thank Stephen Masters for digitally capturing the data of the work's first UK edition. Several members of the Armenian Institute team including Rebecca Jinks, Paula Melville and Anieka Sayadian contributed to the effort. Thank you to Jennifer van Schoor for going beyond the call of duty in designing the cover and pages and David Low for his eagle-eyed handling and reading of the material. Vahe Tashjian at Houshamadyan.org and Boris Adjemian at the AGBU Nubar Library were helpful in providing some of the photographic images at the back of the volume. Thank you to Aras Publishing House in Istanbul — publishers of the Turkish language edition of the work — for putting us in touch with the author's niece, Hasmig Surmelian, who was very encouraging and appreciative of the project. A special debt of gratitude is owed to her for generously providing photographs from the family archive and graciously responding to our various queries. Finally, this publication would not have been possible without the energetic leadership and sponsorship of Richard Mourad Anooshian.

The Armenian Institute
London